The

Complete

Restaurant

Management

Guide

The

Complete

RESTAURANT
MANAGEMENT

Guide

ROBERT T. GORDON and
MARK H. BREZINSKI

SHARPE PROFESSIONAL

An imprint of M.E. Sharpe, INC.

Library of Congress Cataloging-in-Publication Data

Gordon, Robert T.
The complete restaurant management guide / Robert T. Gordon and
Mark H. Brezinski.
p.   cm.
Includes index.
ISBN 0-7656-0305-5
1. Restaurant management.   I. Brezinski, Mark H.   II. Title.
TX911.3.M27G664   1999
647.95′-068—dc21   98-31765
CIP

Printed in the United States of America

The paper used in this publication meets the minimum requirements of
American National Standard for Information Sciences—
Permanence of Paper for Printed Library Materials,
ANSI Z 39.48-1984.

MV (c)   10   9   8   7   6   5   4   3   2

About the Authors

Robert T. Gordon, President, Gordon Associates, Inc., a restaurant and food service consulting firm, is a veteran of some forty years of restaurant operations and management experience. Having been involved, at one time or another, with the operation of restaurants, clubs, hotels, fast-food restaurants, commissaries, and institutional food service organizations throughout the world, Mr. Gordon knows just about everything there is to know about the restaurant and food service industry.

Mr. Gordon has held positions as regional vice president with ARA Services; general manager, Rice Hotel; a partner in several successful fast-food restaurants in Dearborn, Michigan; district manager for Shoney's Big Boy operations in West Virginia; director of dietary administration and instructor at the University of Iowa Medical Center.

Robert T. Gordon graduated from Michigan State University, where he earned a B.A. and completed work toward an M.B.A. He is past member of the Texas Hotel and Motel Association, the Texas Restaurant Association, Food Consultants Society International, and the Society for the Advancement of Food Service Research. He previously taught hotel and restaurant management courses at the Hilton College of Hotel and Restaurant Management, University of Houston, Houston, Texas.

Mark H. Brezinski has over twenty-nine years of experience and practice in the restaurant industry. In 1978 he received a master's degree from Cornell University in Hotel and Restaurant Management. Mr. Brezinski began his restaurant career in various management positions with fine dining restaurants in Houston and Chicago, owned a frozen yogurt franchise, and was a consultant for a nationally acclaimed restaurant consulting company, and taught restaurant management courses at the Hilton College of Hotel and Restaurant Management, University of Houston, Houston, Texas.

He was director of operations of Canyon Cafes, Inc., where he helped grow the company from four restaurants to seventeen; director of opening units and franchise operations director of Macaroni Grill, and opened over thirty restaurants for Brinker International. Mr. Brezinski recently opened his own restaurant project, Tin Star, in Dallas, Texas.

Acknowledgments

The authors wish to thank the following individuals: Michael Dill—for his uncanny sense in menu development; Don Doggett—for his help with the SCORE organization; Denie Breuss—for her great skill in communication; Rich Hicks—for helping to solve current operational dilemmas; Tara Benedict—for her patience and processing talent; John Farquharson—for his input on Food Safety issues; Ted Lefovich—for sharing his experiences with franchising; Carols Martinez—for his investment feedback; Susan Mills—for her help with information from the National Restaurant Association; Ricky Oberoi—for his friendship and advice; Clare Sullivan—for her input on party planning; Linda West—for her strong contribution on professional catering; Sol Kobb, CPA—for his many hours and expertise on tax matters; Gene Gordon—for her patience and help; Jana Hardgrave—for putting up with late hours at the computer.

What This Guide Will Do for You

The goal of this guide is simple: to help you improve your restaurant operations, reduce costs, and increase profits. The *Guide* provides you virtually with everything you need, in easy-to-understand language, to be outstandingly and increasingly successful in this competitive and exciting industry. Used properly, it will give you the edge on your competition and bring you the growing satisfaction and financial return that your efforts deserve.

This is a fast-reading, "how to do it" book, crammed full of effective practices and techniques. It is a storehouse of practical information and proven tips gathered over sixty years of association with highly successful restaurants large and small, and their owners and managers. These tips, which have been used so successfully by others, are accompanied by charts and checklists for easy use and implementation. For the seasoned owner or manager, it is a complete review of steps that must be followed if a business is to realize its full potential. For the newcomer, it is a virtual road map to success. For anyone, its practical advice can be sought and put to instant use whenever a problem arises in any area of restaurant operations.

The *Guide* will take you step by step through the process of increasing your sales and controlling costs. In these times of changing economic conditions, it is imperative that you prepare adequately for the future, whether that future is tomorrow or five years away.

The keystone of more profitable restaurant operations is the menu. In the *Guide*, you will find hundreds of tips that others have used in the development of menus that sell. There are charts and concise introductions to tell you how to price for profit. The *Guide* points out the changes that occur around us, how they can affect your business, how you can stay informed, and how to deal with change before it occurs.

The *Guide* sets down the right techniques needed to control food production with accompanying charts, checklists, and sample records that are absolutely necessary to the control of costs. You will find checklists and tips for avoiding production problems caused by inadequate equipment and excessive preparation time and service. You will also see easy-to-adapt examples of how others have greatly increased sales and profits by employing techniques that are outlined and explained in the *Guide*.

Buying skill is crucial if the restaurant is to earn top money for you. The *Guide* will show you how you can *make* hundreds of dollars with sound purchasing policies, and how to make sure that you don't *lose* hundreds of dollars with poor receiving, storage, and handling practices. There are thousands and thousands of dollars wasted in the storerooms, kitchens, and refrigerators of restaurants and through restaurants not receiving what they ordered. Checking deliveries is often delegated to others who may not use the same degree of care as you would. Although you may assume that those persons or firms who sell or deliver to your restaurant are honest, we do know that there are some dishonest persons who serve our industry. Consequently, and as the old saying goes, "an ounce of prevention is worth a pound of cure." Using the *Guide* will help you to prevent, in your restaurant, the waste and losses that are so prevalent in many others.

There is much talk about how hard it is to find good employees these days. The *Guide* furnishes proven tips and techniques that will enhance and improve your entire labor situation. For example:

- Tips on recruiting and selection of quality employees

- Increasing sales and profits through better training of employees

- How to measure performance and establish reachable goals

- How to communicate with your employees, and how this *will* increase your profits

- How to develop fringe benefit packages that your restaurant can afford, and that pay off for you personally

- How to protect yourself in the face of changing laws and regulations that affect your business

- How unions can affect your business, and how best to deal with them when it's necessary

The *Guide* deals at length with cocktail lounge operations and the merchandising and sale of wine. There are loads of proven money-saving ideas on

- Purchasing and receiving

- Pricing of liquors and wines

- Cash and inventory controls

- Control of sales and securing of profits

Throughout you will find solutions to common and not-so-common problems that may crop up on a daily basis. There is coverage on the kind of accounting you need for adequate control of your money—how to forecast sales and expenses accurately, analyze your labor requirements, and then relate them to a work schedule that will do the job you want. The *Guide* provides a review of tax savings and guidelines that are available to restaurant owners.

Remodeling or expansion calls for expertise and deep soul searching. The *Guide,* with the help of checklists, will help you to make the right decisions. There is information about consultants: who they are, what they do, where to find them, how to evaluate their expertise, and how to be sure you receive the most value for the money you spend. There is also information about SCORE (Service Corps of Retired Executives), a nonprofit organization that works in conjunction with the Small Business Administration. Business counselors, with years of expertise in the restaurant industry, provide their service free for the asking.

Whether you are in the business a long time or not, the *Guide* will provide you with the help you need to run a more profitable restaurant. It has taken the new and the old and blended them into the most practical and useful information source available anywhere at any price today.

Robert T. Gordon
Mark H. Brezinski

Instant Chart of Surefire Ways to Increase Profits

There are thousands of successful restaurants owned and operated by real pros. You, too, can have a restaurant that is as successful and profitable if you will use the practical working tools that are outlined throughout this guide. Here are some quick ideas you can use to help make those profits.

How to Stay Ahead of the Competition		
Every restaurant operator has his or her own ideas about how to sell food and drink. Therefore, it is a good idea to visit other operations, looking for unique ideas that you might adapt in your own restaurant. (In some cases, checking up on your competition might be tax deductible.)	Try to give time to some sort of community service. High visibility in the community will not only help to bring people to your restaurant, but you may also get free newspaper, radio, or TV coverage for your business. In other words, show the community that you support it and it may support your restaurant.	Establish contact with your Chamber of Commerce and with the Convention and Visitors Bureau. Both these groups act as evaluation committees that consider facilities for upcoming meetings and conventions. In addition to suggesting appropriate hotel and meeting facilities, these communities consider auxiliary amenities such as surface transportation, entertainment centers, shopping, and restaurants. Be sure to remain visible with these selection committee, so that you put yourself out in front of your competition for future business when the visiting associations choose your town for their convention.
Be aware of happenings in your town. Visit with your banker, insurance agent, and real estate people. These people are invaluable sources for information about neighborhood transition and longer-range changes that may affect your restaurant.	Employ handicapped persons in suitable positions. Not only is it evidence of community support, but you may also find some loyal, dedicated, long-term employees. (Bookkeeping and cashiering are just two positions where you may readily employ a handicapped person.)	It may be profitable for you to become acquainted with • Hotel front office personnel • Taxi drivers • Tourist bureau people, since they constantly deal with transient people.

How to Make Certain That Your Guests Will Return

Make certain your waiters remove soiled china and silver between courses. Although there's some additional expenses in doing this, treating your customers to a "touch of class" can be well worth it.	Background music can be complementary to gracious dining. However, be sure it is appropriate for your particular type of clientele. Remember, there is a difference between loud music and noisy music. The former is right in some places and actually helps sales. Noisy music can be irritating and may even drive away business.	Visiting and conversing with guests indicate your interest in them. However, it can be overdone and become a negative factor in your business. For instance, servers and managers can become boring when they don't know when to quit talking. This can also mean that if you or your service people are spending too much time at any one table, other guests are probably being ignored. Managers and servers must know how to "hit and run." In other words, the real restaurant pros know how to carry on a conversation with each and every customer who feels like talking. They do it without actually letting it interfere with the job of providing equal service to every guest.
Train, train, train your people. Work to make your employees function like a truly professional team. Graciousness and efficiency will encourage repeat business, which, is of course, the foundation of your restaurant.	Sales incentive plans for servers will help to keep things moving.	Work for consistency in your menu offerings. Guests often turn to a restaurant because they like one particular item. Be sure your offerings remain consistently good day after day.
Keep your restaurant lively and interesting for your guests, e.g., live flowers on each table, place mats for the children. Friendly, caring employees will also help to make it so.	Sanitation and neatness are an important part of good service. Even though your restaurant is basically clean, it can still look messy. So keep tabs on this. In addition, clean, crisp uniforms on smiling, well-groomed servers will surely bring guests back to your restaurant.	

How to Provide an Atmosphere That Says "Welcome—We Want Your Business"

Fit the price to the service or vice versa. Although French service and table-side cooking is lovely to observe and experience, you can't have it with cheese sandwich prices. You must know your market thoroughly and work it carefully. For example, if you were to offer three specials for $6.95, one each of chicken, veal, or shrimp scampi, most people who dine out regularly will know that at $6.95, the only intelligent choice is the chicken. The shrimp would probably be too small, and the veal is a less-than-quality cut or grade.

Don't be so rigid that you can't make exceptions to the menu or provide special items on request. Although requests of this kind are sometime disruptive, you should do everything you can to please your guests. And don't be afraid to charge for extra or special service if the charge is warranted.

Remember, there are a lot of people who can't function in the morning before they have three or four cups of coffee. These people are also in a hurry to get each one of those cups. If you serve breakfast, put the coffee on the table in insulated serving containers. It's a nice touch and will allow your servers to handle more orders, instead of running around the dining room filling coffee cups. Today, it is common practice to provide brewed decaffeinated coffee. The difference in taste is remarkable compared to instant packets—and your patrons will appreciate it. Many people are requesting decaf especially at luncheon and dinner meals. And if necessary, charge extra for it. Your guests know from shopping that it is more expensive than regular coffee.

Other products that should be offered include one or more diet soft drink selections, along with at least one brand of light beer. If you want to find out about additional eating trends, spend some time in the grocery or convenience stores and see what is new.

In-house Selling: The Way to Fame and Fortune

If your service staff presents the menu—or even just the special or specials of the day—orally, be certain they know what they are talking about. Servers should know as much as possible regarding the items, including ingredients used, method of cooking, and style of service. Even if your offerings are described only on a written menu, the servers should be thoroughly familiar with preparation so they can answer questions intelligently.	Some restaurants publish a daily complimentary synopsis of local and national news, with sporting event scores of the season and stock market quotations. It is usually placed on a table or counter in the morning and at noon. This is especially effective if you have a large white-collar business clientele.	Depending on your type of establishment, and if you use place mats, have something of interest to your guests imprinted on the face. It's a good way to advertise your restaurant, town, state, resort, etc. Games and puzzles aren't a bad idea either. They will frequently occupy children as well as adults.
When seating a party, diplomatically inquire who will be paying the check. It will often save embarrassment later on.	The use of clip-ons or tip-ups on the menu for advertising specials can be an aid to sales. There is no denying the fact that they are used successfully in many restaurants.	Funny sayings and unusual descriptions on the menu go very well in some kinds of restaurants. As a rule, they should fit in with the overall theme and decor of the restaurant.
Another sales tool is the dessert and after-dinner drink menu that is presented following the completion of the entire course.		

How to Hold On To Those Hard-earned Dollars

Do forecast your sales, and budget your cost and expense. Also, be realistic in setting attainable goals on cost and expense, and work to make them. However, it's important to put a little "reach" in your sales goals.	Employee theft can be another factor in your profit picture. Richard Ward, former vice president, SAGA Corporation, has studied the in-house pilferage and theft in business. According to him, all businesses lose at least 2.5 percent to 3.0 percent of total sales through theft. Therefore, showing up in the unexpected parts of your restaurant—and at different times—may save thousands of dollars for you.	If a specialized task confronts you, consult an expert. In the long run, you will probably realize a savings—plus you will save yourself a great deal of worry and frustration.
Watch the details of the business with diligence. For example: • Weigh the meat. • Don't buy ice at the price of fish or shrimp. • Inspect the products, and check all invoices for everything you buy.	Don't start a restaurant if it is to be undercapitalized. The days of starting a business on a shoestring are long gone. Present interest rates, plus commodity prices and customer resistance, all make for a difficult situation even in established restaurants. For new restaurants, they add up to a situation that is almost guaranteed to ensure failure.	

How to Build a Responsible Staff

Smooth and efficient running of your restaurant stems from your staff. Building such a staff depends on a good training program.	A good source of labor is the retired person. Some of these people are perfect for particular positions. Even though they may be limited as to earnings, you can still use them on a part-time basis.	Show your appreciation by rewarding your employees for good service. This will ensure that the good ones will stay. Don't forget to compliment your people on a job well done, every day.

Economic and Social Changes That Can Mean Opportunities for You

Fast-food restaurants now account for a high percentage of the total restaurant business in the United States. In fact, today's lifestyle requires people to look for quick meals and food that they can carry off the premises.	The senior citizen population is increasing, and these retired people like to travel. That means more tours and group business. It also opens up an opportunity for box-lunch-type meals for people on the go.	Catering in homes and for such events as picnics has always provided good opportunities for additional business. The need for this service will increase as people continue to enjoy more leisure time.
For those operators who have established a good reputation in the business, there are many opportunities to manage restaurants under contract or by leasehold. Although the opportunity is vast, there are a couple of words of caution in order here: • Be sure you negotiate a deal you can live with and that won't hurt your reputation. • Good management is essential to every business. Don't stretch yourself or your management staff too thin. It is very easy to get greedy and suffer losses in the process.		

Table of Contents

**Chapter 11 How to Make Advertising and Promotion Dollars
Pay Off for You**..247

**Chapter 12 How to Get Top Benefit from Tax Savings and Shelters,
and Build Financial Security**.....................................259

Chapter 1

Magic Keys to Making More Money in the Restaurant Business

Table of Contents

Chapter
1

Magic Keys to Making More Money in the Restaurant Business

Imagine that back in 1990 you had $500,000 to invest and you were deciding whether to open a restaurant of your own or invest in a balanced stock portfolio. Since 1990, a $500,000 investment in stocks within the Standard and Poors 500 would have turned into about $1.4 million in 1998, on an average. In that same period, about 60 percent of all restaurants opened in 1990 are now out of business. Now, how important is profit? Let's explore the relationship further!

HOW TO SET OBJECTIVES FOR MAXIMUM PROFIT

KEY IDEA: The capital assets (i.e., building, land, equipment, etc.) are only valuable to a restaurant if they can contribute to the earnings of profits. Similarly, the staff (cooks, waiters, dishwashers) and the food and supplies are only valuable if they contribute to sales and profits. And it is the responsibility of management to use and direct these various elements properly to enhance the restaurant's profit potential. Therefore, planning and setting objectives are an essential part of every manager's job.

The most basic objective of all business ventures is to make a profit. Capital assets are only valuable if they contribute to or facilitate the making of a profit. Similarly, the staff, raw food supplies, and decorations are only valuable if they, too, enhance the restaurants' profit potential. Believing that merely providing the facility or the staff to serve food is sufficient to set profit in motion is a mistake many restaurateurs make. Although it may be noble to be perceived as a "Mom and Pop" business or have the charm of a helter-skelter operation, there are precious few restaurants that can or will survive without excellent organization.

What constitutes excellent organization? For starters:

- Short-range and long-range planning

- Sales and expense forecasting

- Organizational charting and structure

- Financial control implementation

- Monthly profit and loss statement compilation

- Job performance measurements

- Commitment to training programs

A dear friend and extremely successful restaurateur once said, "In the dining room and kitchen I operate like I've invited you into my home, but behind the office door I'm no different than IBM." The essence of his belief was that he needed to have two very different but essential skill sets, one as a host and culinarian and the other as a businessman who was no different than any other businessman in the community. To survive, or better to thrive, meant having more skills than merely providing a good product.

Perhaps the best organizational starting point is to define your concept and your goal. Mission statements have been all the rage in the nineties simply because they allowed entire organizations to share a common goal. Write down your own description of what your concept is and whom you're attempting to appeal to. It might be as simple as the following:

"Our concept (NAME) stands for high-quality, freshly made Mexican food served in an authentic atmosphere at a check average of no more than $6.00 per person."

It's amazing how quickly your staff and guests will begin to rally around your simple goal. From that simple sentence are born innumerable organizational challenges. To be "high quality" means attention to purchasing standards and production techniques. "Fresh" means making intelligent batch recipes, qualifying vendors, and installing proper product rotation guidelines. "Authentic" implies a commitment to honest efforts in recipe development, service training, and attention to design detail and cleanliness. A "$6.00 check average" means competitive purchasing, invoice reviews, standardized recipes, and portion controls. Notice how many "tools" are needed to back up a one-sentence goal.

And the effort doesn't stop there. Setting the staff up for success, thus setting the business up for profit, implies putting policies and procedures in place that direct your staff in the proper ways to perform their jobs. Guidelines must be formalized so that "interpretation" is minimized. Although you may wince at the sound of the phrase "chain restaurant," the proliferation of successful chains in the '80s and '90s has been predicated on this elimination of "interpretation" through specific and closely monitored guidelines. Although we promote the spirit of entrepreneurialism throughout this book, there is no harm in learning from the success of others. Organization is definitely not a dirty word. There are seminars, continuing education programs, and organizational consultants, all of which will help you become a better competitor. In addition, you will extract many tools from this guide that will put you on the right track.

HOW TO DEVELOP A PLAN AROUND PROFIT

KEY IDEA: Great food without great goals and controls spells disaster, and a festive atmosphere without intelligent management is a doomed recipe as well. Understanding the relationship between profit and developing a plan around profit is no less important than being able to distinguish fresh from frozen food.

There is nothing sinister or negative about starting your plan by stating your profit goal. To begin by saying "I must make a net profit of 18 percent" is not only advisable but it is also becoming more necessary. To compete for excellent locations, to stand up to the deep-pocketed chain restaurants, or simply to be able to hire the best staff, you must be a profitable restaurant, regardless of your concept. If the goal is to be a successful long-term business, then there truly is no honor in being the cheapest restaurant in an area if it makes the profit margin thin. Your guests, your employees, and your landlord all expect you to make money. In a sense, their welfare, especially your employees, is directly tied to your ability to make a profit. Know how much money you need to make and commit to hitting your goal. Here are a few tips.

1. *Develop a yearly budget.* Be very specific in all sales and expense categories. Give yourself reasonable but aggressive targets to hit. There are many schools of thought regarding budgeting and there truly is no "right" or "wrong" way. Many individuals start with sales goals and project sales first before attempting to project expenses. Others start with a net profit goal and work upward on the financial statement using rules of thumb for major expenses and finally arriving at what sales need to be to achieve the desired net profit. Work with your accountant or business plan team to format a budget that works for you but, by all means, have a budget, not just a previous year statement to compare to.

2. *Carefully price your menu to meet a specific cost goal.* If your budgeted food cost is 30 percent then it will only be achievable if your menu items cost out to no more than 28 percent to 30 percent on average. This is discussed in detail in Chapter Two.

3. *Do "mock" schedules for all staff positions.* Write schedules that you think would apply for the business volume(s) you are anticipating. Assign hourly wages and extend all costs for a one week schedule for all hourly positions. When all schedules have been costed for one week you will have a total projected weekly labor cost. Divide that cost by your anticipated weekly sales. That figure should compare favorably with your yearly budgeted labor cost

percentage. Depending on the type of food service operation, your hourly labor cost percentage (not including management or taxes) should be in a range from 15 percent to 20 percent. In other words, if you're projecting weekly sales of $12,000, your hourly payroll cost shouldn't be more than $2,100. If it is, you're in need of some schedule reviews!

4. *Share your profit goal with key management.* It is imperative that all managers who manage expense centers know what their budgetary goals are. Regular progress reports are critical if goals are to be achieved. If necessary, set the management team up on a bonus plan for exceeding the goals, but be careful not to reward behavior that compromises the guest experience. For example, a manager may decide to use an inferior linen product simply because it is cheaper and will minimize this expense. However, we all have used a nonabsorbent napkin and know how frustrating it can be to use.

5. *Never stop promoting your restaurant.* By far and away the best profit margin contributor is increasing sales. Once a break-even level of sales is achieved, extra sales carry only a variable expense against them. Most occupation costs and operating costs like utilities do not increase as volume increases, so generally extra sales dollars flow through to the bottom line in larger percentages. Although many promotional efforts may cost some money to implement, there are numerous community participation and business goodwill practices that cost little to nothing.

HOW TO USE TODAY'S TOOLS TO COMMUNICATE YOUR PROFIT GOALS

KEY IDEA: You must maintain a clear and open line of communication with your employees at all times. Further, you should actively promote communications between employees. Encourage the exchange of information and the flow of suggestions, all for the good of the business.

Once you have accepted the notion that profit is not only good but necessary, it must be communicated to your staff how you intend to reach your goals. Having a common goal is only effective if there is a shared responsibility in reaching those goals. For many years ours has been an industry that has lagged behind in the information age. Communication tools such as point-of-sale system reporting, video training, and seminar attendance for continuing education are available at a more sophisticated level than ever before. Taking advantage of these tools becomes another link in the chain for your success. Specifically, here is how these tools communicate your intentions.

Point-of-Sale Systems

Almost everyone has heard the phrase "Watch the pennies and the dollars will watch themselves." Well, it isn't that long ago that watching pennies was not a computer-aided function for restaurants. Today, point-of-sale systems help track sales down to the minute, the server, and the penny. By installing a point-of-sale system you are communicating to your staff that pennies mean something to you and should mean something to them as well. Sophisticated systems allow for each and every sales by each and every server or bartender to be tracked. Accountability goes hand in hand with profitability. And beyond the ability to monitor all income, systems allow operators to analyze operations in ways that were often left to intuition. Now we understand that the best decisions are those that are made using an intelligent mix of intuition and information. The opportunity to be profitable is enhanced when there is a system by which to analyze information. You can communicate better when your information is accurate, up to the minute, and accessible. A staff that realizes you have this ability is more likely to participate in your profit goals.

This is not to say it is suggested to remove a personal touch, so critical in the service industry. It is simply saying that possessing technical tools that help analyze and at the same time control your flow of information is an intelligent way to achieve profitability goals. Remember, systems are a subset of service, not vice versa.

Video Training

With the accessibility of video tools (cameras, recorders, monitors) there is a great opportunity to improve training communication in our industry. How often does your training program consist of teaming up a new employee with an experienced employee and then simply assuming your experienced employee is capable of communicating all the messages the new person needs to hear? When was the last time you worked a shift side by side with your so-called experienced employee trainers? The point here is that, especially in smaller operations, it is so much easier today to share your message with each and every employee. New cooks not only need to know how to follow a recipe, but also how to properly clean their cutting boards or store sensitive products. Simply ask any restaurateurs who've been closed down by a hepatitis scare or had their restaurants reported in the five o'clock news for poor sanitation scores how important information can be.

Whether you like it or not, this is the video age and people respond to video. Take a video camera and record a ten-minute speech from you personally to be played to all new hires. Follow that with specific training for specific positions. What communicates the need for proper sanitation standards better than seeing the chef or owner on video showing the proper way to store items in a walk-in cooler? A video of a server properly removing dirty dishes from a dining table may seem like an inconsequential detail to some, but are you aware that historically, the second most popular reason people cite for choosing a restaurant is service?

Each and every communication tool you put in place ultimately affects profitability because these tools affect your staff's ability to take care of your guests properly. If your guests receive the type of food you set as your standard and the type of service that you know will be accommodating and professional, then you have given yourself the best chance to succeed. "Repeat customers" is a term that has more to do with your ability to organize and communicate your goals to your staff than any other factor.

Seminars and Continuing Education

National and state restaurant associations have been providing excellent assistance for restaurateurs for numerous years. The sophistication level of assistance has been growing by leaps and bounds. Most states or geographic areas have yearly shows that include seminars, exhibits, and roundtable discussions. Additionally, the National Restaurant Association produces mountains of literature, conducts several yearly conferences, and provides a once-a-year show that brings all the information and support available into one location. Continuing education is now more available than ever with forums on the labor crisis, tax laws, menu trends, and supervisory training, just to name a few of the types of focuses you can find.

Our industry has evolved remarkably in the area of shared information. And although competition is keener than ever, the availability of industry leaders and innovators have never been more accessible. Ours is not an industry of big secrets like so many other industries. Opening a business and providing great food and service is not the type of skill that only intellectuals possess. You should actively participate in associations that offer services like those just mentioned. The communications available to you are vast and there is much valuable information to be absorbed. Through your attendance and your sharing this information with your staff you are also communicating to them how seriously you take your business. A staff that respects your passion is a staff that has a better chance of performing at the level you need them to for everyone to be successful.

WHY YOU SHOULD NOT OVERLOOK YOUR INTUITION

KEY IDEA: Profitability is not possible when decisions are questionable. The best decisions are made by combining information and your intuition. To be intuitive is to be your own best and worst customer.

There must be an assumption made that your intuition for the restaurant business is strong, otherwise you wouldn't have chosen this field. We cannot overemphasize how important it is that you become your own worst critic in this regard. Far too often we see owners who have spent hundreds of thousands of dollars starting a new business stand aside and let someone else dictate the course of that business. We can recall no successful restaurant operator who isn't also on the firing line when needed. There is no better way to develop intuition than to be immersed in the operation, and by our definition, there is no way to make smart decisions without the intuition that comes from the immersion. Profitability is not possible when decisions are questionable. To help you develop critiquing skills, the following three points are offered:

1. *Ask a select few regular guests.* This is simple, easy, and very informative. Sit down, buy them a bottle of wine, and talk to them about what they like and

don't like about what you're doing. Listen, absorb the information, and then factor it into the other points.

2. *Ask your employees.* Again, be selective but not biased. We all know this could be an open invitation for an overwhelming session, but keep it specific. Invite three trusted employees to join you for lunch or dinner and keep the conversation in control by limiting the topics. You might simply ask, "What menu items do you steer guests away from and why?"

3. *Ask new guests.* Pick out a couple who are first-time guests (enlist the help of your service staff since they have the interactions to know) and ask them if it's all right to ask a few questions. Be specific, again, and be sure to approach them after their meal. Buy them a dessert or even buy their entire meal. You succeed in getting "fresh" information and you've pretty much guaranteed yourself some new regular guests!

HOW TO MAKE THE BEST USE OF YOUR TIME

KEY IDEA: In a busy restaurant, it is usually difficult for the manager to find the time to handle all the necessary tasks each day. This is why your time must be jealously guarded and wisely used.

One of the major time-wasters is this: every day sales professionals, customers, other merchants, job seekers, and fund raisers will want to see you. You'll have to pass at least a pleasantry or two with each, and more time than that with some. You must be able to schedule those kinds of visits—and know when and how to close the conversations. In addition, you will want to know and be friendly with other merchants, since it is important to exchange information with them.

With job seekers, you should know whether you are in need of more employees, and if so, what kind and how many. You should be able to move quickly into an interview if warranted, have application forms readily at hand, and have all the information regarding wages, benefits, and schedules at your fingertips.

As for customers, you will find that some of them love to visit with you, or they wouldn't be there in the first place. In such cases, you must remember that there are other customers in the restaurant who deserve the same attention. Therefore, you should learn to move graciously from diner to diner—while conveying the impression that each of them is "the most important person in the house."

How to Get Better Control of Your Time: A Checklist

Preparing checklists that outline the tasks requiring your daily, weekly, and monthly attention will help you to make efficient use of your time. These lists should then be translated into a form of schedule for yourself. For example, the following is a checklist for duties that must be done each morning:

☐   Visit with chef and check availability of items needed for day's production.

☐ Review labor situation and identify any problem areas in preparation and service.

☐ Spot-check entire restaurant for sanitation and security.

☐ Review previous day's business. Check cashier's report and examine bank deposit slips.

☐ Open and peruse mail; take action as needed.

☐ Visit with cashier and/or bookkeeper, noting and correcting problems where necessary.

☐ Review dining-room service with hostess, and preview the day's menu.

☐ Inspect service staff with hostess, and assist her or him in briefing the staff on the day's menu.

☐ Supervise the taste test of preprepared foods appearing on luncheon menus.

☐ Prepare to greet guests and oversee the operation of the restaurant.

Undoubtedly, you will have other items that you will want to include on your own checklist. By scheduling what you can, you will be in a much better position to cope with emergencies and unusual events that cannot be planned for.

HOW SMART SALES PROMOTION PAYS OFF BIG

KEY IDEA: Although there is nothing like word-of-mouth advertising for this business, outside advertising and promotion are desirable and may be necessary in certain situations.

Your overall planning should also include a sales promotion plan to draw customers in for special occasions. Although cost control is extremely important in a restaurant, a sales program and the generation of revenue are even more important.

Some restaurants have been known to make the grade with little or no promotion, but those are the exception rather than the rule. Remember, the restaurant industry is highly competitive and consumers do have a wide choice of places in which to spend their food service dollars.

Promotion in your restaurant will be most effective if you plan far enough in advance to ensure a real "professional" effort. Too often promotions are the result of last-minute thought and, although they bring some increases in revenue, fail to realize their full potential.

Your best approach will be through the use of a planning calendar. This is not some special kind of calendar that you would get at the office supply store, or as a promotional piece from a vendor. Several different kinds of calendars will do, but the important point is the system, rather than the tool. It is a rather simple procedure that requires a minimal amount of research. The benefits will far outweigh the efforts if you put the entire program on a year-long schedule, and allow for sufficient lead time on each promotion for adequate planning and execution.

Before you begin construction of your forecast and budgets for the next year, put together a calendar of events that you want to promote during that year. Suppose, for example, that you want to run one special promotion per month. Procure a desk calendar that lets you see at least one full month at a time, and that has space for writing notes on it each day. Next, go through the coming year and decide on the kind of promotion you want for each month.

For instance, you might wish to promote Valentine's Day in February, and have some sort of Salute to the Newlyweds in June. Mark your calendar accordingly, and then go back at least six weeks from a particular promotion time and signal on the calendar a get-ready time. For example, if Valentine's Day, February 14, was your promotion day, you would indicate a signal at approximately January 1 to begin your preparation. Such a system will allow enough time for design of ads to play up the special occasion, and for the procurement of special props, foods, or whatever might be needed for the promotion. Later in this guide, you will find ideas to use on advertising and promotion, along with how to construct budgets for control of these expenses.

You will also want to establish some guidelines for how much you can afford to spend for each of these promotions during the year. The guidelines or budget for each will even go hand in hand with your planning calendar. Therefore, when you are thinking about a particular promotion and just how it is to be done, try to set some sort of limit on the total amount of money that you will spend for it. The expenses might include such items as cost of food and beverage, advertising, and promotional handouts. This kind of system is excellent for restaurants because this business lends itself so beautifully to promotions of all kinds.

THE GREAT "ATES"

Particip*ate*: Don't Over Deleg*ate*

If you can't be a "hands-on" owner, perhaps you ought to consider another line of work. As with most hospitality-related businesses, the owner plays a major role in setting the standard. A service business relies on the personality of the owner to make a statement to the consuming public. Because of the high degree of social interaction and the nature of competition for dining dollars, the aggressive participant will always have the upper hand. Take a moment and think about the businesses you like to patronize. More often than not you spend your money there because you know the owner or the manger, or you feel that you're simply served better there than at other places. This applies to dry cleaners, bakeries, bookstores, or wherever. The competition is so thick now that price and convenience are often not the most important factors in choosing a place to spend money.

The edge will always go to a business where personal service in evident. Throughout this chapter we have indicated the need to institute a mentality that increased sales means increased profit. There is no better return on investment than the return you realize by being a strong participant in your business.

Anticip*ate:* Stay Ahead of the Curve

Although it is never suggested that your business plan or meetings include the use of a Ouija board, there is great long-term benefit in anticipating trends and movements. This requires you to keep an eye on industry activity and to be a student of the industry in general. We have all seen individual as well as chain restaurants ultimately fail because they have missed opportunities to stay "current" with consumer demands. A once and great steak chain experienced incredible loss in market share, all the while blaming the reduced consumption of beef. Yet, at the same time, a budding steak chain offering a more vibrant atmosphere, more reasonably priced steaks, and more energetic service became one of the all-time restaurant success stories. What was the difference? The new concept simply anticipated consumer needs better. There really wasn't a dying market, there was merely a market dying for something new!

Here's a simple example of a way to anticipate the needs of your consumer. Although the percentage of the population becoming vegetarians is not increasing at dramatic rates, the number of consumers aware of the health benefits of eating better certainly has experienced great growth. How can you reach them? How about simply changing your vegetable offering from a butter-topped medley of overcooked (thus less nutrient rich) vegetables to a quick-grilled and lightly seasoned layer of zucchini, eggplant, and bell peppers. All you've done, without changing your core menu, is made your plates more attractive and more health conscious. The same goes or salads. The trend is toward a wider variety of greens and offerings of fat-free dressings as an alternative. Making salads more attractive and making fat-free dressings available is a win-win situation.

The goal is not to be so trendy that you change your entire personality. Instead, there is great benefit in reading publications, attending conferences and shows, and visiting other popular restaurants so that you keep your finger on what's hot and what's not. There's always a way to incorporate new ideas, presentations, or styles of cooking if you make it a priority! Don't become an ailing steak house, be fresh!

Innov*ate:* Be a Leader Not a Follower

Innovation applies to more than just your menu. Here's a great and current example. At the time of this writing, the restaurant industry is experiencing an incredible shortage of service personnel. The pool of talent for waiters and waitresses in most major cities is dwindling. The days of simply putting a sign up "now hiring" or running a newspaper ad for servers is long passed. Some operators in this pinch have even resorted to recruiting servers by guaranteeing a certain income for waiters and waitresses regardless of volume! Other operators have relaxed hiring standards to include inexperienced servers and then pumped more money into training programs. In essence, in order to compete, there is a nonstop need to look at your business in very innovative ways.

As consumers' time continues to be squeezed, some restaurants have chosen to dedicate sections of their dining room to "express" service, guaranteeing that consumers sitting in that section may dine in as little as thirty minutes or less. A host of successful steak houses paired cigars with steak eaters and developed a whole cottage industry of cigar bars that appealed to a very specific market. All of this occurred at a time when smoking was being banned in more and more restaurants and public places. The point to be made and considered is that innovation can pay great dividends in not only increasing your sales, but in running more effective day-to-day operations. Don't hesitate to innovate, and if it's not your strong suit, put someone who is an innovator close to you in your organization.

Celebr*ate*: Be Proud of Your Success

Ours is an industry of great energy, pace, and festivity. There is nothing more uncomfortable than a dull or boring dining room with little life. A restaurateur once said that he could tell the minute he walked into a restaurant if it had any "soul." There must be a sense of energy and celebration that exists in your restaurant for it to attract and keep a grip on your customers. Look around your dining room. Is your staff smiling, is there a spring to their steps, is there a sense of genuine enjoyment in the atmosphere?

This sense of celebration is powerful enough to keep your customers coming back and retain your invaluable employees. Participating, anticipating, innovating, and, perhaps most importantly, celebrating, is how you will find your own way to make a profit and survive in the restaurant business.

Chapter 2

How to Plan, Choose, and Design Menus to Bring in Bigger Dollars

Table of Contents

Chapter 2

How to Plan, Choose, and Design Menus to Bring in Bigger Dollars

At first glance, it would seem that anyone getting into the restaurant business would know that the menu is the heart of the operation. Choosing a style of cuisine or food is one of the most basic, and at the same time, the most critical decisions that is made. It is somewhat surprising, therefore, that so many people who choose to enter this wonderful industry spend so little time and energy on the one thing that will tell more to their guests than any other element of their operation.

This chapter presents many considerations and steps in formulating a menu as well as rules of thumb, and ideas for effective and eye-catching menus. It is important to understand that there is no scientific formula or guaranteed guideline by which to develop an effective menu. There are successful restaurants that present a rainbow of designs to their guests ranging from menus with as few as ten items to ones with as many as sixty or seventy. Some operations have no menu whatsoever and choose to verbally describe the items available for selection; still others choose to follow an ethnic theme and write menus using foreign languages. There are steak houses that roll carts to the table with the raw products on plates and have the service personnel describe the raw cuts of meat available, and there are buffet operations that invite guests to help themselves to what looks appetizing to them.

In essence, however, all restaurateurs must share a few very simple principles about how they choose to make their decisions. Although it is easy to allow oneself to get carried away with so many other decisions that need to be made when starting a restaurant, one must never forget that the primary reason that guests will choose between restaurants is the menu that is offered and the quality of food that is available. Most restaurants realize up to 75 percent of their sales from food, with many that come close to 100 percent, and keeping that in mind when designing a method by which to communicate that food to your guest is critical. Uniforms, decorations, tabletops, liquor variety, hours of operation, service style, and other decisions like those will get their due in this book. The reason that menus are discussed in Chapter Two, before all other considerations, is that choosing the menu items and determining how to communicate them to your guests is simply the biggest decision you will make.

WHY AND HOW THE MENU DECISION DRIVES THE RESTAURANT

In designing your menu, the decisions being made at this critical time will have a domino effect on all of the restaurant operations. All other decisions will be made in response to the type of items that are selected for inclusion on the menu. Additionally, this process begins to shape the statement that you are going to be making to each and every person that has cause to read the menu. Obviously, therefore, the better planning that goes into the menu choices and design, the better your chance of making the statement to your guests that you desire.

Public Perception Is Based on the Menu

As your guests review your menu, they will begin to form their opinion of the type of restaurant that you are trying to be. Your price ranges, your choices of meat and seafood items, the extent of your appetizer and entrée selections, the use of ethnic ingredients or flavorings, and the degree to which you choose to describe your menu items are but a few of the decisions you will have made that will become the guest's perception of your restaurant. All of these factors will shape opinions long before anyone ever tastes a bite of your food. Be sure to understand that the guests will notice the message that is being communicated to them simply by reading the menu, and often that message will dictate their degree of confidence in your operation.

Many restaurant owners choose to display their menus on menu boards or in weatherproof boxes outside of their restaurants. This further indicates the need to have the menu be a clear and well-presented form of communication to potential guests. Many a guest may choose not even to enter a restaurant based solely on the presentation of the menu alone. Reviewing your menu and having several friends or associates look at your menu before you finalize it is a very good idea; often their feedback will be a good indicator on how others will react.

Restaurant "Categories"

Typically, restaurants have been categorized in one of four categories over the years. These categories are full service, casual service, quick service, or take-out service (also referred to as home meal replacement). Although this may seem like an oversimplification, there is no doubt that decisions made in regard to menu items, prices, and service styles will almost certainly classify your restaurant in one of these categories. Full-service restaurants are generally regarded as those in which guests spend at least $15.00 or more per person; casual service is in the $8.00 to $15.00 range; quick service is anywhere from a few dollars to $8.00; and home meal replacement can range from a few dollars to as much as $12.00 to $15.00 in some of the more gourmet-style restaurants specializing in this area.

Because guests are very quick to recognize prices, they will almost certainly begin to assess the frequency by which they can afford to eat at your restaurant based solely on the prices on your menu. Although it is obvious that higher-priced or full-service restaurants may seem to be able to achieve a higher sales potential, they take the risk of reducing their market by setting prices too high. The pricing decision, therefore, becomes part of the philosophy by which you establish your menu. High-quality, full-service, and more expensive restaurants can be enormously successful in markets where there is a high density of high-income potential guests. Choosing a location for this style or category of restaurant becomes a very critical decision. Casual-service restaurants have achieved great success over the years by providing guests with an opportunity to spend less money because their menus are what is considered more "moderately" priced. The appeal is only consistent if the casual service restaurant can deliver a high quality of food as well. There are considerably more casual-service restaurants in business, and competition is fierce in this category; guests can frequent this style of restaurant more often because the prices allow it. But the fiercest competition and most crowded category of restaurant is the quick-service segment. Choosing this category is attractive because the prices of menu items of most quick-service restaurants allows almost anyone the opportunity to frequent this style of restaurant nearly every day, and sometimes even several times a day. The typical quick-service restaurant does not approach the sales potential of full- or casual-service restaurants because of the considerably lower check average, but quick service operators generally incur less total expenses to operate their businesses, thus making them an attractive option. Home meal replacement restaurants are growing in popularity because they have been able to be more flexible in meeting guests' needs. Spending as little or as much as guests want is the attraction of this category. In most cases, choosing this category means the elimination of wait service that is common in full- and casual-service restaurants, and concentrating on preparing and packaging items more suited to take out.

This discussion has been presented to help you think through the type of menu you choose because that menu will most certainly put you in a category. Knowing that price drives so many of the restaurant choice decisions made by consumers will help you plan a menu that you believe will help you be successful. The restaurant industry is no different than any other in that respect; price and quality drive spending habits.

Equipment and Kitchen Design

Although kitchens vary in size from a few hundred square feet to as much as a few thousand square feet, one factor is common to any size kitchen: the type of food called for on the menu will determine size and equipment needs. In addition, the style of cooking used for preparing the menu items will dictate the size and number of pieces of equipment. Generally, restaurants use the following methods of cooking:

- *Sauté:* Items are cooked on stovetops in pans. Stovetops can be either flat or have open burners. Menus with a heavy concentration of sauté items may require as many as ten to twelve burners. These ranges may or may not be accompanied with ovens.

- *Grill:* Usually some form of grid or grating over an open gas, wood, or charcoal fire. Grilled menu items are popular because they remind people of cooking outdoors, and foods cooked over fires add an extra flavor profile. Grills can be anywhere from a few feet long to as long as ten feet in some restaurants. A menu with an abundance of grilled items will cause more hood exhaust capabilities and will create a great deal of smoke and heat in a kitchen.

- *Fryer:* Items are immersed in vats of heated oils. Fried foods cook rapidly because of this intense immersion, and this is a method of cooking that is used for many types of meats, seafoods, and vegetables. Speed of cooking and popularity of this style of cooking make it a widely used method, though lately there has been scrutiny on the effect of fried foods on one's health. Fryers generally emit some oils into the air, and a large amount of fried items on the menu will cause a ventilation concern.

- *Bake/Roast:* Items are placed in large pans or trays and placed in ovens. Baking or roasting ovens are not unlike those many people have in their homes, only the ones used commercially are made of heavier-duty materials and have greater capacities. Large roasts, casseroles, breads, and items like whole hams or turkeys are roasted because of the size and density of the items. Baking allows for products with density to get heat over a longer period of time to cook them to the center. Almost all kitchens have a least a few ovens because this is an excellent way to cook bulk items.

- *Broilers/Flat Grills/Microwave Ovens/Cheese Melters/Steamers:* There are a variety of other pieces of equipment that can be used to cook or hold products in once they are cooked. Generally, however, these types of pieces are used in a supplementary capacity and can be fit into a kitchen plan without requiring large areas of space. Some can be mounted over other pieces of equipment; others can be placed on shelves below.

Once you have determined the items you would like to have on your menu, it is imperative that you then categorize the style of cooking that each menu item will require. Only after having done that will you begin to see the types and sizes of equipment that you will need. This can be done with or without a kitchen planning consultant or equipment dealer, but it must be done so that you can determine the cost needs and the spatial allocations. Most equipment dealers will gladly supply you with specifications for their equipment (also called "cut sheets") so that you can do some initial rough drawings of your own. Other kitchen considerations such as exhaust hoods, fire prevention systems, counter space, preparation area size, walk-in refrigeration square footage, and dishwasher systems will all be proportionately sized based on the needs dictated by the menu.

Level of Skill Required of Kitchen Labor

No matter what style of food a restaurant might serve and no matter what category of service it may choose, the execution of the menu will be in the hands of a kitchen staff of between six and sixteen people in most restaurants. The complexity of plate presentation, the sensitivity of the ingredients used in cooking, and the need to know the exact temperatures at which foods come together best are all factors the kitchen staff must know intimately to prepare foods at their best. Many foods and ingredients are very susceptible to overcooking and improper preparation techniques, for example, fresh fish will become rubbery and unappealing if cooked as little as a minute too long. Therefore, it is extremely important that the menu be developed with the understanding of how skilled the kitchen staff will have to be to prepare the foods correctly.

The availability of well-qualified and trained kitchen employees should be a strong consideration in the menu decision. Although there are numerous excellent cooking schools and training programs to teach cooking techniques, there is also great competition for skilled kitchen staff members. Strong urban and suburban areas compete for the best of these skilled cooks and chefs, and it is usually an expensive proposition to recruit and train a competent staff. The more delicate or complex the menu, the more difficult it can be to find the number of skilled staff to execute the menu. This does not mean that all menus should be simple and uncomplicated, rather that menus are only as good as the staffs' ability to produce those items as they are described. The guest has the right to expect the food to taste as good as it sounds on the menu. Supervising the kitchen area and making sure that the staff is capable of producing excellent food is a job that starts with the development of the menu.

Profits

To say that the restaurant will be open only as long as it is profitable is not a harsh thing to admit. This business, like all others, must operate with a goal of producing a profit from the sale of its food and beverages. The starting point for this profit goal is the selection of menu items and their subsequent selling prices. Typically, the restaurant business is similar to other businesses in that the selling price of items depends on three major factors: the perceived demand for the item, the raw cost of the products, and the competitive nature of the market. Because it is evident that consumers are well versed in the prices of food products, and because competition is keen for dining-out dollars, the price flexibility of menu items is not very high.

Most restaurants strive to achieve a food cost somewhere between 25 percent and 32 percent (e.g., something that sells for $1.00 should cost no more to produce in raw form than 25–32 cents). For years, the restaurant schools and programs teaching restaurant management have instructed students that the prime costs, food cost, and labor cost combined should not account for more than 50–60 cents out of every dollar taken in. Keeping food cost in the range of 30 percent will usually allow a restaurant to have a chance to keep the prime costs in the acceptable range.

Knowing the raw costs of all ingredients in each menu item allows you to know what each menu item costs to produce. By adding to that cost any "giveaway" items such as bread and butter, you can then simply multiply your total raw cost of each item by 3.3 to see what you would have to sell that item for to maintain a 30 percent cost for that item. As an example, if there was going to be a grilled chicken breast entrée on the menu, served with roasted potatoes and fresh vegetables, the cost of that plate might be $3.00. If there is a salad included with the meal and bread and butter, you might have to add another 75 cents. So the total cost of the meal to you is $3.75. To achieve a 30 percent cost on this menu item, you would multiply $3.75 times 3.3 to get a suggested menu price of about $12.40. The decision must then be made if this is a price you can charge for the plate. Please see the following examples of a few more menu items and how the pricing decision is made.

Profit can only be achieved if these types of steps are taken with each and every menu item, so you can see how important choosing your menu items is to your long-term profitability.

Best Restaurant Location

There is a saying in the restaurant business that the three most critical factors in the potential success of a restaurant are location, location, and location. And although we will not dispute the importance of choosing a great location, it is important to understand that in most cases, the location decision depends on the menu offered. Everyone probably knows one or two examples of restaurants that have defied logic and succeeded in out-of-the-way locations, but these examples are definitely the exception, not the rule. A great little French restaurant in a remote rural town might sound like a romantic endeavor to undertake but it probably is not the best business decision.

One of the best tests of how well a restaurant will succeed in a particular area is to take the time to do a restaurant survey of an area. Once you have chosen what type of food you want to serve, the price ranges of menu items, and the style in which you want to serve it, do some competitive homework. What are the demographics of the area you are looking at? What is the current mix of restaurants? Is there a strong day and evening market? These and other questions like them must all be asked when comparing your chosen menu to the market. For instance, let's say you have chosen to open a higher-priced Italian restaurant. The menu is complete with

Italian names for all the dishes and prices that range from $9.00 to $15.00. Immediately, you should be aware that your location may be restricted to high-density upper-income residential and white-collar office areas. The prices and the sophistication that you have chosen have narrowed your potential locations. Conversely, had you chosen an informal pizza and spaghetti–type Italian restaurant with moderate prices, you'd probably want to look in middle-income neighborhoods and blue- and gray-collar office areas.

Make no mistake about it, location will be the biggest factor in determining your success. You can help make success more probable by being sure to match your menu to that location.

Style of Service

As was discussed in the area of kitchen labor, the menu also dictates the degree of sophistication needed in the dining room. As the industry has evolved into a much more casual one, so has the standard of service. "Professional" servers, meticulously trained and graciously capable, are not as prevalent as they once were. Tableside food preparation and delicate service touches like chilled forks with salads have diminished over the years. As a result, the pool of potential service personnel is probably less skilled than it ever has been. This is not necessarily an awful thing, because it seems that consumers have, to some degree, accepted the new "casualness" that has come with dining in general and the pace of eating in particular. In many ways, "dining out" has been replaced with "eating out." Competent, friendly service is what most people expect and much of the formality has disappeared.

What this means to you as you design your menu is that you must keep in mind the level of service that people will expect once they read your menu. Higher-priced menus raise service expectations. Moderate prices mean that service will be expected to be courteous and prompt. Menus that feature unusual regional or ethnic items bring with them a greater need to have service personnel well versed in answering questions that are sure to arise from guests. It is totally unacceptable to put a very refined and innovative menu in front of a guest and then have that guest served by a person who doesn't know the difference between lemon grass and lemon peel. You will only be asking for trouble if your menu design is above the heads of the staff that you are going to be able to hire. Pay special attention to matching the sophistication of your menu to the labor pool available to you.

WHAT TO CONSIDER WHEN DESIGNING THE MENU

There is no "right" way or "wrong" way to design your menu. Simply go to ten or twelve of your favorite restaurants and observe the differences between menus. What works for some may not work for others. The most important thing that all good menus have in common is that they communicate the personality of the restaurant perfectly, allowing the guest to feel comfortable with his or her surroundings. Achieving that level of comfort does require you to do some planning and some experimenting with your design. Remember, this menu will set your guests' expectations in process long before they taste a morsel of your food. No matter how plain or fancy you may choose to be, your menu must communicate very clearly to your guests the type of dining or eating experience that they are about to have.

Menu Engineering

Menu engineering is another way of saying "careful menu planning." There are consultants and menu planning specialists who will break your menu down into very scientific pieces. Included in their analysis will be research on what style of print is easiest to read, how "shading" certain areas of the menu will attract attention to those areas, where to place the items you want to sell the most of, and how to best list your prices. Menu engineering is primarily used by larger corporations whose profitability can be seriously affected by employing these specialists. Even if you choose to call upon a menu engineering specialist at some point, the following guidelines are provided to help you enrich your own storehouse of knowledge for designing an intelligent and creative menu.

How to Determine the Number of Menu Items

As with so many of the decisions you will be making about your menu, choosing the number of items to put on your menu is not a scientific formula. Your success will not be determined so much by how many items you have, but in how well you execute the items that you have. Traditionally, menus in full-service or casual-service restaurants have at least three or four areas within their menus: appetizers, salads, entrées, and side dishes or desserts. If you choose to list these type of categories, then there must be enough choices in each category to give the guest the confidence that there was serious thought given to the items. Additionally, by offering at least four or five appetizers, for instance, you are giving the guest an opportunity to make a choice of items that may have varying appeal. Although there is no "right" or "wrong" number of items in any of these categories, it is safe to say that your entrée category should command the largest selection of items. It is assumed that although not everyone will order an appetizer or salad, each person at the table will order an entrée.

Some very successful independent restaurants and some popular chain restaurants have been able to execute menus with as many as eighty items. Conversely, some of the most popular chains at the time of this writing have succeeded using the method of simplicity, limiting the menu to no more than twenty or so items. Basically, your own philosophies on variety, execution of standards, perceived value, and the statement you want to make to your guests should determine the number of items you offer. A standard is not really applicable, but an average number of total menu items might be between thirty and forty. Use this as a starting point and add or subtract depending on what you believe you can succeed at executing.

Is the Size of the Menu Important?

At first glance, this may seem like a trick question. You might think that this is pretty much a "no-brainer." But you would be amazed at how many restaurants do not consider the actual physical size of their menu and, as a result, present their guests with a very cumbersome or difficult-to-handle menu. Remember to think of your guests sitting around a three-foot-square table, each holding a menu while trying not to knock over water glasses or inadvertently pushing their flatware onto the floor when they move their menu. No one likes to feel clumsy or uncomfortable in a dining room environment and you must be sure that you don't embarrass your guests by putting them in an awkward position with a large or heavy menu. Picture this scenario: a party of four seated at a standard-size table. The setting is lovely with service plate, gleaming flatware, water and wine glasses, ashtray, candle, condiments, etc., and along comes the captain with the menus. Each guest is now presented with a book of five pages, attractively encased in what seems to be leather-covered, 3/8-inch plywood. Each of theses documents is 18 inches high by 10 inches wide. Add to this scene a dimly lit dining room, and we now have the ultimate in discomfort. And as though this is not enough, this group has also been presented with a multipage wine list in an unwieldy cover. You should be able to produce a menu that doesn't take up so much room that it stifles conversation or creates "barriers" between people when they open the menu at the table. The best way to do this is to develop a menu proof with your printer and then sit down with the proof at a typical table. Have three friends join you at the table and then all of you open your menus at the same time. Be sure to set the table as it would be set for service and then analyze how comfortable you all are with the menu size. A little common sense goes a long way in this business, and this exercise could save you a lot of reprinting costs!

Presentation Medium

We have seen menus made out of bamboo, chalkboard, newspaper, leather, and even glass. We have held menus that were inscribed on butcher knives, wine bottles, and even on pounded copper. In short, if there ever was a material that could be written on, chances are that someone has created a menu on it. Creative expression is not limited to kitchens, it seems, in our industry. Making a statement, be it a subtle one like printing a menu on plain white card stock or as unique as etching a menu in glass, is a decision that only you can make. The only rule of thumb that applies is that the menu must be legible and not too difficult or dangerous for your most fragile guest to handle. Practicality might tend to dictate that the food presentation be your focus instead of letting an elaborate menu set the tone, but there are instances where choosing a more fun or creative menu might be called for. An example would be a restaurant at a seaside resort using a menu that incorporates shells somehow in its design, or a wine bistro presenting a wine bottle whose label is inscribed with the actual menu. Be as creative as you think you need to be to make your statement but do not overestimate the menu presentation and underestimate the food presentation. Your guests will remember your food far longer than they will your menu.

Number of Pages

Obviously, this decision is directly tied to the decision of how many items you choose to have on your menu. Although we would never suggest that you produce a twelve-page menu that is put together with a spiral bind, one of the most successful restaurant chains of the '90s did just that. Sometimes defying logic can be very rewarding and, although it may a risky decision, high risk can yield high reward. In general, however, you should remember that guests are not in your restaurant to read, they are there to eat. Providing them an opportunity to do just that should keep you on a simple track. There is an unwritten rule in our industry that says if you make the guests' experience too difficult, they may not tell you verbally but they probably won't be back. Communicate your menu offerings in as little space as possible, remembering that your servers can provide additional information about menu items, and having your servers "enhance" your menu conversationally is a much more effective tool in the long run. Also, if you've done a good job at building repeat business, many of your guests will not even need a menu after they become regulars.

How to Prepare a Well-Written Menu

The menu should speak to the guests. It should be your "voice" in inviting the reader to sample the taste delights that flow smoothly from your kitchen to table. Your menu should reflect all the good qualities sought by your patrons.

Your menus should always be clean and fresh in appearance. And they should be discarded when they become spotted, torn, or just plain tired. Dirty, unkempt menus, no matter how well written, suggest poor sanitation and overall inefficient operations.

Although adjectives and descriptive phrases are useful, they can be greatly overdone. Take a look at these two examples:

A. Broiled Prime New York Sirloin Steak, 12 oz. ....$_____

B. A tender mouth-watering 12 oz. Prime New York Sirloin, broiled
to perfection as you like it, 12 ounces of beefeater's delight ....$_____

They both offer the same thing. But all the extra verbiage in "B" is probably wasted. No restaurant has to describe further a 12 oz. Prime New York Sirloin. And there is certainly no need to repeat "12 ounces." Further, any discriminating diner buying a prime steak these days assumes that your broiler cook knows how to prepare it. Telling too much, in fact, might even detract by "hiding" the name of the offering in the middle of the description. As far as we are concerned, if we order an item of that caliber and it is not "as I like it," someone is going to hear about it. We believe most patrons feel that way.

However, this is not to say that we are against the use of certain descriptive adjectives on menus. On the contrary, they are necessary to the art of culinary showmanship. Well-written menus will have a mouth-watering and appetizing appeal to your guests, and will be a major contributor to total sales in your restaurant. But there are many successful restaurants that offer menus with little or no description at all. One example is a popular and famous restaurant in Rockport, Texas. The following are excerpts from that menu:

red fish almondine

broiled rib-eye of beef

beef wellington (for two)

baked potato

onion soup à la Française

In some instances, you might want to elaborate on items that have become house specialties or are unique to your menu by writing something like "we use only prime beef" or "a family recipe favorite for thirty years," but you should be careful to not oversell.

Another reason why you should watch how specific you get on your menu descriptions is that most states now have in place "truth in menu" regulations. If you are going to tell people, for instance, that your salmon is "only from the fresh waters of Glacier Bay, Alaska," then you had better be able to prove it. Saying "prime beef" means you use no grade other than prime. And the popular "free-range chicken" had better not be from anywhere U.S.A. Several restaurateurs have paid fines for getting overzealous in their menu descriptions without being able to back up their claims. A suggestion is to put your menu in the hands of several friends before you put it in the hands of your guests. Then simply ask them for their feedback; chances are their opinions will be representative of your typical guests. Sometimes less is more.

Selecting Type Styles, Print Sizes, and Color

One of your most important relationships during the process of designing your menu will be the one you establish with your printer. We steadfastly recommend that you call upon their expertise when it comes to things that will and will not work. Generally, your printer should have had some experience in printing menus and, at the very least, they should be able to advise you on legible typestyles and point sizes for letters. Be sure to take samples of other menus that you like to your printer and be prepared to run as many proofs as necessary until you are satisfied. Some other tips include reading your proof in dim light, giving a proof to an elderly friend to review or someone with poorer vision, spill a little water on the proof to see how a stain might affect the legibility, try different colors of background to see how the print stands out, use a bold print to distinguish menu items from their descriptions, and if you are going to laminate the menu, test the laminate in bright light to see how much glare it produces. All in all, common sense should be your guide in this process.

The matter of choosing colors for a menu is also an important area in which expert advice can be beneficial. Blending colors that are pleasing to the eye, enhance the food, and complement your restaurant is a job for someone who is artistic—and who also understands the hard world of retailing. There have been many studies done by various research groups on the impact of color and color combinations as related to sales. Some of these studies relate to packaging of foods, laundry items, and other products that are found on the shelves in supermarkets. Studies show that certain colors appeal most to men, whereas others have greater appeal for women.

Other studies indicate that many people can't read without glasses, and that some of these folks don't wear glasses in public. Consequently, some people can't read labels. Therefore, manufacturers identify their products with arrows or other easily identifiable marking. (This is another idea you can incorporate in your menu.) If you are interested in finding out more about these studies, you can usually obtain additional information from the psychology and business departments of your local college or university. Your city library is another fine source for information of this kind.

USING MENU SUPPORT MATERIALS TO SUCCESSFULLY EXECUTE YOUR MENU DAY IN AND DAY OUT

Once you have finalized your menu design and you are confident that you have a menu that you and your staff can execute, it is time to provide your staff with the support materials. This section presents the materials you should make available within your restaurant to make sure that the food presentation lives up to the promises made to your guests in the menu. Perhaps the second most critical reason that restaurants fail (after poor location) is that the kitchen does not deliver the food quality so eloquently stated and promised on the menu. Support materials and exceptional training are your best tools to keep this from happening.

Using Standardized Recipes for Quality Tracking

A standardized recipe for each item, salad dressing, dessert, sauce, side dish, or any other in-house prepared item will be your first step in the process of ensuring food quality. For our purposes here, we presume that the recipes you have chosen for your menu items are excellent recipes. A standardized recipe simply lists all the ingredients and their amounts for your cooks to use in replicating the item. Once you have tested all the recipes and have written them in this format, all recipes should be laminated and compiled in a folder or binder for easy reference. This seems like such a logical idea, yet many restaurants try to operate using a chef or cook's memory to reproduce items. There is nothing to lose, however, and everything to gain by backing up all your prepared items with recipes.

Another great reason for having a standardized recipe binder in the kitchen is that you must anticipate some turnover in your cook staff. For whatever reasons, cooks will go on to other jobs and they must be replaced. By having a recipe file available, your training process will be much more efficient and your new staff will have better success executing the menu to your expectations. Be sure to group your recipes by category and separate them in the files by usage (e.g., sauces together, desserts, chicken dishes, etc.). Also, it is a good idea to have several "batch" amounts for recipes that you will use in varying quantities. For example, if you have a recipe for roasted garlic mashed potatoes, you should provide recipes for preparing batch sizes from three to six gallons. That way, you or your chef can direct your staff depending on the volume of business anticipated. Not all recipes are the same when simply multiplied and you should never assume that your staff knows how to interpret a phrase like "recipe times three." It is safer and more user-friendly to list the graduated amounts for different batch sizes.

Pricing Your Menu for Maximum Sales Volume or Lowest Cost

It would be almost impossible to overemphasize how important this part of your work is to your restaurant profitability. You must determine the plate cost of every item that you sell. This sounds like a simple job, but it can be tedious and time consuming. Although different forms can be used for this all-important function, they all do basically the same thing.

Figure 2.1 is an example of one way you can determine the cost of a menu item.

The next step is to evaluate the entire menu as to the cost of the sales target. As stated earlier, you should determine a food cost goal of between 28 percent and 33 percent. Not all items will fall within that range, but remember, you are trying to achieve a balance that lands you in that range. Typically, items such as soups and salads will have lower food costs, and items like steak and shellfish will have higher food costs. The key is to price your items so that the final mix will achieve your food cost goal. And for your menu to contain enough lower-cost items (pasta, chicken, and casseroles) to offset the higher-cost items (shrimp, tenderloin of beef, red snapper). You can only anticipate what the sales mix of the items will be and you must be careful to be realistic on what will sell the most. This is one reason that many restaurant owners change their menus at least once a year after they have enough information and feedback to see how well they have anticipated their menu mix. You are never "locked into" a menu if you've miscalculated, but you must be careful to intelligently anticipate changes in your cost of goods and your menu mix. Customers have a way of knowing what is reasonable and unreasonable because competition is keen; never underestimate their ability to remember your prices.

You will see all types of pricing strategies on menus. Some restaurateurs like to round off all their prices to end in .95 or .99; others are content to have prices covering all odd cent ranges. For simplicity, you should use a rounded-up price once you have costed out all your menu items. For instance, let's say that you have a plate cost of $2.84 for a honey-roasted half chicken, including all side items and "free" bread and butter. If you are trying to achieve a 30 percent cost percentage, you simply multiply the $2.84 by 3.3, or a selling price of $9.37. That becomes the minimum price you might charge. Depending on what you think the market will bear, you might round up to $9.50 or $9.75. If your competitors have items on their menus that are similar

Figure 2.1

Name of Menu Item			*Honey Roasted Chicken*	
Ingredients	Unit Measure	Unit Price	For One Serving Portion Sold	Portion Cost
1/2 Chicken	one	1.25	1	1.25
Honey Glaze	2 oz.	.10/oz.	1	.20
Vegetables–Grilled	4 oz.	.15/oz.		.60
Garlic Roast Potatoes	4 oz.	.10/oz		.40
Spices	1 oz.	.15/oz.		.15
Garnish	one	.25	1	.25
Place Setting				
Other				
			Subtotal	2.85
			Plate Cost	2.85
			Selling Price	9.75
		Plate Cost / Selling Price =	Plate Cost %	29.2%

to dishes like honey-roasted chicken, then you must be tuned in to what your competition charges. The most important point to remember is that you must always start with a multiple that keeps your food cost in your targeted range. Try not to sell items for less than the multiple unless you have a number of items that sell above the multiple.

Photographing Presentations

With all the technology that is available to us today, it would be negligent for you not to record, pictorially, the proper plate presentations. Many of the successful chain restaurant companies actually record their menu items on discs and then send out those discs to all restaurants. All menu items are prepared in a test kitchen and then digitally photographed when the chef is 100 percent satisfied with the look of the finished plate. Once in the individual stores, these discs allow cooks to reproduce the photographs so that the entire kitchen staff can observe the proper plate presentations.

There is no reason why you can't take advantage of that same technology. As you hire new staff members or while you are training your staff prior to opening, these photographs become the standard for all menu item presentations. It becomes crystal clear to all kitchen staff what your level of expectation is and leaves very little room open to individual interpretation. If we agree that consistency and quality are the two most essential goals within your kitchen, then support materials in the way of photographs reinforce those goals to everyone. Keep a complete binder of photographs in your office and in the kitchen, and keep it updated as you change your menu. Even though there is a certain degree of interpretation that you allow for all recipes, once you have established the "perfect" plate, you really do not want your staff to deviate from that expectation.

Using Video as a Tool

Another technological advance that you should consider using is videotaping your chef or kitchen manager preparing the more delicate or elaborate menu items. This tool is available at a very reasonable price, you can videotape it yourself, and it provides an excellent training tool for your staff. Many recipes require that your staff not only be able to read the ingredients, but know how those ingredients are mixed. By allowing your chef to be taped showing various methodologies for combining ingredients or handling delicate items, you are providing your staff with valuable information for success. New staff members view the videotape as part of their training, accomplishing a variety of goals from getting to hear your chef talk about food to becoming familiar with your menu even before setting foot in your kitchen. Remember that your reputation, and your success, is in the hands of every cook in your kitchen. What level of performance do you want them to achieve? And what are you prepared to do to ensure that performance? These are fair questions you should ask yourself when considering options like this.

Training Booklets for Cooks and Servers

Although providing each and every staff member with the proper training materials takes considerable time and effort, it will bring you the best dividends on your investment in this business. Composing brief booklets for your cooking and service staff is an excellent idea that promotes consistency and quality. Using photographs of plate presentations, while emphasizing the importance of consistent presentation, gives your entire staff a standard to match. The cost of such graphic material may come to as much as $25 per staff member, but this is a small price to pay for product consistency, the number one priority in your restaurant. Even the cost of color copies of all menu items is worth the investment if all staff members are able to recognize and produce "perfect" food. This is not a tool available only to the chain restaurants, and you should seriously consider making this kind of investment in your employees.

Product Mix Reports, What's Hot And What's Not

Let's assume that you have followed all the steps previously listed and that your operation is up and running. Intuition will tell you what menu items are successful and what menu items are not. But that information alone is not all you should rely on when attempting to revise your menu. It is important to accept the fact that not all menu items can or will be popular with your guests. Inevitably, you will have a handful of items that are wildly popular for reasons that may vary from price to uniqueness. And you will also have a handful of items that are not popular at all for perhaps the same reasons. Collecting this information on item sales is a simple process of using your cash register or point-of-sale device to help you develop a product mix report. Be sure that when you purchase or lease your system that your installer or salesperson trains you on how to retrieve all of the reports that are part of the system. The product mix report will tell you exactly how many of each menu item you sold in a given period, from an hourly report to a daily and weekly report. Generally, a two- to three-week period is an acceptable span of time from which to draw some conclusions. This does not mean that you are going to change menus every two to three weeks, only that you are committing to analyzing your sales periodically.

In addition to the black-and-white facts produced by such reports, you must also consider other factors. Often you may choose to keep certain sluggish-selling items on the menu because you believe them to be some of your most creative items. One company that we know kept an item on every menu change they made even though it regularly proved to be a mildly popular item. They stuck with that item because they knew that no other restaurant had attempted to sell that particular item. In a sense, they used that menu item to make a statement to the chefs and guests; they were going to serve dishes that they knew were unique (and it was an excellent dish) so as to create a space between themselves and their competitors. It mattered more to them that they dared to be different than that the dish was wildly popular. Of course, they made sure the majority of the menu provided more popular items, but they stuck by their belief that not all menu items could or would appeal to the masses.

Another reason to keep slower-selling items on a menu is because they may serve to provide better variety or choice to your guests. You may know that grilled jumbo sea scallops have a limited market appeal, but you also know that those guests who enjoy sea scallops will always appreciate how perfectly you grill them. Another consideration is your menu price variation. There may be an item or two that helps keep your costs in balance. If you have a popular steak item that runs a high food cost, then keeping that less popular pasta pomodoro on the menu will help offset the higher-cost steak. All in all, keep a healthy balance of reasons why you change your menu items in the same proportion as you determine what those menu items are in the first place. Variety is not only the spice of life, but also one of the essential elements in helping create a successful business.

HOW TO COMMUNICATE YOUR MENU TO YOUR STAFF AND BUILD CONSUMER LOYALTY

It is often said of the automobile industry that, essentially, all car companies are very similar. What separates them is the methods by which they choose to communicate their brands and the degree of success their sales staff has in building consumer loyalty. In some ways, the same can be said of the restaurant industry. Most restaurant owners buy from similar vendors, have the same pool of workers from which to hire, pay close to the same for food products, and have menu items that include the basics of chicken, steaks, seafood, salads, and a variety of other dishes. Perhaps the single most critical variable, then, becomes the way you choose to communicate your menu to your guests, and then, through your staff, build consumer loyalty.

Your Menu Philosophy Drives Training

Your menu has been formulated using countless hours of planning and preparation. You have proofed it no less than five times to be sure you haven't made any silly mistakes, recipes have been tested and retested, plate presentations are as perfect as can be imagined, and your heart and soul are now part of a menu that will drive your business. The staff that you have chosen to help you make this a successful business must somehow be aware of how important this menu is to you. If you fail to make them aware of this fact then you have done a lot of planning for nothing.

Our industry, fortunately, is one that allows great creative expression. At this time in your business development it is imperative that you impart that creativity to your staff and have them know how much time and effort went into your menu. Sharing the philosophies that you used in creating your menu allows your staff to know how much you care and how deeply you believe in your menu.

You must first get your staff to understand what it is you are trying to accomplish, before beginning their technical training. Spend time with your staffs, both kitchen and service, and you will reap dividends. Your first training session should include no less than one to two hours of menu discussion, longer if necessary. Explain why you chose the dishes you have on the menu, whom you used for inspiration, and any little stories behind the menu items that you want to share. This truly is the beauty of our industry; food is a lifestyle and a nourishment in more ways than one. Give your staff a reason to have pride in what they are serving and share with them, so they can go out and share with your guests the things that make you special, the things that will build guest loyalty.

How to Build Consensus within the Sales Staff

Perhaps the simplest way to build consensus with your service staff is to be sure that each and every one of them has tasted all of your dishes. This is a commitment that you should make in the training of all your staff. Have you ever been to a restaurant where you asked your server how good a particular menu item was and the reply was "I don't know because I've never tasted it?" There is nothing more unprofessional than having a sales staff not know what they are selling. No industry misses this essential point more than the restaurant industry. Conversely, nothing is more impressive, and at the same time more confidence building, than to have a server take a full minute to describe a menu item in great detail. And as you must know from being a guest in other restaurants, this knowledge is essential when spending your expendable income.

Another way to build consensus is to have regular staff meetings and solicit feedback from the staff. Ask specific questions about menu items. If you are puzzled at why something isn't selling well, it is guaranteed your staff will tell why the item is not selling. Your service staff, in particular, will hear more feedback in one night from guests than you might hear in a month. They are a smart group and will recommend to your guests only the items they know the guests will like because their gratuity will be based on their service *and* how well the guests enjoyed their meal. If certain items are inconsistent or are too difficult to sell because of the time it takes to cook, unusual flavor profiles, or they are not perceived as having value, your staff will give you that feedback.

Upholding Menu Standards

The best form of controls were as true years ago as they are today. The three best controls are as follows: first, hire the best person for the job, second, train those people as best you can, and, third, be a great supervisor. Those principles apply well in this menu discussion. Let's say that you have developed a great menu by really testing recipes and coming up with only the best recipes you could develop or find. Next, you have trained all of your staff in the proper way to execute and serve all the menu items. The last, or third, step in the process is to take the time necessary to supervise your staff in their work functions. Failing in this last step would put your business at great risk. As good as your recipes are, as wonderful as your people may be, you must personally take responsibility for ensuring that menu standards are upheld.

Success is mostly dependent on how well the menu is executed. You must take responsibility for supervising food production, final plate presentation, and occasional tastings during the shifts. This does not mean that you must plant yourself in your kitchen, but it does mean that you should know your kitchen inside and out and believe that it is the heart and soul of your operation. Enjoy your guests, mingle and socialize, entertain and converse, but never let your kitchen be merely a place you pass through on your way to the office.

Setting Your Servers Up for Success

Here are suggestions on how to equip your service staff with tools for executing the menu:

1. Give them a discount on purchasing menu items and set hours in which they may order food from the kitchen. The more they eat your food, the better they will know it. Place limits on "special orders"; a stipulation should be that the items must be ordered as they appear on the menu.

2. Make up a short menu test and revise the test when you change menus. Each server must pass the test with a minimum score that you determine to keep his or her schedule.

3. Make the menu picture book a part of all new servers training. Seeing the food will help them in their efforts to learn it better. In addition, no new server should be allowed to work shifts in the dining room without having spent at least three shifts in the kitchen observing final plate presentations. Most restaurants have an expediter or food runner position, and that is a great way to become familiar with the food.

4. Be sure that you don't overload servers with large or oversize stations. This is a mistake many operators make, and it forces servers to cut their service short and not spend the time needed with your guests. Depending on the type of menu you have and the service philosophy you employ, there should be no need for a server to be given more than four to six tables to serve. Experienced servers and some restaurant managers may overload you with reasons that servers can handle larger stations, but experience shows that the guest is the one who suffers when servers take on too large a station.

HOW THE PURCHASING/RECEIVING/STORING CYCLE AFFECTS MENU SUCCESS

Control aspects of food cost will be addressed in Chapters Four and Eight. Because the decision as to what items to include in the menu affects your ability to control costs in the long term, the following guidelines are provided to help keep costs that affect the menu in line:

1. Try not to use too many food items on your menu that are difficult to procure. Although it may be unique to offer some unusual items such as white truffle oil, their availability and supply may cause you headaches, making it difficult to execute your menu. By all means be creative, but try to limit those types of items.

2. Purchase from vendors who have good reputations for service. Generally, by asking around you will get great feedback on who can keep you well supplied. Show your menu to prospective vendors and be sure that they can keep up with your needs.

3. Try as much as possible to "cross use" as many items as possible. In almost all restaurants, except for perhaps the most exclusive ones, menus should not be full of items that are not used in several dishes. For example, it may sound like a great idea to serve a salad with slices of cranberry glazed duck breast, but if that is the only item on the menu using duck, you will probably have a hard time keeping your quality at a high level because you may not serve a lot of duck. The same can be said of some more common items like shellfish, which typically have a short "shelf life." Sautéed bay scallops may sound great, but if they are not popular sellers then you may find yourself throwing away mose than you care to believe. It is a good idea to use these types of items as specials, serving them only on occasions when you believe they will be popular sellers.

Don't strap yourself with items that are difficult to project sales volumes of. Go with known winners.

4. Remember your storage area capacities when designing your menu. If you plan, for instance, to serve a lot of fresh seafood, be aware that you may need a separate walk-in refrigerator for fresh fish. Your kitchen equipment specialist or designer can tell you what foods should not be stored together (dairy and seafood are a bad mix) and you should be sure not to put your chef in a bad position by making it difficult to organize storage space. In addition, health departments are generally very stringent on how adequate and properly controlled storage areas are, so plan your storage spaces when planning your menu.

5. Be aware of what food items have seasonal fluctuations that affect their quality. This is especially important when you are matching words on your menu that are specific like "fresh" or "Gulf lump crab." If you are in an area that cannot get excellent fresh corn year round, then it's probably not a good idea to list on the menu something like "fresh grilled sweet corn" if you might be forced to use a frozen or inferior fresh product. Remember, your guests have a right to expect the menu items that you describe to be just the way you list them; if you can't do that all the time it's a good idea to reconsider some of your choices. Many vendors will tell you they will have no problem supplying you with all of your needs, but you must do your own homework to be sure.

6. As you finalize your menu and test your recipes, be sure to separate items into categories to make sure you have a good variety of foods. It is amazing how this simple task will help you identify if you have "overlooked" or "over-booked" certain items. You might be surprised to find that you have used chicken in a total of twelve dishes, using everything from whole roasters to boneless breasts. Perhaps there is a way to consolidate or purchase chicken in ways that will make your buying more effective or cost-friendly. Maybe all of your vegetables are of the green variety and you've neglected to add more color by using items like yellow bell peppers or purple eggplant. Food is as much a visual experience as it is a culinary one, and this exercise will help you round out your menu.

7. "Shelf life," mentioned earlier, bears further elaboration. Be aware how long certain items will keep their fresh appearance, texture, and flavors when designing your menu. Delicate items have a place on your menu and you can't avoid them altogether, but be careful not to overload yourself with items that turn bad in short periods of time. It is a fact of life that your staff may not "rotate" the food items in your refrigerator properly and the more delicate the food, the more likely you may have rotation problems. This is especially important because many times delicate foods such as fresh clams and lamb are more expensive to purchase.

HOW "SPECIAL MENUS" CAN BRING IN EXTRA $$

Special menus can mean extra sales by satisfying certain groups of people's needs. Adding special menus to your operation can be adding dimensions to your market. Actually, almost all restaurants already offer some form of special menus. In some instances, you may incorporate some of the ideas that follow on your regular menu; others may require you to print separate menus.

"Heart-Healthy" Descriptions

As little as ten years ago, "heart healthy" menus were unheard of in our business. It was thought to be something that only hospitals needed to do, and no one wanted to be associated with hospital food! But in the present era of a growing vegetarian population, cholesterol counting, fitness awareness, and countless television programs that remind us to watch our saturated fat intake, ignoring the need to be more health conscious could be disastrous. Although some restaurants may choose to dedicate either their whole menu or a large part of it to providing only heart-healthy foods, we are not yet surrounded by a society clamoring for more health-conscious foods. *Balance* is a word that you should keep in mind when assessing your overall menu selection. It is not just vegetarians who look for lighter entrées without meat protein, it is also a wide variety of people who simply think it's smart to limit their intake of meats. Additionally, as consumers become more aware of the wide variety of foods available in supermarkets and at your competitors' establishments, mixing in lighter meals on your menu is wise.

Designating these lighter meals can take many forms. Some restaurants choose to set aside a special section of their menu and list that category as "Lighter Meals"; others may simply add a heart symbol in the margin to highlight the lower-fat items. You may even see some restaurants actually list not only the calories for a particular dish, but also a breakdown of the calories from fat. Several large chain restaurants also experiment with categories that are listed with catchy names like "Guiltless Grill." The extent you may choose to use these types of designations really depends on the type of restaurant you want to be. A vast majority of restaurants do not choose to make this an issue on their menus; it is advised that you thoroughly survey your market before deciding what course to take. This type of attention can only become more acute as time goes on and your awareness can put you in a position to broaden your customer base.

Children's Menus

This is another area that has changed dramatically over the last ten years or so. In the past, children either ate off their parents' plates or they ordered smaller portions of items on the regular menu. The whole attitude of full-service restaurants changed when the fast-food restaurants started to appeal to families with children by offering meals that kids desired at sizes and prices that made it easier for parents to justify. In addition, these fast-food feeders offered playgrounds, cartoon characters, coloring books, and all sorts of little goodies to keep kids entertained. Happy, preoccupied kids helped making this choice an easy one for parents. Slowly, full-service restaurants saw the need to appeal to children, and children's menus became commonplace.

A typical children's menu might offer from four to six items, mostly simple and popular foods that kids like to eat, with price ranges from $2.95 to $4.95. The menus are often presented with games, crayons, and other "participation" type ploys that keep the kids occupied. Depending on the style of restaurant you are planning, you can survey restaurants in your local area to see what they are doing and then choose to do something similar. The percentage of meals that you will serve to children will probably be quite small, so this is not an area that you need to spend a great deal of time on, simply one you want to include in a competitive way.

Holiday and Special Occasion Menus

There will be several opportunities throughout the year for you to present a special menu to your guests. Here is a list of some of the days you may want to consider:

1. New Year's Eve

2. Valentine's Day

3. Easter Sunday

4. Mother's Day

5. Father's Day

6. Thanksgiving Day (if you choose to be open)

7. Christmas Eve and Christmas Day (if you choose to be open).

Although this is a choice that is purely personal, it is a good idea to be aware that many restaurants look forward to these days to offer their regular guests a little something different and more special. Some restaurant chains choose to offer only their regular menu regardless of the day, while others (especially ethnic restaurants) take full advantage of promoting holidays that pertain to their nationality. Traditional New Orleans style restaurants, or Cajun style, take full advantage of celebrating Mardi Gras week, for instance, in the same way that Mexican restaurants may celebrate Cinco de Mayo. At the very least, you should consult your chef or kitchen manager and plan ahead for special occasions so that you don't scramble around at the last minute trying to decide what to do. And while your guests may appreciate the different menus, be careful not to try to take advantage of their "holiday spirit" by charging prices that are not in line with your regular menus.

FOUR THINGS YOU CAN DO TO ANTICIPATE HOLIDAY BUSINESS AND VOLUME CHANGES

When business volume changes by as little as 10 to fifteen percent, it can cause major upheavals in business. Subconsciously, your employees have fallen into a kind of routine and without you there to manage volume swings, your business can be negatively impacted. Most of the time you sit back and pray for more business and the last thing you want to do is to be caught unprepared. Consider the following ideas to keep you ahead of the curve:

☐ 1. At the beginning of each month, produce a calendar that depicts the holidays in that month. On the day the holiday falls, pencil in the sales you achieved the previous year on that day, including the number of guests you served. Be sure to note what day of the week the previous year's holiday fell on so that you don't miscalculate. There is a substantial difference in your preparation for a Valentine's Day that falls on a Tuesday than there is when it falls on a Saturday. All managers and chefs should receive a calendar or there should be one posted for everyone to view.

☐ 2. Create a "holiday checklist" that steps you through the different preparations you take to handle the holiday. Perhaps you see linens on your tables for Mother's Day when you normally don't, be sure to give yourself plenty of time to order them. Special menus take a while to create and print, staffing levels must be adjusted, and all of your vendors will be very busy, take the time to write a complete list that you can monitor as the holiday approaches.

☐ 3. Be specific with your delegating of special projects and develop a follow-up system so that there are no surprises. You cannot do everything yourself so your assignments must be clear and direct. Hold a manager meeting at least a week before the holiday to review responsibilities and be sure that you are available to help.

☐ 4. Don't forget that the day before the holiday is an important day of business to the guests who frequent your business on that day. We have seen far too many examples of "looking ahead" and losing sight of the guests that are spending their money while you and your staff are busy running around to get ready for the "big day." It is a great idea to have pre-shift meetings on the days leading up the holiday to remind your staff to take care of the business at hand. Please don't be putting up decorations while someone is in your dining room trying to enjoy his or her meal, don't laugh, we've actually seen this being done!

Catering Menus

Catering menus come into play at the same time you are developing your regular menus. Some restaurants have realized as much as 20 percent additional sales volumes by emphasizing catering, and you should not take this area lightly. Although companies may view catering offerings differently, depending on the perceived market for catering events, it would be a good idea if you selected several items from your regular menu that you think can be produced in larger volume amounts, and begin to formulate a menu or menus that you can present to prospective clients. To compete in this arena, your menus should look like you have taken the necessary time and considerations into account to be viewed as a serious alternative.

In this section, you will find several examples demonstrating effective elements of a catering menu along with basic catering aspects for you to consider.

1. *You Need to Determine What Your Market Will Be.* Will you cater for social events such as weddings, christenings, family reunions, and private parties? Or will you see corporate customers who will need catering for special events such as office parties, seminars, business luncheons, and so on? Some caterers specialize in large-scale events such as convention banquets, benefits, and other large-scale, sit-down or buffet-type lunches or dinners.

2. *You Need to Determine How Profitable Catering Will Be for You.* (Not only is there competition from other restaurants, but from catering businesses as well.) How is the catering portion of your restaurant business controlled from portal to portal? How much and what kind of equipment is needed? What kind of liability? Is insurance necessary? How much and what kind of coverage should you have?

Personnel

There must be adequate and competent supervision at all off-site events to provide the service expected by the client. The staff must be dressed in a neat and appropriate manner and they must handle themselves as professionals. They should understand that they are not just performing a catering function but are also representing a restaurant that is dependent on customer attraction and retention.

Food and Beverage

There should always be some sort of agreement between client and restaurant as to the quality and quantity of food and beverage to be served. This agreement may or may not be in writing, but a written contract is the most businesslike way to proceed. Unfortunately, some businesses do not exercise the kind of administrative effort that is necessary and neglect to reduce understanding between the parties to writing. Such a practice can result in disagreement and lead to loss of profit. Professional and successful caterers use contracts that spell out any and all arrangements between client and caterer.

The following "Proposal" lists items to be included in a signed agreement with a client. This material was developed by Melange Catering and is reprinted here with the permission of Linda West, owner.

PROPOSAL
all proposals based on xxxx guests

FOOD: @

BEVERAGE:

> *Premium Liquors, House Wines, Domestic Beer, Soft Drinks, and Sparkling Water @ $10.50 per guest . . .*

> *Well Liquors, House Wines, Domestic Beer, Soft Drinks, and Sparkling Water @ $8.50 per guest . . .*

> *House Wine, Domestic Beer, Soft Drinks, and Sparkling Water @ $6.00 per guest . . .*

STAFF:

> *Amount listed is inclusive of all staff charges for event lasting from xxxx to xxxx, including delivery, set-up and breakdown of event and return to Melange warehouse. Overtime is charged at $20.00 per hour per staff member for an event running past xxxx.*

RENTALS:

FLORAL/DECORATIONS:

VALET:

ENTERTAINMENT:

MANAGEMENT FEE:

> *Subtotal*
> *Tax*
> *Total*
> *Deposit Due*

Final total dependent on selections chosen.
All sales subject to 8.25% sales tax.
50% deposit necessary to book event date.

Please read and sign a copy of the attached policies. Please fax or mail them, along with your deposit, to our office to ensure booking of this event.

Figure 2.2A is the agreement used by Melange Catering. It includes a cover letter, a proposal based on a specified number of guests, a suggested menu, and a policy statement constituting the official "contract" with the client.

Equipment

It is important to have neat, clean, and good-looking equipment. How your food and beverages look to the client and their guests will have a direct bearing on how it is received. Good well served will always taste better than when it is not. The appearance of the equipment will also reflect on how your restaurant is perceived. You must be careful with the security of your equipment. It is easy to "lose" equipment when it is taken off the premises. Major caterers have specially designed bays where equipment is temporarily stored while waiting for transport to a function. Everything is inventoried and inspected before being sent out of the restaurant. Copies of the inventory should accompany the food, beverage, and equipment to the function. It is the responsibility of the supervisor for the function to see to the return of all items on inventory. Your restaurant may own or lease equipment for the catering service. If you lease it, you must have a clear understanding with your client if the charges for leasing are included or are add on-items. Keep in mind that menus are severely limited when food is to be transported, because some foods do not travel well.

Pricing the Service

Most functions will carry a price for food and beverage that is designed to return a predetermined profit to the caterer. There must be a guarantee by the client as to the quantity ordered and provided. In addition the caterer will usually be provided sufficient food and beverage so as to minimize running out of products. Providers will usually charge on a portal-to-portal basis to cover transportation and labor costs. Extras provided to the client are added on to the base costs. It is wise to include as much in the base charges as possible because too many add-ons can confuse and upset a client. When planning the function, the caterer will generally negotiate with the client to ensure that each side is clear on what is to be provided and at what price. There must be a guarantee by the client for the service, with a signed contract and a cash retainer.

Marketing and Sales

Restaurant catering will probably not require any special advertising. Most restaurants will have some sort of advertising program for the business, and catering can be a part of that expense/ This component of the restaurant business is usually a sideline and it is doubtful that it would support an advertising budget.

MELANGE CATERING AND SPECIAL EVENTS*

Date

Thank you for your interest in Melange Catering. We are pleased to submit a proposal for a Holiday Cocktail Buffet Dinner in your home on Saturday, December 6 for 75-90 guests

Melange Catering is a full service catering company prepared to handle all the Client's needs to the smallest detail including linens, china, silver, glassware, flowers and entertainment.

Distinctive food and flawless service define Melange as one of Houston's finest caterers. Every facet of Melange Catering is designed to reflect the impeccable taste of the Client and to relieve them of the many details that accompany any successful party.

I have enclosed for your consideration suggested menus along with our estimates. If you have any questions or suggestions please feel free to call.

Again, we appreciate your interest in Melange and I look forward to working with you.

Sincerely,
Melange Catering

*Reprinted by permission of Melange Catering, Linda West, owner, Houston, Texas.

Menu Selection

Passed Appetizers

Chiquita Medallions
breast of chicken wrapped around jack cheese and peppers,
encased in smoked bacon, grilled and served as medallions with
tomatilla sauce

Mushroom Crostini Tarts

Cocktail Dinner Buffet
Dining Room

Perfectly Roasted Beef Tenderloin
served with sour cream biscuits, horseradish cream
and ancho chili sauce

Herb Crusted Pork Loin
served with petite rolls, jalapeno mayo and
bourbon mustard

Grilled Vegetables glazed with Balsamic Vinaigrette

Fruit Cheese and Pate Boards with
French Bread Toasts and Condiments

Artichoke Braids

Chef Station
(located in kitchen)

Margarita Salmon with Cilantro Aioli
accompanied by black bread triangles

Shrimp Risotto prepared by our Chef, tableside
(vegetarian version available)

Warm Crayfish Cakes with Spicy Remoulade

Cocktail Dessert Trays
an assortment of holiday favorites including decorated sugar cookies,
gingerbread men, cranberry and date bars, chocolate crinkles,
thumbprints, gingersnaps, and lots more

Reprinted by permission of Melange Catering, Linda West, owner, Houston,
Texas.

PROPOSAL
all proposals based on 85 guests

FOOD @

    Passed Appetizers @ 4.00 per guest   *340.00*

    Cocktail Dinner Buffet with Desserts @ 35.00 per guest   *2975.00*

BEVERAGE:

    Coffee Service for 60 guests   *90.00*

    Ice for beverages and icing wine & beer

        (5 coolers @ 10.00 each)   *50.00*

    All liquor, wine, beer, mixers, sodas and bar condiments

        furnished by client.

STAFF: *850.00*

    1 Party Maid

    1 Bartender

    1 Chef

    2 Waiters

    Amount listed is inclusive of all staff charges for event lasting a maximum of 4 hours, including delivery, set up and breakdown of event and return to Melange warehouse. Overtime is charged at $20.00 per hour per staff member for an event lasting longer than 4 hours (includes travel charges for The Woodlands).

RENTALS: *500.00*

    Silver Buffet Table Service-ware

    Clear acrylic plates and glassware; stainless flatware

    Silver Coffee Urns

    All utility equipment necessary to produce event

FLORAL/DECORATIONS:

    Holiday greenery to decorate buffet tables   *20.00*

    Melange would be happy to have our floral designers

        provide suggestions for table centerpieces or holiday décor.

        Please let us know if you would like more information

        regarding this service.

MANAGEMENT FEE: *135.00*

    Subtotal   *4960.00*

    Tax   *409.20*

    Total   *5369.20*

    Deposit Due   *3000.00*

Please read and sign a copy of the attached policies. Please fax or mail them, along with your deposit, to our office to ensure booking of this event.

Reprinted by permission of Melange Catering, Linda West, owner, Houston, Texas.

POLICIES OF MELANGE CATERING

GUARANTEES:

Food and Beverage charges will be based on Clients' final guarantee. If no guarantee is submitted the original estimated guest count will act as the final number. If the final guest count drops 20% below estimated number, the price per guest may increase. Guest count will be guaranteed NO later than *five working days* prior to the event. Melange will make every effort to accommodate last minute increases in guest count but client acknowledges that this is sometimes impossible and agrees not to hold Melange responsible for this increase.

DEPOSITS:

A deposit of 50% of the estimated total will confirm the booking of this event, 20% of which is non-refundable. Events will not be produced with a deposit. Deposits are refundable as follows:

- 45 days prior to event, the remainder of deposit is refundable*

- 30 days prior to event, 50% of the remainder of deposit is refundable*

- Cancellation less than 30 days prior to event date, deposit is non-refundable*

ESTIMATE:

Melange will submit a proposal which will include a billing estimate for the Client's approval. The estimate is not a final guarantee of price. The final invoice will reflect charges according to the final guaranteed guest count and any additional charges incurred as approved and discussed with the Melange representative and the Client.

STAFF:

Our professionally trained staff will be dressed in black tie unless otherwise requested. There is a three hour minimum charge for all staffed events. Melange reserves the right to increase or decrease the estimated number of staff should the Final Guarantee vary more than 10% of the estimated guest count. Overtime is charged at $20.00 per staff member per hour. No overtime should be incurred if event runs as scheduled.

RENTALS:

Melange Catering will handle the ordering of all rental equipment. Rental charges included in final invoice.

LIABILITY:

The Client assumes all liability for rental items damaged, broken, or removed from the party location. Although the Melange staff will execute with the greatest of care handling personal and/or rental china, glassware, flatware, and other party equipment, Melange Catering assumes NO liability for loss, damage, or breakage unless proven negligent. Any charges incurred for rental losses will be included in the final invoice.

* Less any portion Melange has placed with sub-contractors for services

BEVERAGE SERVICE:

Melange Catering is fully licensed by the Texas Alcoholic Beverage Commission.

Mixed Beverage #MB 22189; #LB 221190
Beverage Cartage #PE 22191
Caterers Permit #CB 221192

Melange carries full Liquor Liability coverage. Melange staff reserves the right to refuse beverage to a guest if necessary.

TIPPING:

Melange Catering believes that tipping should only occur when the Client wishes to show appreciation to party staff for excellent performance. However, if you would like to tip staff, to ensure tips are distributed fairly please choose one of the following options:

- Melange prefers that you include tips in your final payment, allowing our accounting department to distribute them with scheduled paychecks.

- Please tip all or none of the staff at your event. Please divide the tip evenly between all staff, including any staff that may have been dismissed prior to the event conclusion.

- Please do not give one staff member a sum of cash and expect him to distribute it to other staff members.

PAYMENT:

A 50% deposit (based on our proposal estimate) is necessary to confirm event booking. Clients will be invoiced for the remaining balance within five days of the executed event. TERMS ARE BALANCE DUE UPON RECEIPT OF INVOICE.

Upon acceptance of this proposal, please sign and return one copy of this document with your 50% deposit.

DATE_____   EVENT DATE_____

_____   _____
MELANGE REPRESENTATIVE   CLIENT

Melange Catering   6803 Wynnwood   Houston, Texas 77008   713-869-0066

Reprinted by permission of Melange Catering, Linda West, owner, Houston, Texas.

Event Planning Companies

A good source for your catering business is an event planner. These companies are involved in planning, negotiating, and operating various kinds of events from meetings (large and small), company picnics, and many other functions for association and corporate clients. They use different modes for advertising, including newspapers, the Internet, and telemarketing. Most do not have facilities for food service operations and rely on restaurants, hotels, and catering companies for that service.

They develop contracts with their clients and will subcontract for those services such as physical facilities, food and beverage, display equipment, and so on. These firms are an excellent source for restaurant catering because the only requirement needed for a restaurant would be the development of an ongoing relationship with the planners and providing acceptable service to the planner's clients. One such event planner, Clare Sullivan and Associates, is located in Houston, Texas. A sample contract used by the firm is printed here with their permission.

Restaurants must exercise care in the business of catering. It requires special licensing and close attention to food safety for the clients and guests. As noted previously, food does not always travel well, and what is finally set out on the buffet line or individual plates may not meet with approval if care is not taken to ensure quality. In addition, the old maxims that one must keep hot food hot and cold food cold is a necessity for any caterer. More importantly, hot food and cold food must be transported, stored, and served at optimum temperatures by workers thoroughly schooled in sanitary procedures to protect against food-borne illnesses.

Wine Lists and Special Drinks List

The two most critical questions you must ask yourself in this area are

1. How many wines do you want to offer?

2. Do you want to list them on a separate menu or include them in some way on your regular menu?

Unfortunately, there is no rule of thumb or standard answer. There are as many philosophies and opinions in this area as there are restaurants. In your own market, you will see wine lists with as few as ten wines available and some lists with well over one hundred available. Lists are often presented with all the pomp and circumstance of a papal visit in some restaurants; others choose to merely leave the list lodged on the table between the salt and pepper shakers. Your own decision process must truly start with the level of formality you personally believe that wine will take in your restaurant. The more emphasis you want to bring to wines, the more you must be prepared to be compared with similar style and philosophy restaurants. Here again, you must know your market and your competitors. This does not mean that you must play "follow the leader" or that you can't choose to be innovative, but it is imperative that you know, to some degree, what your guests' expectations will be.

CONTRACT FOR SERVICES*

AUTHORITY

Clare Sullivan & Associates (CS&A) will act as exclusive agent for (CLIENT). It is understood that CS&A will provide consulting and planning services and will communicate with all third parties to organize the event(s) as set forth below.

DATE:

EVENT(S):

COST:

CS&A shall not be liable should a supplier be unable or fail to perform. However, CS&A will use its best efforts to replace such supplier's goods or services and, to the extent possible, will notify CLIENT in advance of the substitution.

SCHEDULE OF PAYMENTS

1. Upon acceptance of this CONTRACT, CS&A requires a deposit in the amount of $_____.

2. The remainder of the fees and any additional charges or credits will be due as invoiced and payable NO LATER THAN _____ 1999.

3. Additional charges incurred will be invoiced separately and due fourteen (14) days after the event.

4. Any amount not paid when due shall bear interest at the rate of 18% per annum. In the event that any collection activity becomes necessary, CLIENT agrees to pay CS&A its court and/or collection costs, plus reasonable attorney's fees.

GENERAL

1. CLIENT agrees that it is CLIENT'S sole expense to procure all permits, licenses, and approvals necessary and to comply with all local, state and federal laws, ordinances and regulations which may effect this CONTRACT or the activities which are the subject matter of this CONTRACT.

2. CS&A will not be liable for any loss, damage or injury of any kind resulting from acts of God, accidents, illnesses or other matters beyond the control of CS&A. In the event that performance of this CONTRACT is prevented by any of the above, then this CONTRACT may, at CS&A's option be canceled without penalty or charge to either party for any portion not complete.

3. If the property or equipment of CS&A or any subcontractor of CS&A's equipment is lost, stolen or damaged under any circumstances, regardless of fault, CLIENT shall be responsible for all charges including replacement charges, if equipment is lost or stolen, and labor and materials required to replace or repair the equipment.

4. This CONTRACT and any addendum hereto sets forth the entire CONTRACT

between the parties with respect to the subject matter and supersedes all prior representations, warranties, agreements and understandings whether written or oral.

5. Any provisions in any purchase order, quotation, acknowledgment or other forms of contract documents applicable to this CONTRACT which are inconsistent or in conflict with any of the provision of this CONTRACT will be deemed inapplicable to this CONTRACT.

CANCELLATION

Should CLIENT find it necessary to cancel the event(s), such cancellation must be in writing. Any deposits made by CLIENT to CS&A are non-refundable if the event(s) is canceled less than thirty (30) days prior to the scheduled date of the event. If the written cancellation is received at least 30 days prior to the event(s), CLIENT agrees to pay CS&A a coordination fee in an amount equal to 10% of the proposed cost of the event(s).

LIABILITY

CS&A shall not be liable for any acts or omissions on the part of suppliers or their failure to perform. CS&A will not be liable for any loss, damage or injury to persons or property arising in connection with this Contract EXCEPT ANY SUCH LOSS, DAMAGE OR INJURY WHICH IS DUE TO THE DIRECT AND SOLE NEGLIGENCE OF CS&A. CLIENT AGREES TO INDEMNIFY, DEFEND AND HOLD HARMLESS CS&A, ITS OFFICERS, EMPLOYEES AND SUBCONTRACTORS FROM ANY LOSS, DAMAGE OR INJURY TO PERSONS OR PROPERTY ARISING OUT OF OR OCCURRING IN CONNECTION WITH THIS CONTRACT SAVE AND EXCEPT FOR SUCH LOSS, DAMAGE OR INJURY THAT IS THE RESULT OF THE DIRECT AND SOLE NEGLIGENCE OF CS&A.

In all events, CS&A shall not be responsible for any incidental, special or consequential or other similar damage in any way connected with the performance of this CONTRACT.

COMPANY NAME   CLARE SULLIVAN & ASSOCIATES
By:_____   _____
Signature   Claire L. Sullivan, CSEP
Title:_____   President
Date:_____   Date:_____

ALL PRODUCTIONS/PROGRAMS INCLUDE CS&A'S
COMPREHENSIVE GENERAL LIABILITY POLICY

*Reprinted by permission of Clare L. Sullivan, Clare L. Sullivan & Associates, Inc., Houston, Texas.

CS &A EVENT CONTRACT

CLIENT: _____

ADDRESS:_____

CONTACT: _____

TELEPHONE: _____

FAX: _____

E-MAIL: _____

EVENT DATE: _____

EVENT TIME: _____

EVENT LOCATION:_____

EVENT DESCRIPTION:_____

ESTIMATED GUESTS: _____

GUARANTEE DUE: _____

INVITATIONS

CS&A will provide theme invitations per client approval.

*Approval signature*_____

SECURITY

CS&A recommends & will provide one off-duty HPD or Sheriff's department officer per 100 people for duration of event.

  NUMBER OF GUESTS _____

  NUMBER OF OFFICERS _____

PARKING

Self-parking   [   ]   CS&A provide Valet Parking   [   ]

TRANSPORTATION

CS&A will provide the following ground transportation.

PRICE QUOTED INCLUDES TAX AND DRIVER GRATUITY

RENTALS

CS&A will provide the equipment and purchases necessary to produce the event.

TENTING

    TYPE _____

    SIZE _____

TENT FLOORING _____ yes _____ no

TENT AIR CONDITIONING/HEATING _____ yes _____ no

STAGING

DANCE FLOOR

LIGHTING

POWER

WATER SUPPLY

TABLES:

    REGISTRATION _____

    BUFFET & BEVERAGE _____

    DINING _____

    CATERERS _____

CHAIRS

    COLOR _____

    TYPE _____

LINENS

    CHAIR COVERS _____

    CHAIR SASHES _____

    SIZE _____

    QUANTITY _____

FOOD & BEVERAGE SERVICE EQUIPMENT

PLASTICWARE/PAPER PRODUCTS

GLASS PLATES/SILVERPALTE & FLATWARE

WAITER TRAYS & STANDS

COAT CHECK RACKS & TICKETS

<u>RENTALS, cont'd.</u>

VOTIVE CANDLES

ASHTRAYS/NO SMOKING SIGNS

TRASH CANS & LINERS

RESTROOM FACILITIES

SPECIAL TRASH REMOVAL

STAFF

ICE TRUCK

EASELS

PIPE AND DRAPE

*****PRICE QUOTED IS BASED ON DELIVERY AND PICKUP DURING NORMAL BUSINESS HOURS.*****

<u>STAFF</u>

CS&A will provide the following uniformed staff to set-up, service and break-down the event:

SUPERVISORS

BUFFET & BEVERAGE ATTENDANTS

BARTENDERS

FOOD & BEVERAGE SERVERS

COAT CHECK ATTENDANTS

REGISTRATION

RESTROOM ATTENDANT

DISPATCHER/TRANSPORTATION COORDINATORS

MISCELLANEOUS STAFF

PRICE QUOTED IS BASED ON _____ HOUR EVENT.

<u>DÉCOR</u>

ENTRANCE SIGNAGE/CUSTOM SIGNAGE

PROPS

SPECIALTY LINENS

FLORALS/PLANTS

CEILING TREATMENTS

STAGE DÉCOR

WRAP TENT POLES

CENTERPIECES

LIGHTING/POWER

******PRICE QUOTED INCLUDES DELIVERY, SETUP AND BREAKDOWN DURING NORMAL BUSINESS HOURS.******

ENTERTAINMENT

MUSIC
    DEEJAY

    BAND

    TAPED/PRE-RECORDED

VARIETY
    ARTISTS   ***CHARACTERS***

    MISC. PERFORMERS

LIGHTS & SOUND

SPECIAL POWER REQUIREMENTS

    EACH ONE IS PRICED PER PERFORMANCE TIME.

PHOTO OPPORTUNITY

MEMENTOS

BEVERAGE SERVICE

TYPES OF BEVERAGE SERVICE:

SOFT BEVERAGE ONLY _____

BEER, WINE AND SOFT BEVERAGES _____

FULL BAR SERVICE _____

NOTE: BEER: KEG _____   CAN/BOTTLED _____
IMPORT _____
DOMESTIC _____

SODAS: CAN _____   GUNS _____
BRANDS:CALL _____   PREMIUM _____

MENU DESIGN

BUFFET _____
SEATED MEAL _____
PASSED _____

NOTE: signify # of hours or time frame which food is to be served.   _____

Wine pricing is also a wide variable. Some restaurants try to mark up their wines as little as 50 percent (a bottle that costs them $10 may sell for $20); others try to mark up between three and four times. Keeping prices lower may encourage higher sales of wine, thus putting more dollars in the register, but there is a school of thought that says guests expect to pay more for wine and the service that comes with it. A reasonable cost percentage to have as a goal for wine is between 30 percent and 35 percent.

Here is a wine pricing formula that some managers have used. These operators strive for a market mix of sales that yields one-half as wine and beer, and one-half from "hard" liquor. To reach their goal, they mark the low-cost wine up from 3 to 4.5 times the cost per glass or bottle. The more expensive wines are marked up 2 to 2.8 times the cost per bottle.

Note: The state of Texas requires a payment of 10 percent of gross sales from all mixed beverage permit licensees. This tax is not an add-on—which means that the house realizes 90 percent net of all sales of liquor, wine, and beer. The following example accounts for such a tax.

One glass

Cost—$0.35 × 4 = $1.40

Selling Price (rounded up)—$1.50

Cost—$1.50 −.15 (tax 10 percent) = $1.35

.35 / 1.35 = 25.9 percent COS

One bottle

Cost $6.00 × 2.5 = $15.00

Selling Price—$15.00

Cost—$15.00 −1.50 (tax 10 percent) = $13.50

$6.00 / $13.50 = 44.4 percent COS

If you sold seventy-five glasses of wine

Sales—$112.50 −10 percent tax = $101.25 net

And twelve bottles

Sales—$180.00 −10 percent = $162.00 net

The yield on wine sales would be:

Sales $101.25 + $162.00 = $263.25

Cost $26.25 + $72.00 = $98.25

$98.25 / $263.25 = $37.3 percent cost of sales on wine

The above example would meet the stated goal of cost of goods on wine at between 35 percent and 40 percent of net sales. Try this formula, making whatever adjustments are necessary to fit your own particular situation, for example, your own desired mix of beer and wine sales.

You should solicit the advice of your wine sales representatives before committing to any printed wine list because wine bottle prices and availability can be very volatile. Also, your representatives are a good source of information on wine pricing, supply problems, wine descriptions, training techniques, and offering tastings for you and your staff. The service of wine has become more informal over the past decade, but your guests will still expect a well-rounded list and a high degree of professionalism in wine service owing to the prices that you will be charging for bottles. Many wine suppliers can also help design and pay for your wine list printing. (Be careful to weigh the amount of obligation this may put on you to continue to use their wines.) Be prepared to change wine lists at least once a year because prices and supplies may cause you to make many changes in selections.

Offering a wide variety of specialty alcoholic drinks is a practice that varies greatly depending on the style of restaurant that you are planning. Usually it is ethnic restaurants, resort-setting eateries, very exclusive restaurants, or heavy "theme" restaurants that choose to make a big occasion out of specialty drink menus. A truly authentic Mexican restaurant may have a margarita list offering up to ten varieties, a beach resort may have a multitude of frozen daiquiris, and a fancy steak house may have a martini list that comes to the table separately. Once you have determined where you want to "position" your own restaurant, then you can decide if a separate drink list will be an advantage for you to have. Further, don't let your bartenders make this decision for you because, invariably, many will tell you that you absolutely *must* have a drink list, regardless of the type of restaurant you are.

HOW TO DECIDE WHETHER TO HAVE SPECIAL LUNCH AND DINNER MENUS OR ONE ALL-DAY MENU

If you are choosing to open a restaurant that serves both lunch and dinner, then this is a very critical decision for you. It is not uncommon to hear of restaurants going from separate menus to one menu and then back to separate menus in the space of just a few years. There truly is no right answer when it comes to making this decision, and you must allow yourself to admit that you may have made a mistake if you feel you've made the wrong decision. Guests will forgive you as well as long as you don't continue to confuse them with continued indecision. Here are the major factors that will help you determine the best course of action.

1. Look at your competition and see what they are doing. Generally, restaurants that have been around your area for a while have a pretty good feel for the pulse of your market base. The demographics of your area should be pretty well established, and your competitors may have helped you make this decision.

2. If your goal is to have a wide variety of items available for lunch and dinner, then you have answered this concern. Changing menu item selections will dictate that you have separate menus. However, if you want to offer the same

items at lunch and dinner, then you have to decide if the prices you will charge at lunch are reasonable to charge for dinner. Many times, the market flexibility for lunch prices can be considerably more rigid whereas dinner prices are more "relaxed." Because more people eat out for lunch more frequently than for dinner (the nature of the marketplace in a 9 to 5 world), it stands to reason that price is a big factor in choosing where to eat lunch. Many, if not most, chain restaurants choose to serve one menu all day because it is easier to train and manage. All-day menus must offer a good variety of items in many price ranges to appeal to a broad market. Many independent operators and full-service restaurants in the higher price category offer different menus because this helps distance them from chain operators.

3. Your specific location will also help you make this decision. If you think that your lunch clientele and dinner clientele are totally different, you may decide to change menus. For instance, you may be located in a market that has, on one side, a very strong office population of moderately salaried employees, and on another side a community of higher-income households. To attract and satisfy both potential clienteles you may have to have separate lunch and dinner menus. Much of this type of analysis should be done while you are planning your restaurant, not after you buy the business or sign the lease!

4. The strength of your kitchen staff, and your chef or kitchen manager in particular, may dictate how successfully you can achieve separate menus. The implication with separate menus is that you will be serving a wider variety of items, and as soon as you do that, the skill and retention level of your staff must be taken into consideration. For you to double the number of items you ask your staff to execute perfectly means that you must have extremely strong supervision. Be very realistic in assessing this area of concern because your philosophy may backfire if you can't perform the menus.

5. Simply ask yourself, "What is the image I want to project?" This question will help you drive this decision. If it is extremely important to you to separate yourself from your competitors if all of them are offering one menu, then be an efficient planner and gear up to execute two menus. If you are comfortable trying to attract your share of the pie without assuming too much risk, then go with a single menu that covers your bases. Like the menu items themselves, your philosophy will be portrayed by this decision.

SPECIAL NEEDS OF DISABLED OR HANDICAPPED GUESTS

The Americans with Disabilities Act had a large impact on how our industry viewed the handicapped. As a direct result of many new laws and changed attitudes in our society, the special needs of the handicapped should play a part when making your menu decisions. This is not necessarily a factor when choosing menu items, but more so when choosing menu design. More and more restaurants are offering menus in Braille to their blind guests, equipping some menus with clip-ons that will attach to the arm of a wheelchair, or printing a few menus with extremely large and boldfaced print for the visually impaired. These are just a few of the considerations you might make. It would be a good idea for you to contact agencies that work directly with handicapped people to see how you might be able to better accommodate this part of our society. Our industry is commonly called the "hospitality" industry, and to be truly hospitable means that you are prepared to accommodate anyone that has a need or desire for your services.

OTHER CONSIDERATIONS FOR MENU PLANNING

How Many Menus Is a Good Quantity to Print?

The two main factors that enter into your decision here are cost and the number of seats in your restaurant. If you have chosen an expensive medium on which to print your menu, chances are your budget may only allow you to print so many menus. Typically, a card stock paper menu that is nonlaminated and is a reasonable size can cost between $1.00 and $1.50 per copy to print. Sometimes it can be a bit less and frequently it can be a bit more depending on the detail of print and the number of color separations you have. Try to choose a reputable printing company that will work with you as a new operator and is equipped to handle small business accounts. Menus can cost upward of $10 each and unless it was critical to your concept, you should not start with something that elaborate.

The supply of menus you will need ranges between 2 and 3 times the number of seats in your restaurant. If your menus are frail and disfigure easily, you may need more to start off with to see how they wear. The last thing that you want to be doing is scavenging around your restaurant to find menus to give to your guests. Have a safe but reasonable supply on hand and always check them to make sure they are clean and presentable. If you have separate lunch and dinner menus, then have the same number available for both meal periods. It is also a good idea to print "To Go" paper menus (in a smaller size) at the same time you are printing your regular menus because you will want to pass out as many of the smaller menus as possible. A reasonable amount of "To Go" menus is about five times the number of seats in your restaurant. Your printer can help you determine the exact number to print because there are generally price breaks at different intervals. Please do not get carried away here because you will be changing menus at least every eighteen months or so.

Proofing Your Menu

It may take two to three months to finalize your menu items, and when you have finalized the menu and had it typeset be sure to proofread it carefully. It is always a good idea to have one or more persons proofread it as well. Remember that your menu is the most important tool of communication that your business has and, hopefully, it will be read by hundreds of people a day. A professional presentation gets you off on the right foot.

How Often Should You Change Menus?

Typically the time frame varies from one year to eighteen months. Although you are certainly not restricted to making that your own goal, you may want to change it more often. However, you should not go longer than eighteen months to make price adjustments. As an example, a massive weather system called El Niño severely affected the supply of produce and some seafood items. Crops that fed beef cattle also took a hard hit and prices for red meat were extremely variable. Several of the large restaurant chains have whole departments that keep an eye on these changing supply patterns, and El Niño forced many independent and chain operators to adjust their prices. Your suppliers are an excellent resource for you to use in these matters and you must be prepared to anticipate and react to changing conditions that affect your cost of goods.

Should Your Menus Be Laminated?

This should be a relatively simple decision for you. Laminate is available in both a high gloss and a matte look, and both will help protect your menus from wearing out too quickly. However, cost is not the only consideration when making this decision. Many people regard laminated menus as a sign of a more casual dining restaurant, because the "feel" of laminate is not as authentic as the feel of paper or other nonlaminated card stocks. Whether it is considered acceptable to you is the most important issue. How you view your menu should decide if you choose to laminate. Again, it is a good idea to have a few nonlaminated menus and laminated menus prepared so that you can judge the difference. Look at the menus in both dim and bright light since a glossy laminate will be highly reflective and a nonlaminated menu will tend to absorb light much better.

How to Prevent Costly Mistakes When Adding New Items to the Menu

The following short story is an example of how checklists, accompanied with careful consideration, can often prevent costly changes that don't pan out.

Sam has a nice restaurant with a menu that is pretty standard for his kind of business. After a trip to a competitor's place, he decides that adding prime rib would put him even with the competition. To surpass that competition, he further decides that carving from a cart in the dining room would really add some "pizzazz." (You are probably starting to get the picture.)

Anyway, in comes the new cart—pretty, but it takes up considerable aisle space and really slows down the rest of the service. Well, that can be solved—take out a table or two; however, seating was "tight" before, and not having those seats means lost sales. Further, coordinating the serving of the accompaniments to the beef meant a further disruption for the service staff.

This scenario has no ending, but the point has been made. Actually, the addition of the prime rib may have been good, but the method of service with insufficient planning was disastrous. In all probability, what really happened was that the expensive cart was relegated to the storeroom where it still sits today—even though the storeroom was too small to begin with.

Often an owner or manager will see a new item somewhere and, without too much thought, add it to the menu. This is like adding a fifth wheel to an automobile without studying the process and retooling the assembly line. Anytime you introduce a change in your menu, you must first be sure that the service staff can handle it. It is also a good idea to use checklists when planning new ventures or changing old ones. Before you change your menu, use the following checks to see if you are on the right track.

☐ *Kitchen*

Can the present staff handle another change, or must you add another person? Do you have to remove something else from the menu to add the item? What?

Will the present equipment stand an extra item? Do you have sufficient and proper storage? Is there a ready supply of these items, or is it the "special order" variety?

☐ *Service*

Is your china properly sized and shaped for this service? Or must you buy some new type of dish?

Can this item be "held" and still be served fresh and attractively? Can you keep it hot? Cold?

If it is of the "gourmet" variety, can your service staff handle it smoothly and with flair? Do you have the proper cart? Table-side cooking or serving equipment?

Will it sell? Or is it out of character with the balance of your menu?

How to Develop a Menu Pattern That Will Sell

This is where it all begins, and where you "separate the men from the boys." Because the menu is the backbone of business, developing a good one will take some experience, as already outlined. Here are the important ingredients that go into a winning menu:

- The menu must be attractive and interesting. This requires flair and imagination in the writing and the layout. A dull menu won't sell much.

- The menu must have balance. This means it must include a sufficient mix of items (i.e., taste, shape, size, texture, etc.). It also must offer an adequate range of prices to satisfy the widest possible market available. For example, when a party of six comes to your restaurant, chances are the group will include those who are able and willing to spend freely, and those who are not. If your menu is constructed so as to offer a variety of items with an acceptable range of prices, the group can solve the problem by asking for separate checks, and everyone in the party is then satisfied. If not, next time that group will go elsewhere.

Only Ride the Winners

Make sure that you watch your sales records carefully so that you know when to move the slow sellers off the menu. There is no profit in items that don't sell. When to change an item is largely a personal matter. But one way would be by watching inventory turnover by item. If, for instance, you are turning your inventory four times per month or about once each week, but a certain item lies in storage without movement for, say, two weeks, then it should be checked for salability. Here is where a good inventory system really pays off.

Copying a competitor could be a mistake unless you have a very good idea that the "hot" item down the street will be equally "hot" in your place. Further, copying others will often lead to a mishmash of items on a menu. That condition may destroy the theme of a restaurant and make the total environment uncomfortable for the patrons. If you think you need to make a change, exercise caution and research the matter carefully.

One sure way to monitor your menu is to keep clear, open lines of communication with your service staff. They know what the patrons are saying about your restaurant. They also know what your patrons say about the competition. This is just one more good reason to hold regular staff meetings during which you listen.

Spending time with your patrons and listening to their comments is also very educational. There are too many restaurant managers who don't spend enough time in the dining room. That is a bad habit to fall into, because it isolates management from the point of sale.

Watch Out for Changing Economic Conditions

There will be changing conditions in the economy and in the community that will have an effect on the items you sell and the prices that you charge. Commodity prices will fluctuate with supply and demand. An example of this is the price of beef. If supply is plentiful and demand moderate, then wholesale prices will tend to be down. But what usually happens then is that the producers trim their herds, thereby shortening the supply. In the meantime, consumers have increased their consumption owing to the lower prices, and at that time, wholesale prices tend to climb. So you must watch these cycles and know when and how to buy. Sometimes it may pay to carry a heavy inventory on a particular item to protect your price. But that will only be true if you do not have to borrow money at high interest rates to carry the supply.

Then too, the neighborhood in which your restaurant is located may undergo economic changes. Such change may bring demand for new items on your menu. You must be alert to what goes on around you. Your restaurant must interface with the community and if the community undergoes change, it may be wise for you to make some changes also.

A good way to keep up with the "outside" world is by reading your local newspaper, and bulletins and periodicals from trade associations. Both the National Restaurant Association and your own state association publish information that is very important to you. There are also many magazines and journals published for the food service industry, and one or more of these may be helpful in identifying changing patterns and trends in the business.

Chapter
3

Money-Making Secrets
of Food Production

Table of Contents

Chapter 3

Money-Making Secrets of Food Production

Do you have sales of $400,000 per year or more in your restaurant? Would you like to make about $20,000 more? You don't even have to increase your sales to do that. If you do the things recommended in this chapter, you can improve the management of your business, and in the process, probably increase your income by at least 5 percent.

Too many operators leave the detail of planning production to others, and in most cases, sacrifice profits in the process. Expecting a busy working chef or salad person to monitor sales trends, manage inventory levels, and guess how many customers will be served on a given day is inviting trouble. Because you are in a business of producing food for sale, controlling production may well be your most important job.

There are certain steps that must be taken to manage production levels of menu items properly in a commercial kitchen. Overproduction of food has helped to put more than one restaurant out of business. Also, raw food prices are high, and those cost dollars must all be converted to sales dollars if you are to survive in this business. Underproduction is the counter to overproduction, because it means that you don't have enough food prepared to satisfy customer demand. Remember, if you don't have it, you can't sell it—and if you don't sell it, you won't be in business very long.

In this chapter, you'll learn the tools and techniques needed to control the amounts of food to be prepared by the kitchen staff. In addition, the value of recipes in stabilizing the quality and cost of food will be covered. In other parts of this guide, forecasting, purchasing techniques, and the need for an awareness of economic changes that might affect the business will be discussed.

HOW TO USE STANDARD RECIPES TO STABILIZE YOUR FOOD COST

The standard recipe is one of the most useful attention-getters and profit-builders you can use in your restaurant. The largest and most successful food service companies in the world use them—and swear by them. No matter what the size of your operation, you too can benefit from using a standard recipe. For example:

- Consistent use of standard recipes insures that the proper ingredients are used in the correct amounts when preparing a menu item. Control of these factors is a must if you are going to stabilize your food cost.

- Mr. John Farquharson, retired president of ARASERVE Sector of ARA Services (operators of commercial restaurants and food service installations in colleges, ballparks, etc.) and the past president of the National Restaurant Association, and currently president of the International Food Safety Council, states that standard recipes may be worth as much as ten percentage points of food cost. If yours are worth as much and you have a yearly food cost of $200,000, then your potential savings could be as high as $20,000 per year. That amount, if saved, will drop right to the bottom line as profit.

- Another plus from the use of standard recipes is the advantage of producing items that are consistent in quality. Customers come to your restaurant because you have certain things they like. Sometimes it is decor, or service, but usually it is a particular food offering.

- The best way for you to ensure that customers received what they want is for you to have control over how the food is prepared. All of us—including your employees—have good days and bad days. Therefore, if you don't use a written guide (recipe), then your food quality will probably vary. If that happens, there may be days when your customers become dissatisfied. And when customers experience inconsistency, they begin to look for different restaurants.

- So if you want to make big profits, be sure you run a consistently good restaurant. If customers can trust the high quality of your food day after day, they will keep coming back. And when they come back, they will bring others.

WHERE TO FIND STANDARD RECIPES—AND HOW TO DEVELOP THEM FOR YOUR RESTAURANT

Good Standard Recipe Sources

Quantity recipes can be found in various places. For example, one good source is *Food for Fifty* by Fowler, West and Shugart, published by John Wiley and Sons,

Inc., New York. In addition, the Educational Department of the National Restaurant Association sells a quantity recipe file, as does the Cornell University School of Hotel Administration. These sources will provide the basis for starting your own file. Furthermore, take advantage of the hundreds of cookbooks that are for sale. These will most likely provide you with a recipe or two. Magazines and newspapers are also good sources.

Test First and Modify

In constructing your own file, you of course need to research and test the recipes before you offer them for sale. Your kitchen at home is every bit as good as any large research facility for this job.

After you have tried the recipes at home, you can then experiment in the restaurant kitchen. When recipe quantities are changed from small to large, they will require some adjustment in the ingredient ratios. For instance, if you have a recipe for six servings and you want to increase it to twenty-four, you first divide twenty-four by six which gives a ratio of 4:1. You then multiply the individual ingredients by four, to increase the total recipe yield to twenty-four. Once that is done, you must experiment with the recipes until you find the proper ingredient balance, because not all ingredients will require increasing in the same proportion.

When you are working with recipes, be sure to keep a good set of notes. In that way, you will be able to add and subtract, adjust and readjust, until you have the product you want. Once you have worked out the final adjustments, that formula (recipe) can be added to your standard recipe file.

Keep a Recipe File

It is a good idea to spell out all cooking procedures. For example, there are two schools of thought on roasting meat. One recommends a fast initial searing at a high temperature (500°), and dropping the oven temperature immediately to about 325°. The other school recommends a slow roasting at 275° for a longer period of time. Once you have tried both methods to see which you prefer, prepare your recipe and adopt the method as standard for your restaurant.

The form of the recipe file is a matter of personal taste. Some operators have their recipes in loose-leaf notebooks; others use 5 inch by 8 inch file cards. We prefer the latter. The recipes can be filed by categories (e.g., soups, entrees, desserts, etc.). Such a file is easy to use when scheduling production, and planning food and supply purchases. To protect the cards in the kitchen during production, clear plastic shields can be used.

Recipes should never be left lying around. They should only be removed from the file when they are being used and returned when finished. Carelessness will result in lost recipes and a breakdown in the system.

HOW TO SCHEDULE PRODUCTION—AND SAVE MONEY BY DOING IT RIGHT

Production schedules are built on sales forecasts. Once you have projected your sales, you are in a position to forecast the production needed to satisfy your customer demand. Here is how you do it:

Step 1—Enter on your production record the name of the dish to be produced, and the number of portions that will be needed.

Step 2—Go to the recipe file and pull the necessary recipes for production. Check them over and deliver them to the various departments, along with the production schedule that you have prepared. It is a good idea to deliver them personally a day ahead of time, so that you can have a short meeting with the people responsible for the actual production. During the meeting you can discuss the day's menu, and if there are any potential problems, attempt to solve them early.

Step 3—Watch the production process. Be sure that you supervise for compliance with your instructions, and that everyone is working to the standard you have set.

Step 4—Follow through by checking on the number of portions that were yielded by the particular recipe. If production was either short or long, find out why—and make every attempt to see that it doesn't happen again.

The production record form is simple and easy to use (see Fig. 3.1 for a sample form that you may find useful in your restaurant).

These records will refresh your memory on what happened the day you last served a certain item or combination of items, such as

- Day of the week and month of the year

- What the weather was (e.g., sunny, rainy, etc.)

- Outside temperature

- Any special happenings on that particular day (i.e., local election, strike at nearby plant)

- Total dollar sales per meal

- Total number of customers per meal

- Total portions or items sold by category (e.g., twenty-six New York sirloin, fourteen baked stuffed pork chops)

Figure 3.1

FOOD PRODUCTION RECORD					
Department	**Day**	**Date**	**Meal**	**Special Conditions**	
Hot Food	Thu	4/17	Lunch	Holiday today, many stores closed	
Menu Item	**Recipe Number**	**Portions to Prepare**	**Raw Ingredients Needed**	**Portions Left/ Time Ran Out**	**Comments**
Oyster Stew	S-14	40	See rec.	Ran out 12:50	Good seller, maybe could have sold 20 more portions
Roast beef	L-5	20	See rec.	4 left	OK seller but poor bus. today
Chick Pot Pie	C-12	10	See rec.	7 left	Poor seller, discontinue
					Total Portions Sold Today 58

Whether or not your menu changes frequently, these records can still be of great value to you. Watching well-kept sales records will not only show what sold today, but also what is apt to sell on another day in the future.

How to Keep Production Costs under Control

All costs are best controlled before they are incurred whenever it is possible to do so. The key to that kind of control is called *planning*. The plan to be used in the control of food production cost relates directly to the use of a sales forecast. It is important to have an accurate history of past sales for comparative purposes when forecasting future sales. Actually, the history provides the starting point from which you work on the forecast.

The most basic ingredient in controlling production costs is the sales forecast. Although there is a certain amount of intuition involved with any forecast, the use of good sales records will certainly minimize the guesswork.

Different kinds of restaurants have different problems related to menu preparation and production control. If you were to establish broad categories, they might be grouped as follows:

- Restaurants having menus that change daily as in cafeterias and buffets.

- Restaurants having menus that are fixed but offer specials that change periodically. Dinner houses and hotels are examples.

- Restaurants that have menus that infrequently change (e.g., the so-called fast-food group).

The first group relies heavily on sales records and, in many cases, develops cycle menus in its operations. These are menus with items that repeat on a preplanned, cyclical basis. Generally the cycles change with the seasons.

Making Meal Planning a Breeze with the Popularity Index

A popularity index computed for each item on the menu can be a big help in meal planning. Such an index is derived by dividing the number of portions sold by the total number of items in the same category (meat, fish, etc.) that were sold. For example:

Roast beef portions sold—62 percent total portions sold = .31. The popularity of roast beef as a percentage of the total sale.

Menu Item	Portions Sold	Popularity
Roast Beef	62	0.31
Broiled Haddock	49	0.25
Knockwurst/Kraut	86	0.44
Total Portions Sold	197	100.00

Next, the popularity index is applied to the forecast for the business day in question. The planner will know that last time there were 197 portions sold. The sales record will also show whether that was a good day or a slow day, and why. The planner must then forecast the number of customers he estimates there will be. At that point, he can determine how many entrée portions are expected to sell. The next step is, of course, to calculate how many portions of each menu item will be needed using the popularity index. (In actuality, that was probably determined for purchasing beforehand.)

Forecast—225 entrée items needed

Menu Item	Popularity Index	To Be Prepared
Roast Beef	0.31	70
Broiled haddock	0.25	56
Knockwurst/Kraut	0.44	99
Total	100.0	225

Obviously, there are also other factors that enter into this process. For example, poor sellers should have been eliminated and new items added.

This technique can be useful in any kind of restaurant. If you offer a set menu, except for changing specials, you can still index the special against the balance of the menu. Even if your menu changes infrequently, you will want to forecast your sales based on past history and present trends. All restaurants should forecast for purchasing information. (Too many operators buy from habit and, as a consequence, are either over- or understocked.) That same forecast is then applied to production to avoid leftovers and "run outs."

HOW CHECKLISTS CAN HELP YOU AVOID PROBLEMS

You can ease many of your production headaches, help your kitchen run smoothly, and head off potential problems if you use checklists of equipment needs, plating, and food service. Here are some examples:

Checklist to Determine Equipment Needs

FROM THE MENU—

- List those items requiring oven preparation and length of baking time.

  _____   _____

  _____   _____

  _____   _____

- Will the oven capacity accommodate this production?

- Is the broiler capacity sufficient? The grill?

- Are there enough pots and kettles for the soups, sauces, and gravies?

- Will the bain-marie, or steam table, hold all the hot items?

- How many pans are needed for holding purposes? What size?

- Is there any need for special equipment? Sauté pans? Skillets?

- Stockpots?

- How will the food be portioned and dished up? What size ladles? Serving spoons? Tongs? Food scoops?

- Will a scale be necessary for portion control? Do we have one?

- What is the general condition of the kitchen equipment? Oven thermostat? Cold spots?

- Is the person on staff who will do the preparation sufficiently skilled to handle new items?

Furthermore, when scheduling production, you must be aware of how the items are going to be served. You will also need to know if the items can be produced with efficiency and served to the customers in the same way.

With few exceptions, owners and managers want to "turn their seats" as often as possible. (For the uninitiated, one turn of a seat means one customer. The more turns, the more customers—and the more customers, the more cash in the till.) Diners, for the most part, don't want to be pushed, but they do want attention. Therefore, to make a good profit in your restaurant, you must work every possible angle to deliver smooth, easy, and fast service in a comfortable and attentive manner.

Proper Plating and Food Service Checklist

Check the following points in regard to your own restaurant. These all have to do with how well your service staff can procure food from your kitchen.

☐ Is the china properly sized in relation to the portions offered?

☐ Are the right dishes available for attractive and speedy dishing up in the kitchen?

☐ Are the serving trays properly sized to handle the kind of parties that most often frequent the restaurant?

☐ Is the kitchen properly equipped to keep dishes either hot or cold as needed?

☐ Have you studied the work area to see if the kitchen personnel are accommodated with dishes, supplies, etc., within easy reach? Or must they constantly move out of their stations for equipment?

☐ Is the service pickup area adequate in size and layout? Can service personnel quickly pick up and move out?

☐ Is the food check control station organized and equipped for fast and accurate checking, to ensure against unnecessary time delays in service?

How to Minimize Those Constant Nagging Repair and Maintenance Problems

Murphy's Law was probably written by a frustrated restaurant manager who was tired of being in the business of managing equipment and facility problems. Sometimes it seems that producing excellent quality food and service takes a back seat to trying to keep your restaurant up and running. And while we know of no way to eliminate those headaches, here's some advice on how to minimize the pain:

☐ 1. Produce and keep handy a comprehensive list of repair and maintenance contractors. The last thing you need is to pull out the yellow pages to try to find someone to help you in an emergency. Chances are you have called upon the assistance of various trades people, including electricians, plumbers, equipment repair specialists, tile repairmen, and others, and keep their numbers in a separate binder. Conspicuously label the binder and be sure your entire management team knows you have it and where it can be located.

☐ 2. This sounds so simple yet we know of many operators who have not done it: Get yourself a well supplied tool box and keep it available. You might be amazed at some of the skills your staff may possess if you make the tools available.

☐ 3. Consider hiring a handyman and putting him on a retainer. A close friend who owned several restaurants actually had a full time handyman on staff who was an accomplished carpenter, plumber, and electrician. For about the cost of a mid-level manager, he had an on-call technician whose hourly rate was considerably lower than the $60–$90 rates that most trades charge. The handyman also had signing privileges for his meals, and there was a certain comfort in seeing him sitting in the dining room during busy times!

☐ 4. Get yourself set up on a preventative maintenance program for all of your refrigeration and air conditioning/heating equipment. Most HVAC companies are glad to set you up on a monthly or quarterly program where they come out and change your filters, clean your compressors, and do routine checks on motors. Even having the lighting company come on a monthly basis to change lightbulbs in hard to reach places is suggested.

☐ 5. Create a list of all of your equipment that includes serial numbers, model numbers, and manufacturer. List the date of installation and then the warranty information beside that date. Within the same list, write in the service company who is approved to fix the piece of equipment, or if it isn't warrantied, write in the name of the company you use. As with the list of service contractors, keep this list in a conspicuously labeled binder in the manager's office.

☐ 6. It may be silly, but, check to make sure a piece of equipment is plugged in before you call out an electrician or service company. It may not be working because somehow it got unplugged.

Chapter
4

How to Buy Food Right for Maximum Profits

Table of Contents

Chapter
4

How to Buy Food Right
for Maximum Profits

Every restaurant operation, no matter how large or small, should have purchase specifications. These "specs" represent the plan under which you buy merchandise for preparation and resale. They spell out the quality standards by which you purchase. For instance, beef stew specs will indicate the cut from which the beef cubes are to come, the size of each cube, and possibly the grade of beef from which they are cut.

Every restaurant is vulnerable to such uncontrollable problems as disruptions in supply and skyrocketing wholesale prices. In addition, all owners must cope with pilferage, spoilage, and delivery shortages. But here are some things you can control to keep your enterprise profitable. You can take a great step toward better profits by determining what and where you want to buy well in advance of actually placing any orders. Preparing a set of purchase specifications for your restaurant will help you to buy well in advance of actually placing any orders. Preparing a set of purchase specifications for your restaurant will help you to buy "right"—and buying "right" is the first step toward selling for profit.

THE ADVANTAGES OF HAVING PURCHASE SPECIFICATIONS

One benefit of having purchase specifications is the fact that most of the decisions related to product grades, cuts, yields, etc., have been made in advance—when you were not under pressure to buy. Another benefit is that you'll be able to determine which purveyors are best for your business.

If you are knowledgeable and decisive in your buying, the purveyors will quickly notice the fact. That means that they will supply you with only those goods that you demand, In turn, you will soon find out which dealers you can trust and rely on for the kind of service you want. Keep an eye on things and supervise your receiving function to be certain that what you ordered is what was actually received.

The "specs" or guide for purchasing is of course developed from your menu. Development requires thorough research into many areas including price, product yield, market conditions, portion control, and "proper" quality of merchandise. It is not something to be drawn up and then shoved into a desk drawer, never to be seen again. Rather, it is a very important management tool that should be used daily when contemplating or actually purchasing food, beverages, and supplies. Furthermore, it must be constantly studied and modified as follows:

- When menu changes are contemplated, the market for new items must be researched for price and availability.

- Once decisions regarding new menu offerings have been made, the purchasing guide must be adjusted to reflect any changes necessary to support the menu modifications.

Because one of the biggest problems encountered by restaurant owners or managers is finding enough time in a day to do all of the many tasks, the job of purchasing is often delegated to someone else. When there are no written policies or guidelines for the delegates to follow, there is little or no control over the activity that requires the highest expenditures. But if adequate control is exercised over purchasing, your gross profits will increase and inventory levels will decrease.

How to Develop Keen Purchasing Skills

The two most important ingredients of good food buying are buyer education and maintaining good records.

Smart purveyors know that the best road to a long-term relationship is through buyer awareness. So don't be afraid to take advantage of the opportunities available to you to learn from them. For example, you should visit the produce terminals, meat processing plants, wholesale grocery warehouses, etc., asking lots of questions and taking notes for future reference.

Another way to better educate yourself is by checking with your local restaurant association for books and articles on the subject of food and beverage procurement. Here you will uncover a wealth of material for your file.

In addition, most trade shows have some exhibits related to food and beverage products. It is a good idea to attend several of these shows to stay current on new products and changes that are occurring in the industry. Restaurateurs who go to these shows repeatedly find that they give a far greater return than the money and time spent attending them.

Your best source for information, however, is found right in your own restaurant, as follows:

- Your customers are the ultimate critics of your buying, preparing, and serving skills. So if you are good, they will let you know by coming back to your restaurant again and again. But if you fall down in any of these areas, they will usually tell you first by offering criticism, and if that fails, by not coming back.

- Your employees can be top-notch assistants if you use them properly. Therefore, take your people into your confidence regarding purchasing decisions. Discuss the merits of various products with them and let them offer advice. Try their ideas when possible, and let them be party to the testing of same. Then follow up by discussing the results.

Final decisions as to what to use, and how, are of course up to you. However, you can learn a great deal from your staff and, at the same time, make hundreds of points by letting them be team members instead of uninterested workers.

USEFUL TIPS ON PURCHASE SPECIFICATIONS

Simply put, you should know *why* you are buying certain products. Good operators don't just buy "ground beef." They buy according to their needs. Many restaurant operators, for example, buy ground chuck over ground round—although it's less expensive—because they find it to be a juicier final product. Some like a ratio of 80 percent lean to 20 percent fat; while others prefer a ration of 85:15. And there are also operators who prefer beef patties with a small percentage of soy added. Prices will vary, of course. But what you have to do is strike a balance between what will satisfy your customers and what will provide maximum return to you.

When considering meat items, for instance, you should be looking for maximum yields of cooked items, as well as palatability. An example of how this can affect your bottom line would be the difference in grades of a roast beef cut. Generally speaking, the higher end of the grade, or "Prime," will have more fat than the lower, or "Good." In between is "Choice." These grades will vary as to quality and yield. And what you should buy will depend on your customer's tastes and pocketbooks, as well as your own particular profit requirement.

Testing the Products You Buy

Selection of the best buys for your own specific needs will be the result of study and diligence on your part. In the case of roast meats, much will be learned if you run yield and taste tests on the products you buy. This is a relatively simple matter of weighing the roast before cooking, and weighing it after cooking, to determine the net cooked weight. Further, the number of portions yielded should be counted to determine the amount lost during the slicing process. The same testing procedure is used regardless of whether the roast is boneless or bone-in. Just be sure, however, that when testing, you measure like items one against another.

The following is a sample test procedure:

Case 1

1 Top Round Beef Roast	
Raw Weight -	10 lbs.
Roasted at 325° for	
- hrs.	
Cooked Weight	7 lbs.
Yield 25 - 4 oz. portions	

Case 2

1 Top Round Beef Roast	
Raw Weight -	10 lbs.
Roasted at 425° for	
- hrs.	
Cooked Weight	6 lbs
Yield 20 - 4 oz. portions	

Using the above example, if the price per portion was a $5.95 luncheon special, you would have lost five luncheon sales, or $29.75, cooking the meat at a higher temperature—thus decreasing the number of portions available for sale.

Selecting the Best Method of Cooking Meat

Most experts agree that the lower the roasting temperature the higher the yield of cooked product. They also tend to agree that the palatability of the final product is enhanced by the lower roasting temperatures.

The cooking of meat, as well as poultry and fish, is a broad subject, however. Understanding the technical changes that take place through cooking requires some study and research. Further, the "best" method for roasting in one restaurant may not be the "best" method for you. All of these factors—yield, palatability, waste, etc.—are further complicated by the recent steep increases in energy costs. In addition, cooking times may vary due to the different kinds and the physical conditions of ovens in use.

As mentioned, it is in your best interest to study this subject further because any increases in yield and quality of product will likely mean higher profits for you. Material on this subject is found in many cookbooks. In addition, there are several textbooks available that address the subject:

Food Service in Institutions
West, Wood, Harger and Shugart
John Wiley and Sons, Inc.
New York

Cooking Meat in Quantity
National Live Stock and Meat Board
Chicago, Illinois

What about Canned Fruit?

Another area where money can be spent needlessly is in the selection of canned fruit. Different grades are available, and each of them can of course be used for different menu items. As with most products, the price differs between grades. Therefore, in addition to the price consideration, you must consider the product yield and intended use. The following lists the grades of fruit and when to use them.

Grade A or Fancy—When appearance and flavor is of first importance.

Grade B or Choice—Very good for most uses.

Grade C or Standard—When cooking is necessary for further preparation, or as one of several ingredients in a preparation formula or recipe.

Substandard (sometimes called D)—For the same uses as Grade C or Standard, but when appearance is of still less importance.

"Pie" grades of fruit, usually canned in water, can also be used in these instances, and may or may not be of the same grade, depending on the particular commodity.*

THE BENEFITS OF MAINTAINING GOOD RECORDS

Keeping a good accounting of prices and product yields is a must. With such records at hand, you will be able to explore the markets and search out the very best buys for your restaurant. These records will also help you decide what quantity to buy.

Keep in mind that your suppliers are in business to sell, and they will be pleased to sell you as much as you care to buy. Often restaurant owners and managers forget that they too are in business to sell. Therefore take a hard look at your inventory. If it is too heavy in relation to your sales, cut it down—and put yourself back in the selling business.

How to Keep Track of Suppliers' Prices

Because suppliers are in competition with each other, it follows that prices for similar items will probably vary among them. To keep track of what they're charging, you can prepare bid sheets for each food category. (See Figure 4.1.)

When comparing items, don't be fooled by the lowest price on a bid, as it may not be what you wanted. Anyway, if a low-priced product turns out to be unsuitable, the "real" price you pay will be much higher.

---

*Adeline Wood, *Quantity Buying Guides,* Vol. 2 (New York: Ahrens Publishing Co.)

84

Figure 4.1

Bid Sheet

Specification of Food Items	Vendor		Vendor		Vendor		Vendor		Vendor	
	Price	Amt	Price	Amt	Price	Amt	Price	Amt	Price	Amt
Total of Quotes										

Should You Use One Supplier for All Items?

Some operators prefer to use one vendor to supply all items, if possible. In many areas of the country this is not only logical, but necessary. Because the cost or running and maintaining delivery vehicles today is high, most suppliers are no longer willing to make deliveries with less than full truckloads. Further complicating the overall situation is the fact that suppliers are shrinking in number—with the remainder growing in size and volume. With this volume growth has come centralized ware-housing, which uses sophisticated inventory control systems and delivery vehicles that carry more tonnage per trip.

All of this means that small and medium-size restaurant owners are often com-pelled to buy larger amounts of merchandise. They must do this to qualify for delivery from companies that require orders exceeding their established minimum amounts for delivery. These developments have caused inconveniences of operators in major cities too, and some have had to change their buying habits. But it has had a much greater effect on restaurants located in outlying areas and small towns, where many low-volume restaurants are located. Storage also becomes a critical problem for these people, because their facilities are often very limited.

It is wise for today's operator to seek out and deal with suppliers who will deliver the quality and quantity that fits into the operation. That may mean buying like items from one or more sources.

It is also possible to save money by cutting off deliveries when possible. Years ago, restaurant owners went to market themselves and saw what they bought. Some still do. If you are close to a produce market, you can go there as often as you like, buy and carry your own. That cuts out the distributor's profit, and the difference between their delivery charges and your own transportation cost is profit to you. These savings can be substantial. In addition, the education gained through selecting your own produce and negotiating prices will be notably rewarding.

EFFICIENTLY STORING YOUR FOOD AND SUPPLIES

Improper storage of food and supplies is a wasteful practice that will cost any operator big dollars. To purchase sensibly, you must first determine your needs. Need can only be determined accurately if you can readily tell what you already have on hand.

There are many restaurants in which taking an inventory is virtually impossible. Their storerooms are in a shambles, with boxes piled on boxes, and all piled high in front of open shelving that is also full. In addition—as if that weren't bad enough—everything is all mixed up. You are probably familiar with these types of restaurants. They're the ones that order a case of #10 sliced pickles because they can't find the bottles they were sure they had. The suppliers love these people, because it is no work at all to sell to them. They just fill out the order blank while they try to work from memory or witchcraft. This may be profitable for the salesman, but it is obviously very unprofitable for the restaurateur.

Four Steps You Can Take in the Event of Vendor Inconsistencies

As with any relationship, the road between supplier and user is definitely a two-way street. Sometimes the problems between you and your vendors will occur as a result of the vendor not living up to his or her end of your agreement, and sometimes your payment or loyalty will dictate vendor performance. It is critical that you both understand that each of you is trying to run a successful business and that integrity is the foundation of your mutual success. If you feel that you are holding up your end of the agreement but your vendor is not performing on his or her end, here are a few ideas that might help you get things back on track:

☐ 1. Request a face-to-face meeting with your salesperson and his or her sales manager. At this meeting have any and all information gathered that indicates that your vendors has provided inconsistent service or prices. Have your G.M. or chef participate in the meeting and take whatever time is necessary to achieve a resolution to your problems. This presumes that you are current with your account with the vendor and that you have made a conscious decision to attempt to resolve the problem and continue doing business together. A good vendor really is like a business partner and it is a smart decision to have them help you solve problems. It truly is a short-sighted decision to change vendors on a regular basis because there are too many opportunities for inconsistencies with whole-sale changes, and, ultimately, inconsistency finds its way to your guests.

☐ 2. Having said that it is a good idea to work with your vendors, it is also a good idea to invite new suppliers in to show you their products. Competitive purchasing and knowing what else is available on the market is simply a good business decision and you should never get too comfortable with all of your suppliers. Attend trade shows and keep a reasonable library of trade publications in your business so that you know what is available to you.

☐ 3. Be prepared to refuse products that vendors send you if those products don't meet your expectations or standards. If you are serious about "holding the line" then you must occasionally be prepared to reject orders that aren't correct or that are delivered at inconvenient times. There is no delivery truck driver that we know of who likes to go back to the loading dock with product to be re-distributed. The message to your vendor is loud and clear and will become the subject of discussion at the warehouse. Of course, there is an implication that you have an alternate source for product.

☐ 4. In some instances, it may be necessary to write a letter to the owner of the company you are dissatisfied with. Letter writing has become a lost art in our business, but it can actually work in your favor. Since most people do not receive personally written letters, their effect is that much more powerful!

You must know the storage capacity of your restaurant. And, if possible, you should place your food and supply orders with such frequency as not to overload the facilities. Next, you should categorize all items and devise a system, so that each item has a specific place for storage. If you develop and maintain such a system, you will be able to make spot checks and take regular inventories with ease—lessening any danger of over- or underbuying. When you can't closely monitor your inventory (meaning monitor "with your eyeballs"), then you risk waste by overuse or pilferage. And there is plenty of pilferage in restaurants! Set up your storerooms and walk-in refrigerators and freezers so that everything has its place—and then make sure that your staff keeps them that way.

How to Prepare an Inventory Record System

You can easily set up a storeroom by first preparing an inventory record that categorizes the various items to be stored. Within each category, items should be alphabetized. The order of items in storage must be in the same order as found in the record. The records on page 88 will illustrate how this might be done.

The dry storage room would be set up in similar fashion with the items alphabetized if space allows. When space is insufficient, then this plan should still be followed as closely as possible.

It doesn't matter whether you arrange the storeroom and refrigerators to fit the record or vice versa—the main point is to arrange inventory in such a way that it is easy to count items and that you have a plan for storing merchandise when it is received. In this way you will always know how much of any item is on hand and what quantity should be ordered for production. You can also leave space for the purpose of making notes about items you notice are in short supply and which should be replaced shortly. The above samples are titled FOOD, which is the general name for these particular samples. The subtitles are for the categories within the total food inventory. If a categorized food cost system is desirable, then those subtitles become major categories. For example, the first category could be Meat, which would also be a separate category on the Restaurant Operating Statement and would allow for the purpose of separating food cost into various cost categories as depicted in Chapter Eight, A Model Statement of Costs. *What must be noted here is that such an operating statement is impossible to develop if the inventory record, along with a breakdown of invoices, does not include the same categories.* How this matter of food cost is reflected as FOOD or by categories is a personal choice; however, the opportunity to manage those costs by being able to analyze fluctuations by item can be invaluable.

HOW PROPER HANDLING OF FOOD SAVES MONEY

You must make sure that your staff is thoroughly trained in the handling of food and supply items. Fresh fruits and vegetables must be handled with care to avoid damage. In addition, they must be examined on receipt, to determine if they are the same fresh

Figure 4.2

Inventory Record

FOOD

Beg Inv	Item	Unit	M	T	W	T	F	End Inv	Price	Amount
	Meat									
25	Beef Stew	lb						10	2.39	$23.92
50	Chuck, Ground	lb						20	1.79	39.80
10	Round, Ground	lb						5	1.99	9.95
	Pork									
20	Bacon, sl 22/26	lb						20	4.12	41.20
25	Chops, Whole Loin	lb						15	3.49	52.35
	Lamb									
15	Chops, 3/1	lb						10	8.79	87.90
	Poultry									
30	Chix, cut up	lb						15	0.99	14.85
	TOTAL									$269.95

GROCERIES

Beg Inv	Item	Unit	M	T	W	T	F	End Inv	Price	Amount
	Canned									
6	Gr beans	#10						5	3.78	$18.90
4	Cauliflower	#10						3	4.26	12.78
5	Catsup	#10						4	4.66	18.64
13	Catsup	btl						12	1.79	21.48
14	Chili sauce	btl						10	1.69	16.90
5	Pears	#10						3	3.97	11.91
	TOTAL									$122.09

and wholesome products you ordered. Meat purchases must be weighed and closely examined.

Every restaurant has a certain amount of prepreparation of foods that is necessary before actual start of production. However, the strongly established trend toward "cook ready" foods has eliminated much of that work. But cleaning and cutting of fruits and vegetables and trimming of meats still must be done. In doing this, people sometimes get careless, and in the process "trim" a sizable amount of foodstuffs that could be used and *sold*. For instance, tomatoes can be cored and sliced, which allows for the entire tomato to be used. Although this may seem trivial, it is just one area where proper training will serve not only in the preservation of tomatoes, but will carry over into the proper handling of other items as well.

How Special Equipment Can Help You

You should carefully analyze your food handling and preparation techniques to make certain that waste is eliminated wherever and whenever possible. If special equipment helps, and if it will increase your profits and preserve your quality standards, then use it!

There are many companies that make a variety of kitchen aids. One such tool is The Frugal Gourmet, distributed by Robinson Knife Co., Buffalo, New York 14225. This utensil will core tomatoes, loosen grapefruit segments, remove potato eyes, remove apple and pear seeds, form melon balls, score cucumber rinds, and stem strawberries.

Again, such items will help your staff better prepare your food. They are worth considering, not only for their time- and money-saving advantages, but also because they can help to make food more attractive and appetizing.

KEEPING IN LINE WITH SANITATION REQUIREMENTS

All cities have a public health department that is organized for the purpose of safeguarding the health and welfare of their residents. Those bodies, in conjunction with the various state and national organizations devoted to maintaining high standards for food handling, have developed the guidelines to be used in public restaurants. There are many publications available that will furnish the information you need to maintain your restaurant operations at an acceptable level. These publications can be obtained by contacting your local Food Service Sanitation Department, or through the offices of your local or state restaurant association. There is no shortage of information available, and the material you get will form the foundation for much of your employee training programs.

Although you must of course adhere to the city health codes—there is also the matter of your own sense of loyalty and responsibility to your restaurant customers. Remember, your customers place their trust in the hands of you and your employees every time they come to your restaurant. Therefore, it is your responsibility to take every precaution necessary to protect the food and drink served.

How Improper Storage Results in Loss of Profits

In addition to the losses that you can suffer through improper prepreparation of foodstuffs—mentioned earlier in this chapter—is the loss that can be incurred with bad storage technique. For example, refrigerators that are improperly regulated as to temperature will cause:

- Spoilage that necessitates *discarding* food instead of using and *selling* it.

- Loss of poundage in meats due to shrinkage. That kind of loss translates into money that comes straight out of your pocket.

When dry storage rooms are improperly planned and maintained, it means:

- Broken containers resulting in spilled contents that become unusable.

- Items actually "lost" in the storeroom, resulting in the need to spend your hard-earned dollars for items that you can't find due strictly to carelessness.

If your restaurant has too much space dedicated to storage, you may want to consider using some of it for additional sales activity, if possible. If, on the other hand, you have insufficient space, the first thing you should do is to examine carefully your purchasing and delivery techniques to be sure that you are not overbuying. In addition, be certain that racks, pallets, etc. are properly sized and used. And make sure that refrigerators are equipped right for storage. If you have a walk-in type, make sure that you are efficiently using it. For example, the coolest parts of the interior should be used to store those items that need the coldest holding temperatures.

Although it is not possible to address completely the matter of proper food handling and sanitation in this guide, suffice it to say that all sorts of help are available to you in the form of books, pamphlets, films, slides, lectures, etc.—and you should take full advantage of them.

The following is a source that can provide further information:

> Educational Materials Center
> National Restaurant Association
> 311 First Street NW
> Washington, DC 2000

It is in your best interest to enroll your restaurant in the National Restaurant Association. This organization is one that can be most helpful to you as well as any and all restaurant owners and managers. They provide a whole host of services to the membership and these services are oriented toward the restaurant business.

- There is a communication department that deals with issues affecting the industry.

- They provide technical services regarding equipment specifications, food safety, and many other subjects of importance to your business.

- There is a department that handles government affairs including lobbying the government on behalf of the membership.

- The list of published articles available to the membership is endless and encompasses all sorts of subjects including employee training, security, media relations, and many other items.

- There are statistical studies about the restaurant business around the country, and the results of these studies are also available to the membership.

It is important to know what the restaurants in your locale and in other parts of the country are doing about business to measure your own performance. The National Restaurant Association will provide information and the resource for you to do so.

The City of Houston Health and Human Services Department publishes "The Food Ordinance," which spells out the requirements for food service establishments in the city.

This same type of publication is prepared in your city and is a document with which you should be completely familiar. They have inspectors who periodically visit restaurants for the purpose of ensuring compliance with health regulations as stated in the ordinance. Although you may be familiar with this procedure, it is in your best interest to review the ordinance from time to time.

In addition to the above, the Health and Human Services Department requires that all food service establishments are properly licensed. In addition, they require certification of all management and supervisory personnel employed in restaurants. This certification is secured through a mandatory training program for all of the above employees. It is probably safe to say that your city has a similar program. These procedures are in force for the purpose of protecting the health of your patrons. All restaurant managers and owners should be strongly supportive of these programs.

Additional resources:

The National Sanitation Foundation
Ann Arbor, MI 48105

College of Hotel and Restaurant Management
Michigan State University
East Lansing, MI 48824

Cornell University
School of Hotel Administration
Ithaca, NY 14853

The Culinary Institute of America
433 Albany Post Road
Hyde Park, NY 12538–1499

Checklist of Steps for Handling a Food Poisoning Complaint

There are few worse feelings as a restaurateur than receiving a call from a guest who claims to have gotten food poisoning at his restaurant. The first step in any such conversation is for you to realize that you absolutely cannot approach the issue in a confrontational way or attempt to prove the guest wrong. There simply is no way of "winning" by appearing to doubt the caller. Instead, the following course of action is recommended:

☐ 1. Politely ask the guest how they came to the conclusion that it was food eaten at your restaurant that made them ill. It is not unreasonable to ask if they have seen a doctor or been to a clinic to have the illness diagnosed. Again, you are merely seeking information about the diagnosis. If they have seen a doctor, inquire if you may call him or her to obtain more specific information so that you may better isolate any problems that may exist in your restaurant. Try to ascertain what food item the guest suspects may have caused the illness.

☐ 2. If you do not have a "Guest Incident" report it is a good idea to design one or get a copy of one used by a fellow restaurateur. The report allows you to document all the pertinent information about the guest's complaint and have it available if and when needed. Be sympathetic with the guest but never acknowledge any agreement with his or her diagnosis, you are merely trying to gather information.

☐ 3. Ask the guest what it is that you might be able to do for them. This is where it can become interesting. You conceivably could get responses that range from "I just wanted to let you know that I had a problem" to "I want you to pay for all my medical bills as well as for my pain and suffering." Depending on the severity of the problem you may choose to simply ask the guest to forward all medical bills associated with the illness to you or you may choose to seek legal counsel or contact your insurance agent to determine the course of action. The key issue here is to deal with the problem expeditiously and to try to diffuse any further actions on the part of the guest. In our experience, most guests simply want reimbursement for their pertinent medical expenses and a sincere apology. A follow-up letter and an invitation to return to the restaurant as your guest are certainly in order. If it appears that the guest will not be satisfied after you have taken these steps, you should contact your attorney and insurance agent and let them intercede on your behalf, giving them instructions to not alienate or aggravate the situation.

☐ 4. At all management meetings you should discuss this procedure and review any calls you have had of this nature. It cannot be overemphasized how important it is to avoid putting the guest on the defensive. The bad press you could receive and the legal bills that could ensue greatly outweigh the cost of settling the complaint early and effectively.

FOOD SAFETY AND THE EFFECTS OF FOODBORNE ILLNESS

A subject that all restaurant operators either know or should know about. Do you know enough? Have there been changes that can have an effect on our business? Yes, there have been changes—they have occurred in the production of many of the foods that we have on our menus. There have also been changes in the pathogens that affect our foods. These have resulted in mutations that are now resistant to the antibiotics that have been used in the past.

Food safety is a subject that rightly belongs in the realm of quality control of a food service program. And that is something that all food management people, whether in restaurants, hotels, contract food service companies, hospitals, etc. should be acutely aware of. It is obvious that the health and welfare of the customers is an all-important ingredient to the continuing success of any restaurant. Events like the *E. coli* incident with the West Coast restaurant chain and the Mid-West meat processing plant have highlighted the increased possibility of our encountering contaminated foods. It is virtually impossible for you to tell by visual examination if purchased products might be contaminated. The only safeguard is to practice good food management. While the government is doing a good job of identifying problem areas, it is the restaurant manager who must train and supervise employees in proper food handling techniques in order to ensure against harm to the customers.

Checklist of Food Safety Signposts

☐ Do you spend sufficient time in the dining room with your customers? Do you listen to what they say about your establishment? They can tell you about how they see your floors, windows, walls, light fixtures, and the overall condition of the restrooms.

☐ Is your staff uniformed? Are the uniforms fresh and clean? Do employees in the kitchen wear hair coverings?

☐ Do the servers wear plastic gloves?

☐ Do you use serving trays? Is care taken to prevent hair from falling on the food that is carried on trays?

☐ How do customers perceive the management personnel? Does their appearance and the overall appearance of the restaurant say to customers, "this is an inviting place to eat and one that obviously practices food safety at all times?"

☐ Is the exterior of the building and the parking lot as clean and neat as possible?

☐ Is there anything more that I can do to prevent food borne illness?

The following material was prepared by John R. Farquharson, FMP, President of the International Food Safety Council and is reprinted here with his permission.

"The time in which we now live may well be the most critical time we have experienced when it comes to the very important issue of food safety. The manner in which we approached food safety in the past is just not good enough today. New pathogens that are food borne and newly recognized are predominating in the United States in the last two decades have, because of their complexity and their adaptability, the ability to cause acute illness, chronic or secondary complications, and in some instances, the ability to cause death.

"If you and your staff are educated in the proper handling and preparation of food, you may prevent serious cases of illness and may even save a life or lives.

"Illness is caused by natural organisms that occur in most foods. If you wash the product, your hands and utensils and cook them thoroughly, your chances are greatly increased that you won't have a problem. You must also chill the product correctly for storage.

"My father ate soft boiled eggs every morning for breakfast and to my knowledge *never* had a problem with the food borne illness salmonella enteritidis—today, he well might.

"As a family, we ate very rare hamburgers at picnics and cookouts and never had a problem with the food borne illness *E. coli*—today, we might. Why might we have a problem with food borne illness today involving these issues, yet not in the past? Because they're new!

"These 'new' pathogens are mutations of ones that were apparently controlled in the past by nature, sanitary practices, or by antibiotics given to the source at feeding time. But, these practices don't seem to work anymore.

"Today faced with these new issues, it becomes vitally important that the people preparing food in kitchens are properly educated in the area of food safety. We must know how and why to properly wash our hands with an antibacterial soap to prevent cross-contamination. We must be educated in order to know what cross-contamination is and how to prevent it. We must be educated to know what temperature to cook foods to and for how long a period of time, and why.

"Education and training are the only answer to the issue of food safety today. The way it was done in the past is just not good enough today. We must be made aware just how critical proper food safety practices are. We need to know where education and training are available and be motivated to become educated. And, to also be motivated and disciplined to practice these learned standards.

"We have about 250 million people living in the United States today. The approximate consumption of each and every person in our country eats:

    126 pounds of potatoes
    100 pounds of other vegetables
     90 pounds of fresh fruit
    110 pounds of red meat
    230 pounds of dairy products

"The nation's food consumption is gigantic each and every year. It is absolutely phenomenal that the United States has the safest food supply in the world today, taking into consideration how much food is produced, transported, processed, packaged, stored, and prepared. There are many places along the food chain that it can become contaminated.

"The cost of food borne illness to the United States in medical expenses, the loss of wages and productivity, along with industry loss of contaminated food products is estimated between $1 billion and $10 billion every year. Infections cause millions of illnesses and thousands of deaths. Most of these infections go undiagnosed and are not reported.

"Food poisoning comes from tainted or contaminated food, caused by organisms that naturally occur in most foods. A bacterium is the culprit in most cases. Bacteria are found everywhere and live in each and every one of us. There are thankfully, only few strains of bacteria that are insidious. Viruses can also cause food borne illness. Shellfish and salads are susceptible to viruses. Another source of food borne illness is mold, and there are a few that are deadly. Spoiled fruit and spoiled vegetables are easy to see and smell. Some tainted food is not always that easy to identify.

Bear in mind, organisms can travel from raw to cooked food, so be careful not to allow raw food to touch cooked food. Wash all utensils, the cutting board and your hands between each prep procedure in hot, soapy water. Cooking food until 'hot' (165 degrees F to 212 degrees F) will kill most food borne organisms. And, NEVER leave prepared food out of the refrigerator for over two hours. Bacteria that causes food borne illness grows quickly in warm temperatures.

Remember, just one incident of food borne illness can be the most devastating thing that can happen in a foodservice operation—it can put you out of business."

The International Food Safety Council, with national headquarters in Chicago, Illinois, publishes literature containing continuing important and timely advice. One such publication is a quarterly magazine, *Best Practices*. You can obtain a full year's subscription by calling their toll-free number: 1–800–773–1455. The mission of the International Food Safety Council is to create awareness in the industry of the importance of food safety education. The following information is reproduced by permission:

"Whether you're in the foodservice industry or taking your family out to dine, you want to feel safe about the food you serve and eat. The International Food Safety Council, a coalition of thousands of restauranteurs and foodservice professionals certified in food safety, is dedicated to heightening awareness of the importance of food safety education.

The International Food Safety Council strives to present a unified, recognizable voice to inspire public confidence in the industry's commitment to provide safe food. Council participants display a logo decal on the doors of their establishment to show their customers their commitment to safe food. Industry leadership has determined educating and training foodservice managers and employees is the most effective method for providing safe food. The Council takes several key steps to promote food safety:

➡ Each September, the International Food Safety Council sponsors National Food Safety Education Month to raise awareness of the importance of safe food preparation in professional kitchens and homes.

➡ The International Food Safety Council is a founding partner in the Partnership for Food Safety Education, a coalition of industry, government and consumer organizations. The Partnership is part of President Clinton's 1997 National Food Safety Initiative, designed to enhance food safety from the farm to the table. In November 1997, the Partnership launched its nationwide consumer education campaign developed to educate the public to handle and prepare food safely.

➡ The Council publishes *Best Practices: The Professionals' Guide to Food Safety,* which is a quarterly magazine, that delivers important food safety information to those who need it most: Foodservice facilities, restaurant managers and chefs.

➡ Organized by the National Restaurant Association's Educational Foundation, the International Food Safety Council promotes food safety by encouraging training at all levels throughout the food service industry. Through its awareness and educational campaign and information publications, the Council is leading the way in raising the bar on food safety.

➡ By supporting the International Food Safety Council, you show your dedication to food safety and the safety of your customers. As a non-profit organization, the Council is supported entirely by the industry we serve and represent. With the help of the International Food Safety Council, your customers don't have to imagine enjoying a delicious meal without worrying about unsafe food. They can!"*

The following material covers the important topic of cross-contamination and provides helpful guidance in dealing with one of the leading causes of foodborne illness. The article entitled, "Cross-Out Cross-Contamination," appears in the Winter, 1998 issue of *Best Practices* and is reprinted here with the permission of The International Food Safety Council.

Cross Out Cross-Contamination

Remember when cross-training foodservice employees became an established trend? If it were as easy for employees to learn one another's jobs as it is for microorganisms to cross-contaminate a kitchen, then all the industry's kitchen personnel could cook as well as Paul Bocuse or Paul Prudhomme.

Cross-contamination, in homes and foodservice operations, is one

---

*Product of Educational Foundation of National Restaurant Association.

of the leading causes of foodborne illness today. As many as four million food-related illnesses a year are the result of cross-contamination, according to the U.S. Centers for Disease Control & Prevention estimates. Of those estimates, about 18 percent of reported cases can be linked to contaminated equipment and up to 35 percent linked to poor personal hygiene.

Cross-contamination happens because people don't realize how easily bacteria can move around a kitchen," says Dr. Elizabeth Scott, a food and environmental hygiene consultant in Newton, Mass.

Foodborne pathogens—microorganisms like salmonella, *E. coli*, and campylobactor can hitch a ride on anything with which they come in contact. Cross-contamination occurs when raw foods come in contact with other foods, hands, utensils, and dishtowels, rags or sponges.

Though cross-contamination can start at practically any point in an operation, from loading dock to front door, the source of most cross-contamination is raw meat, poultry or seafood. While most of these products will eventually be cooked to the proper temperature—killing any pathogens that might be present—these pathogens can end up in other foods if the proper precautions are not taken. Awareness of what cross-contamination is and how it occurs is the first step in preventing it.

"All raw meats have bacteria, so you have to assume they're potentially hazardous," says Joe Rubino, senior technical director for bio sciences at Reckitt & Colman, Montvale, N.J.

Putting Up Barriers

Cross-contamination is one of the easier problems to rectify in a foodservice environment, according to Jack Kennamer, president of KatchAll Industries, Cincinnati. "One way to think of it is to create food production highways that never intersect."

The idea is to handle raw foods in such a way that they're not likely to come into contact with foods that will not be cooked. That means creating barriers-physical, chemical and systems-related-between food products.

Prevention starts at the back door. Deliveries of raw meats, poultry or seafood should be handled first among all deliveries. Once checked, store product separately from other foods under refrigeration. Potentially hazardous product also should be stored wrapped or in containers on a lower shelf, not above other foods, to prevent any juices from dripping down on foods below. Placing a drip pan beneath the product also can prevent potential cross-contamination and make it easier to keep walk-ins clean.

"We now have a receiving department that's just responsible for receiving and storing all product," says James Larsen, executive chef at Delaware Park Racetrack & Slot Casino, Wilmington, Del. Products for the facility's 10 restaurants now are received in one place and stored in a new commissary or the central kitchen. All products are stored in their own walk-ins—one for produce, one for dairy, one for meat and poultry, and one for everything else.

Operators also can reduce the risk of cross-contamination by separating food preparation by time and space. In other words, designate a separate time or a separate area of the kitchen to prepare such items as meat, seafood and poultry that are well spaced from product prep so that the foods do not cross paths.

Buffets, Inc., Eden Prairie, Minn., also puts up physical barriers to cross-contamination in its units. "We actually design our restaurants to help prevent it," says David Goronkin, executive vice president, operations. In addition to separate walk-ins, HomeTown Buffet units have separate prep areas for poultry, produce, and so forth. The Physical design of the restaurants, including delivery, storage and prep areas, coolers, cooking areas and pass-throughs, also is safer and more efficient because of input from kitchen staff, according to Goronkin. "They have the best understanding of food processing and flow," he explains.

An Ounce of Prevention: Cross-contamination occurs when pathogens in one food—usually raw meat, poultry or seafood—are transferred to other foods that are not cooked or will not be cooked further. The most common carriers are:

- Raw foods to ready-to-eat foods

- Food-to-food contact (including food touching or stored under dripping raw meat and poultry in a walk-in)

- Cutting boards

- Utensils and dishes

- Work surfaces and prep areas

- Cleaning rags and dish towels

- Hands

Prevention is a matter of common sense once you know these common causes. Institute practices like these:

- Store and prepare raw meats in separate areas from cooked and ready-to-eat foods.

- Dedicate specific cutting boards, utensils and containers to each type of food product.

- Finish one task, clean up and sanitize before staring another.

- Use dedicated, color-coded or disposable sponges and cleaning rags.

- In addition to soap and water, use approved sanitizers.

The Right Tools

Having the space for separate prep areas may be a luxury for some operators, but there are other ways to keep food production "separate." One is to always use tools that are dedicated to a particular type of product. Color-coding is one way to tell them apart. Buffets, Inc.'s units use color-coded cutting boards in each of its prep areas—yellow for chicken, green for produce, red for meat, and so forth. Some operations also use utensils, especially knives, with color-coded handles. Designating each color for a specific food minimizes the danger of cross-contamination.

Delaware Park's Larsen trains employees to use specific containers for each product as well. Containers are clearly labeled—"Raw Chicken" or "Tuna Fish Salad," for example—so they're not mistakenly used for something that could cause cross-contamination. Larsen also says having enough cleaned and sanitized containers on hand is key to making sure employees don't use them for something else.

KatchAll even manufactures a container specifically designed for ice. "Ice is a forgotten food," Kennamer says. "It's used for everything—in drinks, to chill shrimp or salad—but too often it's moved around in whatever container is available."

Gloves are another tool that helps minimize cross-contamination when used properly. "There are lots of misconceptions about gloves," says Doug Marquis, president of Handgards, INC., Northbrook, Ill. "Just because you're doing things properly, you have to teach people the right way to use gloves to avoid cross-contamination."

In operations where gloves are used, employees should first wash their hands. Gloves should only be used for the job at hand, and changed each time the employee starts a new task. And, employees need to wash their hands each time they change gloves and especially when handling food that receives no further cooking. To avoid cross-contamination, discard punctured or ripped gloves.

Other tools to help prevent cross-contamination include disposable aprons, which also should be changed between tasks, and non-absorbent versions of the pads used to prevent cutting boards from slipping on wet countertops.

Keeping It Clean

All of these tools can be incorporated into a HACCP-based system that will help prevent employees from taking short cuts. But no matter how many tools you use, if they're not clean and sanitary, cross-contamination still poses a dire threat.

Utensils and cutting boards should be run through a properly operated dishmachine after going from raw to cooked or raw to ready-to-eat food prep. Work areas such as countertops also should be cleaned after each task, but need to be sanitized as well.

"For hands, anti-bacterial soap with a good 20-second scrub and running water," says Rubino. "That rinses off the bacteria. Surfaces are harder to rinse, so you have to clean them, then sanitize them."

The most common sanitizers in the foodservice industry are chlorine and quaternary ammonium compounds. Cleaning compounds that make a disinfectant claim must meet Environmental Protection Agency (EPA) standards. Chemical sanitizers and other antimicrobials used on food contact surfaces must meet the requirements of the Code of Federal Regulations, which can be found in your state health code. Employees must be careful to use the right cleaners and sanitizers for each job.

"It takes different chemistry to remove soil from floors versus countertops," says Dan Flesher, assistant vice president of new business development at Ecolab, St. Paul, Minn. "But employees also need to take care to use an appropriate *sanitizer* on the surface of countertops."

Cleaning rags and dishtowels can be common sources of cross-contamination. To prevent the potential spread of pathogens, one option is color-coded cleaning rags that correspond to a specific food prep area or task. Another is disposable towels. If cleaning rags must be used again before being laundered, then they should be rinsed or stored in sanitizing solution between tasks.

Containers of sanitizing solution also should be kept handy for disinfecting utensils and thermometers. You can use a sanitizer specifically designed for that purpose, or prepare a diluted solution of chlorine bleach and water (about 3 tsp. chlorine to 1 gal. water or 50 to 100 p.p.m. of chlorine).

Finally, hands are the most common carriers of microorganisms from place to place in a kitchen. Not only do employees need to wash their hands between tasks and especially after using the restrooms, but they also need to be aware of what they touch throughout the operation.

It's not uncommon even for careful employees to prepare raw meat, then carry it to the oven and touch both the oven door handle and thermostat dial without thinking about it. The next person to touch the oven can transmit pathogens to ready-to-eat food somewhere else in the kitchen.

Automatic faucets at hand sinks also help prevent cross-contamination caused by people turning on the faucets with contaminated hands. Otherwise, employees can use paper towels to turn faucets off and open doors.

Ultimately, awareness of what causes cross-contamination is the first step in putting up barriers to prevent it. Employee training is key to raising that awareness.

What To Watch For: There is no complete list of foods that can be potential carriers of dangerous pathogens, "We want operators to look at broad categories in case something doesn't fall into a checklist," says Bob Harrington, former vice president of technical services at the National Restaurant Association.

In general, employees should take the greatest care when working with

- Raw meat
- Seafood
- Eggs
- Poultry
- Shellfish

Raw produce also can potentially carry pathogens, but they're most likely to be on the outside. Removing the outer layer of leafy vegetables and washing under running water, or peeling other fruits and vegetables usually suffices. But again, if employees touch the peel, they need to wash their hands before prepping the produce.

INVENTORY CONTROL METHODS THAT WORK

There are two basic inventory control methods with variations that you can effectively use. Many restaurants never take an inventory during the course of a fiscal year, estimating their inventory at year end. Such a practice can be very costly. No matter how big or small your business is, you must have a system for controlling your inventory.

The Perpetual Inventory System

Very simply, this particular system requires that "pars" or inventory levels be established for all stock or standard items on hand. Each item has an individual record, often referred to as a bin card. These cards are updated constantly from purchase records to reflect current cost. As units are used, a running record is maintained of units left in inventory and the cost of items transferred to production. Each item also has a reorder point or a level of units on hand, at which time a purchase is made to bring the total units back up to par. Theoretically, with this system, inventory is being taken constantly as items are moved into production and eventually sold.

The Physical Inventory System

This system is simply a matter of maintaining an inventory record of all items on hand. It should be broken down into units that are actually transferred to production. For instance, if #10 cans of tomatoes are transferred as individual units into production, then the inventory of that item should be by the can rather than by the case.

At the end of each predetermined period, you take a physical inventory by counting *all* items on hand. The items are then priced as purchased, extended, and a total cost of inventory determined. This inventory record is generally kept in a book or on separate sheets of paper. It includes spaces for item name, price, amount on hand, and totals. See "Preparing an Inventory System," pages 87–88.

The basic difference between the two systems is in the actual counting. With the perpetual system, counting of items on hand is constantly going on, whereas with the physical system, all counting takes place at one time and only at the end of a fiscal period. That period might be weekly, monthly, or annually as decided by the owners.

It is very difficult for a small business to use a perpetual inventory system because of all the necessary paperwork involved. Even though such a system can be computerized, there will still be a considerable amount of paper to handle—and the cost may be too high for other than the very high-volume places to handle.

Selecting a System That's Right for You

If you don't already have a good system, you will profit greatly by installing one now! In our opinion, there is only one good way to control the costs in a restaurant, and that is by having a weekly cost control system that includes a physical inventory and an operating statement. The key lies in the system itself and how well it works for you.

Because food can easily spoil when improperly handled, and because food and liquor can "walk away" if you turn your back, you must keep track of both at all times. Remember that *watching* and *counting* are the keys to any system's success. As mentioned earlier, when you don't know how much inventory you have on hand, you are apt to either underbuy or overbuy. If you underbuy, you will have "run outs" and lose sales. If you overbuy, the following might develop:

- Spoilage can occur because your sales were insufficient to use up the perishables in time.

- Pilferage can occur because you have more on hand than you need. And if you didn't know what was there to start with, you won't know if anything is missing.

- It costs money to carry excessive inventory. And if you do, you are either borrowing working capital at high interest rates, or losing interest by not investing the money that is tied up in excess stock.

So if you want to have a profitable restaurant, *watch your inventory!*

How Best to Calculate Your Inventory Turnover

Restaurant inventories, because they consist in large part of perishable items, must be "turned" (used) often. You should strive to turn your inventory about once a week, or four times a month. Doing so will ensure your diners fresh, wholesome food.

You can measure your own effectiveness by calculating your inventory turnover ratio on a regular basis. This ratio is calculated by dividing the cost of goods sold by the average inventory cost.

Example:

ABC Restaurant takes inventory and prepares a statement each month.

Average Monthly Inventory—$4,000

Yearly Cost of Sales—$180,000

$180,000 ÷ $4,000 = 45 turns/year

45 turns ÷ 12 months = *3.75* turns/month

Your inventory must be taken at the close of each fiscal period whether weekly, monthly, or yearly. Inventories cannot be taken before the designated date, nor can they be postponed and taken at a later time. Doing so will distort the figures and make statistical comparison with past periods erroneous and, in some cases, totally useless.

How to Make Sure That You Receive What You Ordered

There are lots of "eagle-eyed" people around who are constantly looking for a way to pick up a fast buck. Therefore, you must keep a very sharp watch on your business—including the people who work for you, delivery people, repair or maintenance persons, customers, and security persons.

The best way to do this is to check your incoming merchandise carefully. For instance, it would be a very simple matter for someone to take out a few pounds of meat from any one delivery. And if you don't weight in your merchandise, you will never notice the difference. But you will notice the difference in your food cost if these kinds of people get into your pocket often enough.

Several years ago, there was a restaurant company that took extra pains to check incoming goods. And the purveyors they dealt with knew how closely they checked their deliveries. Even so, the restaurant caught the following neat little tricks:

- Bags of potatoes clearly labeled #1 Idaho Bakers that turned out to be California potatoes.

- Fresh parsley that was rebundled into smaller than standard size.

- "Sealed" cases from which a few bottles or cans had been taken.

There are lots of ways that dishonest people can find to pilfer your goods. "Short weighting" deliveries is one of the easiest.

Case History: The Importance of Keeping Tabs on Inventory

Charlie Shortor had a nice little family restaurant that he was able to handle pretty much by himself. Over the years, the restaurant prospered. Then the kids went off to college and Charlie decided that he should invest in a great big restaurant and make lots and lots of money. Well, Charlie found a place that he could purchase, and he took the plunge.

There were many good features about the new restaurant. Most of all Charlie liked the fact that the storeroom, back bar, and all refrigerators were equipped with locks.

Charlie's restaurant was very busy and sales were strong. But what was puzzling was why the food and beverage costs were high—so high that Charlie was not making any profit. He kept everything locked up, but still items were missing from inventory. Evidently there were pilferers in his organization. Charlie didn't know how all of this could be happening.

One day, while Charlie was hard at work trying to figure this out, he heard the porter with that often-heard restaurant cry, "Hey, who's got the keys?" Right then Charlie realized that, although he had locked up all his merchandise, he had not locked up all the keys.

Moral of this story: "You can't be too careful in this restaurant business"*or* "It's the little things that will do you in." More specifically, keep the keys in your pocket, and know who has them when you are not there.

How to Control Storage Areas

It is sometimes difficult to forecast restaurant sales on a day-to-day basis. But if you estimate your sales with your production supervisor, you will be able to relate those sales to the raw product needs of the restaurant. Once that is done, you can proceed with an actual issue of products to cover the day's production.

This method will never be 100 percent accurate, but the more you use it, the closer you will come. The result will be the prevention of people running in and out of storerooms and refrigerators all day long. Such a practice will help you control your inventory, and will also aid productivity by making the jobs of food preparation and service as easy and convenient as possible.

Access to storage areas should be limited to authorized persons only. One reason for this is obvious—to control pilferage in your restaurant, as in the example above. Another reason is the need to maintain order so that inventories can be categorized and merchandise stored by category in a prescribed manner.

Allowing free access to storage areas means that you will have no control over your storage plan, and it will be ineffective. Remember, people tend to throw items around carelessly, open cases unnecessarily, and generally cause disruption, especially when they are in a hurry. This is particularly true in the restaurant business. So guard your storage areas carefully!

■ ■ ■

On the following pages are checklists for purchasing, receiving, storage, and issuing, to help you rate your restaurant.

CHECKLIST FOR PURCHASING

✔ Who does the purchasing?

✔ Are purchase orders used?

✔ Are budgets for purchasing of food and supplies developed from operating history and forecasts of future business? Or are orders placed by habit or the "guess we need some more" technique?

✔ Are purchase specifications in written form?

✔ Do specifications provide enough information for evaluation of merchandise received?

✔ Are bid sheets used, and are all purchases made on a competitive basis?

✔ Are some items purchased in advance for future needs? What items?

✔ Are these future needs carefully forecasted?

✔ Is there sufficient and safe storage for future use inventory?

✔ Has the cost of money to carry the extra inventory been carefully considered?

✔ How often are the following categories of foodstuff purchased?

> Meat
>
> Groceries
>
> Produce
>
> Baked items
>
> Dairy

✔ Are they bought often enough? Too often?

✔ Do you qualify for trade discounts? If so, do you take all of them?

✔ Do you make petty cash purchases? How often? What is the average dollar amount of a petty cash purchase?

✔ Who checks invoices for payment? Does anyone?

✔ Who writes the checks or disburses the cash? Are they double-checked against vendor invoices and statement?

✔ Are any comparisons of prices paid made with other restaurants?

✔ Is the quality of merchandise closely monitored to ensure that "merchandise received" is the same as "merchandise bought"?

CHECKLIST FOR RECEIVING

✔ Who receives food and supplies?

✔ Is it always the same person?

✔ Where is merchandise received?

✔ Can you depend on the person receiving the merchandise? Will that person check the merchandise carefully? Will that person make sure that you get your money's worth?

✔ Do you have a scale at your receiving point? Is it used for weighing in merchandise? Or do you have empty boxes or unusable equipment stored on top of it?

✔ Is your scale adequate for your business?

✔ How often is it checked for accuracy?

✔ Are "merchandise quality guides" available to the receiving person?

✔ When weighing merchandise—

Are wrappers removed?

Do you buy ice at the price of red snapper shrimp?

✔ How are foods judged as substandard rejected?

✔ How are the invoices handled?

✔ Are invoices verified by signature?

✔ If you are on a cash basis, do you pay in cash or by check at the time of receiving?

✔ If by cash, do you have a "tight" system that will prevent fraud and theft?

CHECKLIST FOR STORAGE

✔ Are foods *properly* and *promptly* stored after delivery?

✔ How are meats handled? Are they stored in the best possible manner so as to prevent spoilage and shrinkage?

✔ Are your walk-in refrigerators equipped with wooden platforms to keep food items off damp or wet floors?

✔ Are fruits and vegetables in shallow trays to retard spoilage from pressure and lack of air circulation?

✔ Do you have sufficient refrigerator and storeroom space for the volume of business you do?

✔ Are those fruits and vegetables that are stored at room temperature properly handled?

✔ What is the temperature in

	*Should Be**
Your produce room	36°–40° F
Your refrigerator	30°–40° F
Your freezer	0–(–10°)F
Your storeroom	50°–70° F

✔ Are they too hot? Too cold?

✔ Do you have adequate locks on your refrigerators and storerooms? Do you use them?

✔ Who controls the keys to those locks?

✔ Do your employees bring packages or carry above-average-size handbags, etc., into the restaurant? Why?

✔ What procedure do you use for checking packages or handbags of employees going off duty? Or do you bother to check at all?

✔ Are vendor drivers carefully watched and checked to prevent pilferage?

---

*M.C. Warfel and Frank H. Waskey, *The Professional Food Buyer* (Berkeley: McCutchan)

CHECKLIST FOR ISSUING

✔ Do you have a procedure for issuing, or are refrigerators and storerooms open to everyone?

✔ Is any food given or sold to employees for removal from premises? How do you control this procedure?

✔ How often do you examine your inventory?

✔ How often do you count and price your inventory?

✔ Are food items that are transferred to the cocktail lounge properly charged and credited?

✔ Are beverages such as wine, liquor, and beer that are transferred from bar to kitchen properly accounted for?

✔ What is your inventory turnover ratio? Does it make you happy?

It is impossible to say too much about inventory control in a restaurant. When an operation is properly controlled, the storerooms and refrigerators are locked, deliveries are closely checked and weighed if necessary, the back door is secured in keeping with fire regulations, and all the proper steps regarding purchasing and production are taken on a consistent basis.

Chapter
5

How to Get More and Better Work from Your Employees

Table of Contents

Chapter 5

How to Get More and Better Work from Your Employees

Although many firms in the food service industry have become large enough so they can afford a specialist to handle personnel matters, there are many others that cannot. If you are financially able to carry such a person, hiring one will save you many hours of detail work. Either way, this chapter will brief you on steps you must take for the effective management of your employees.

In the restaurant business, high employee turnover seems to be a continual problem, with someone always leaving and needing to be replaced. This usually has little to do with how well you manage your restaurant—but it's a serious problem, all the same. Let's consider these reasons.

FIVE REASONS FOR HIGH STAFF TURNOVER

1. Most restaurants hire some part-time people in an effort to control labor costs. For the majority of these people the job is temporary, and they will move on to something else.

2. Some restaurant employees look unfavorably at their jobs, even though those same jobs are performed with dignity by thousands of people.

3. Working in a busy restaurant can be rough and tough. Only the hardy survive.

4. Because restaurants are busiest when the rest of the world is at leisure (holidays, nights, weekends), many people who want those times for themselves don't stay on for long.

5. Generally speaking, many restaurants pay smaller salaries than other kinds of

businesses. In many restaurants prices must be held at the lowest levels possible to protect sales and ensure customer acceptance. Although some restaurants are able to maintain high prices owing to their position with the status-seeking portion of the public, *not all can do that*. But that does not mean that restaurant employees don't make a good living. On the contrary, many are highly remunerated—through either salary or gratuities.

There are, of course, many other reasons for employee turnover and some certainly relate to poor management practices, such as failure to train new employees. Therefore, it is in your best interest to develop and maintain a formal personnel policy.

The Key Steps to Hiring Employees That Are Right for the Job

The important things you need to know in hiring the right people are

- whether you even need to fill the position.

- what the job is all about.

- what kind of person is best suited for the job.

Once you've answered these, there are many ways to find good employees. Here are six recruiting sources:

- Having one's own employees recruit from among their friends and relatives

- Advertising for help in various local and regional periodicals. Even though there may be many organizations advertising in the same paper, your particular restaurant may have special appeal for some individuals.

- Through the placement services of local high schools and colleges

- From the local Labor Department placement service

- Other restaurants or food service establishments, such as school or college food service and industrial plant cafeterias

- Through your own friends, acquaintances, and activities such as church and other community functions

It is wise to look in the neighborhood in which your restaurant is located. Transportation today is expensive and not always convenient for some people. Anything that you can do to minimize inconveniences and cost for your employees will pay big dividends for you. One example of this is the Triple A Restaurant in Houston, Texas. This establishment has been in business for many years and some of their employees have been with them for over thirty-five years. It is located adjacent to the Public Market and is a very busy restaurant. It is in an old neighborhood and many of the employees come from the general area around the market. Although it may not be possible for all restaurants to be located in areas where there is a pool of employees, it is wise to do some exploring to see if such a pool exists when it appears that there is none. Keep in mind that our society is mobile and that changes can easily occur.

Part-time help is important to the restaurant industry. We use many retired persons as well as college and high school students in a variety of jobs and it makes good sense to do so. It is also a fact that the immigrant communities from Asia, the Middle East, Mexico, and Central and South America have made a strong impact on the employment picture in the restaurant industry. As one successful owner states, "If it were not for the immigrants there would be no restaurants in business today." Although language may be a problem it can, in his opinion, be overcome because immigrant communities are both hard-working and intelligent. Training may present problems because of language differences, but these obstacles may be overcome by the opportunity to work with intelligent, desirous persons who want employment in your restaurant.

How to Develop a Better Application Form

Before considering your interviewing technique, you will need an application form, because you must maintain records in your business. Having such an application form, in itself, will tell you much about a particular person, such as

- Can the applicant read and write English?

- Can the person follow simple written instructions?

You'll get the answers to these questions merely by having someone use the form.

There are probably more kinds of employment application forms than there are pages in this guide, but they all have certain parts in common—previous experience, education, and so on.

Caution: There are some questions that you cannot ask an applicant. So before designing your form, you should consult with your local Labor Department office for guidelines.

The length and complexity of the job you are attempting to fill will dictate the kind of application form you will need. There is, however, the following standard information on all of them:

- Applicant's name and address

- Social Security number

- Telephone number where person can be reached

- Previous work record, rate of pay, and name of supervisor

- What form of transportation does the applicant rely on? Have own auto? Take bus? Walk?

You must take care in the construction of your application blank, to avoid trouble through violation of Equal Employment Opportunity Regulations. It is wise to seek counsel from knowledgeable persons regarding the law and what you can or cannot do. The following are some of the topics that you should not discuss.*

✔ Race

✔ Religion

✔ National origin

✔ Sex

✔ Age

✔ Marital status

Actually, applicants will usually volunteer most, if not all, of the information you need without any prompting on your part.

HOW BEST TO INTERVIEW PROSPECTIVE EMPLOYEES

Interviewing is a skill that comes from educating oneself in accepted techniques, and then from actually doing it over a period of time.

Key Point: **Your profits will be directly related to how good a job you can do in the selection and retention of employees. It is almost certain that substandard, noncaring employees will soon drive you out of business—and just as certain that good, caring employees will help you prosper in business.**

When interviewing candidates, keep in mind that the applicant has a need. Maybe it's a need for a change in employment, or maybe the person is unemployed and the need is basic. Your job during the interview process then is to explore these needs. And this can be done through skillful questioning.

How to Ask Result-Getting Questions

It is wise to avoid those questions that invite an abrupt "Yes" or "No" answer. It's better to use open-ended or suggestive questions that elicit conversation from the applicant.

---

*The list is only partial. You should do your own investigating as to the rights under law of employers and employees.

Examples:

Bad: Did your boss at the ABC Restaurant treat you well?

Better: Who was your supervisor at the ABC Restaurant? How would you describe this person?

Bad: Did you graduate from high school?

Better: Can you tell me something about your education? How do you think it might help you in the restaurant business?

Bad: Do you like this kind of work?

Better: What prompted you to enter the restaurant field? Do you find that work pleasant?

Bad: Do you enjoy serving food to diners?

Better: What do you most like about serving diners? Most dislike?

Bad: Do you like night work?

Better: What are your feelings about working nights?

If you study these questions, you will note that the objective is to give the applicant every opportunity to talk. When you encourage the applicant to do the talking, you will be able to listen and form your opinion of the interviewee. When an interviewer remains silent at times, the applicant often will become impatient and talkative. As a result, many of the answers the interviewer is looking for will evolve in the conversation without further questions.

How to Put an Applicant at Ease

If there is sincerity and truth in the interview process, then each person will put his or her best foot forward and attempt to reach the objective at hand.

The first step is for you to put the applicant at ease. Therefore, you should

- Provide as much privacy as possible.

- Have your telephone calls held.

- Instruct others that you are not to be disturbed unless there is an emergency.

If your restaurant doesn't have a private office where interviewing can take place, you can take the following steps to facilitate the interview process:

1. If you have a private dining area, it can be used for this purpose during off hours. However, avoid using a busy area, such as when your staff is trying to set up for a function—even though there are no customers in the house.

2. Select a table in a remote section of the dining room or lounge. Be sure, however, that there is sufficient light for reading and for observing the candidate.

Privacy is very important during the interview. You both want to be able to talk freely with no fear of being overheard. The more private you can make the interview, the more apt you are to elicit meaningful conversation. By doing this, you establish a businesslike environment and convey to the applicant that he or she is important, and that the interview will be conducted properly.

A proper interview is done after each party has completed the homework and has a knowledge of the other. Unfortunately, there are many situations when people are badly needed and little or no investigation takes place before the interview. It is in this kind of situation that "practice makes perfect." If you have "honed" your interviewing technique and if your application form is properly constructed, you will be able to move quickly into the process of evaluation.

How to "Size Up" an Applicant

When first sizing up a prospective employee for any position, "the eyes have it." Because sanitation is so very important in a restaurant, try to see the prospect in that light. Check the following:

1. Is the person neatly dressed? Remember that it is not necessary to have expensive clothes to be neat and clean.

2. How about grooming? Is hair combed? Neat? Clean? How about hands and face? If the applicant is sloppy and uncaring during the interview, he or she will probably carry the same habits on to the job.

Probably the greatest fault in all of us is our desire to be heard. It is a fact that, for the most part, people do not listen well. It is very important for the interviewer to listen carefully to what the prospect has to say, so as to make the right hiring decision.

A good interviewer is one who has the skill to encourage the applicant to talk, and who also has the patience and intelligence to *watch* and *listen*.

Some points to watch out for are the following:

1. Does the person seem overly nervous? Are the eyes steady? Check the position of hands and feet.

2. Does the applicant appear to be indolent? Sleepy?

3. Does the applicant appear healthy? How about complexion? Posture?

If you practice, you will become very adept at spotting these signs of potential trouble. The end result will be a high-quality employee who is interesting in making a profit for your business.

HOW TO DEVELOP A SUCCESSFUL TRAINING PROGRAM

Once you have developed all the techniques necessary to finding good employees, you will want to take steps to ensure that they stay with you as long as possible.

One sure way to keep employees on the job is through the development and consistent use of training programs. It is very important for people to feel confident of their own ability to do a job well. More than one operator has played down training because "they just get trained and someone else hires them away." This, of course, may happen. But a positive way to view such a situation is that, if your employees are so good and in demand, then you will surely have a thriving business—because of the great service they are giving your customers.

Another excuse, which is equally unfounded, that mangers use for not having training programs is that employees "turn over so fast" there is no time to train them. Well, that kind of thinking is dangerous, because owners do not realize that turnover is often the result of no training and little or no orientation on the job.

Employees like to be welcomed and smoothly integrated into the work group. Their skill on the job has much to do with how they are accepted by their peers. If they carry their weight, there is a good chance they will win acceptance of the group. Therefore, having contented, skillful employees who are able to work together will mean additional profits to you. And training programs, even if modest in design, will help bring this attitude into your restaurant.

You can develop your own training programs that fit your own particular needs. Consider, however, that because time is at a premium in most restaurants, the short, ongoing training sessions will probably be the most effective.

Model Training Session for Waiters and Waitresses
(fifteen minutes)

How to load and carry a tray: Select one person as the "doer." Select one person as the "learner." By working with the "learner," have the "doer" demonstrate how the tray can be loaded for balance. Demonstrate how the tray is lifted, and how the hands, arms, and legs all play an important role. Then have the "learner" go through the exercise. Stress to the group how the job is easier and safer if done properly.

Training will best be accomplished by those persons who understand and practice the principles of teaching. These principles are time honored and practiced by all good instructors. Below is a guide for instructing trainees from a book that was originally copyrighted some thirty-five years ago. You will quickly grasp the technique, and you will be a successful instructor if you will adopt and practice it.

The following has been excerpted from Lester Bittel and John Newstrom, *What Every Supervisor Should Know,* Sixth edition, pp. 227–229, Copyright © 1990. Reproduced with permission of the McGraw Hill Companies.

How Do You Get Down to the Real Business of Training Employees to Do the Job the Way You Want Them to?

Training can be either a very simple and highly satisfying task or a very difficult and frustrating one. If you can grasp and apply just four fundamentals, you can be a superior trainer. If you don't buy this approach, you'll spend the rest of your life placing blame where it doesn't belong, arguing that employees are unreceptive, untrainable or unmotivated, however, the problem will lie with you.

The foundation of systematic structured job training, commonly called Job Instruction Training (JIT) has four cornerstones:

Step 1. *Get the workers ready to learn.* People who want to learn are the easiest to teach. So let the trainees know why their job is important, why it must be done right. Find out something about the employees as individuals. Not only does this make them have more confidence in you, but it reveals to you how much they know already about the job, the amount and quality of their experience, and what their attitude toward learning is. This familiarization period helps the trainees to get the feel of the job you want them to do.

Step 2. *Demonstrate how the job should be done.* Don't just tell the trainees how to go about it or say, "Watch how I do it." Do both—tell *and* show them the correct procedure. Do this a little at a time, step-by-step. There's no point in going on to something new until the trainee has grasped the preceding step. This is basically a reverse show and tell routine, with your role then repeated by the trainee. You would begin by telling the employee how to perform the first step (and why) and demonstrating the procedure by doing it yourself. Next you would ask the trainee to tell you how and why it is done (to check for comprehension) and then to demonstrate it to you (to check for proper procedure). In effect, this is a double process—tell and show (by you) followed by another tell and show (by the trainee).

Step 3. *Try the workers out by letting them do the job.* Let the employees try the job—under your guidance. Stay with the trainees now to encourage them when they are doing right and to correct them when wrong. Then praise them when they are doing well and provide constructive feedback when they are wrong. The mistakes they make while you're watching are invaluable to both you and the trainees since they show you where they have not learned, and their mistakes will be useful to you as indicators of the things the trainees have not fully learned.

Step 4. *Put the trainees on their own gradually.* Persons doing a new job have to fly alone sooner or later. So after they have shown you that they can do the work reasonably well while you're standing by, turn them loose for a while. Don't abandon them completely, though. Make a point of checking on their progress and workmanship regularly. Perhaps three or four times the first day they are on their own, then once a day for a week or two. But never think they are completely trained. There's always something the employee can learn to do, or learn to do better.

■ ■ ■

The following are some short instructional sessions that can be scheduled with service people:

- Setting up a table

- Stocking a service stand

- Clearing between courses

- Proper service of food

- Preparing the guest check

- Presenting the guest check

- Serving of all beverages

For the bus people:

- How to clear the table

- Presorting china, glass, and flatware

- Setting up a table

- Serving water, rolls, butter, etc.

- Delivering soiled dishes and flatware to the dishwashing station

- How to fold a napkin

For the back-of-the-house sanitary workers: These are the people who wash dishes, pots, and pans and perform the chores necessary to the maintenance of a clean, safe, and healthful establishment.

- Show and demonstrate the proper technique for using the dishwashing equipment.

- Many of the equipment companies have videos that can be used for training.

- Carefully cover the proper use of chemicals used for these tasks.

- Carefully explain the need for care of the equipment used and constantly supervise for compliance of proper usage of some of the most expensive equipment in your restaurant.

- Stress the need for safety at all times and schedule safety-training sessions for all the employees on a continual basis.

- MOST IMPORTANT—make a strong effort to make these sanitary workers feel the importance of their jobs and recognize any job well done.

For the prepreparation and salad people:

- How to core a tomato before slicing

- How to core a head of lettuce the right way, instead of cutting off and discarding usable leaves.

- How to store produce properly

We can all think of hundreds of small, seemingly insignificant tasks that are performed daily in all restaurants. If you select from these tasks, you can develop a fine ongoing program that will produce the following very worthwhile results:

1. Your people will feel more important and closer to the business.

2. You will promote teamwork.

3. You will be constantly working toward increased sales and lower costs, thereby putting more money in your pocket!

One last word on training: keep the sessions short so that people don't lose interest. And be sure you pay your people for the time spent in these sessions. In addition, there are many fine programs that can be obtained that use film and recorded dialogue. However, these take somewhat longer to use, and that may present a problem. If so, try short, ten- to fifteen-minute sessions. Then, if you have enough time, use both kinds. Whichever you choose, we guarantee that you will be absolutely amazed at the results.

If you are in need of additional ideas or prepared and ready-to-use programs, you can contact your local restaurant association office for information on programs available through the Educational Office of the National Restaurant Association. If you are not a member, you may want to consider joining, because the organization is most supportive of its membership.

How to Measure Employee Performance

To ensure that your employees receive the raises and promotions that they deserve, you should institute and maintain an EMPLOYEE APPRAISAL PROGRAM.

Properly organized and done in a consistent manner, this is not at all burdensome. The following steps will help you to organize and handle this very important function:

1. Set up a file with a separate folder for each employee. You will use this file to maintain all personnel records.

2. In the file, you should have an appraisal form with spaces for the following information:

- Employee's name

- Date of appraisal

- Notes you have kept regarding the person's performance on the job, and notes to be taken as you talk to the employee. You will also want the notes from any previous sessions with that employee.

- Space for signatures that signify your acceptance, and the employee's, of the contents of the session.

Although some evaluation forms have room for other data, the foregoing will suffice for most of the appraisals you will need to conduct.

When and How to Do the Appraisal

You will need a calendar or tickler file to alert you when an appraisal is due. The length of time on the job or time between appraisals is of course your decision. Generally speaking, though, the first appraisal or review should be after the first three to six months of employment, and yearly thereafter.

Of paramount importance is the need to be consistent. If you establish an Employee Appraisal Program, make sure you follow through and do it on a regular basis.

The following are some suggestions that will help to make your program successful:

1. When giving an appraisal, make sure you do it in a place where you will have privacy. Make the employee feel at ease. Hold your telephone calls and do not allow interruptions. In other words, make the employee "king" for the hour.

2. Be prepared for the session. Be sure to give ample notice to the employee, so that he or she can also be prepared.

3. Be fair and forthright, and make every attempt to encourage a give-and-take conversation.

To sum up, when giving an appraisal, be consistent, be on time, listen, and evaluate. Remember too that appraisal time is a time to discuss the employee's performance. It is also a time for you to listen. By listening carefully, you may find out some very worthwhile information about your business. More important, the appraisal may help to turn a marginal employee into a good one, or cause a good employee to change his or her mind about looking for a different job. Either way, you win!

What about Salary and Wage Reviews?

There is some difference of opinion about whether salary or wage reviews should be given at the time of appraisal. Our preference is to schedule the appraisal review separate from any discussion about wages or salary. Remember, a performance appraisal is carried out for the purpose of discussing how well the employee has performed his or her duties during the stipulated period. Therefore, if you include a salary or wage review during the same interview period, you will likely find that the employee has little or no interest in discussing the job. And because money is so important to everyone, the employee will likely be preoccupied with whether or not there is a raise in the offing, and how much it will be.

Another difficulty that can be encountered during simultaneous reviews is the perception of the employee as to whether or not the salary review fits the appraisal. If the performance has been good, you will want to say so. Even if you offer a raise that is proper in your mind, it may be perceived as too low and inadequate by the employee. *Result:* a disgruntled and unhappy employee who may no longer perform to the same high standard.

Similarly, when you are appraising an employee whose performance has not been up to standard, your goal is to try and make him or her understand why you have such an opinion. Furthermore, you should be attempting to turn this person around so that a marginal employee can become a good one. Therefore, if you couple such an appraisal with the statement that no increase in salary is warranted, the entire session is almost sure to become totally negative. In the process, you will probably lose an employee who might have been good if properly handled.

In most restaurants, everyone seems to know exactly how much money everyone else makes. For this reason, you *must* have a wage and salary policy that sets the rate and range for all jobs in the restaurant. When you do this, you introduce and maintain consistency. You also eliminate all the speculation and suspicions that people have regarding how much money each one makes.

How to Communicate Effectively with Employees

Communication can be defined as our most constant activity, but the one to which we contribute the least thought. Our communications skills have much to do with whether we succeed or fail.

When considering how best to communicate with employees, one must focus on the status levels of the participants and the goals and desires of each. For example:

- The goal of the owner or manager is to develop and maintain a successful business, thereby earning more money to enjoy whatever he or she values in life.

- The goal of the employee is to perform in a manner acceptable to the management, so as to advance his or her position and earnings so as to enjoy whatever that person values in life.

How to reach those goals is a problem that you are constantly facing as a restaurant owner or manager. If you are to succeed, you must develop and maintain a high degree of skill in communications.

The ability to communicate effectively with employees has a lot to do with your "track record" as a good manager. If you are consistent in the way you deal with your people, they will know what to expect from you. As a result, they will develop security and confidence, and will perform better on the job.

It is not enough to speak of consistency of management. We have many words in our English language that go well with consistency:

✔ Firm, yet always fair

✔ Honest

✔ Forthright

✔ Friendly

✔ Courteous

✔ Generous

✔ Truthful

✔ Thoughtful

You can take any one, or all of them, to use with consistency—and you will go a long way toward communicating effectively with your employees.

Remember, all of your actions communicate something to others. For example:

- If you walk around with a scowl or a long face, someone will sense unhappiness and feel apprehensive.

- If you are impolite or discourteous with a person, he or she may take it personally and feel insecure and unwanted.

- If you are dishonest with your employees, they will develop the attitude that they must also be dishonest to protect themselves.

- If you are not forthright or "up front" with your people, you will probably encourage them to treat you—and each other—the same way.

How to Handle a Customer Complaint on the Telephone

These types of telephone calls are no easier to handle than the calls that are about a possible food poisoning incident. And as with the food poisoning example, there really is no reason to approach this call with an attitude that you need "win." No one likes to hear someone tell you what's wrong with your restaurant but you're far better off having them tell you than countless other potential or regular guests. Listening to someone recount a bad experience in your restaurant is simply a skill that you will have to learn because it is going to happen no matter how hard you try to prevent it. There are some things you will want to ascertain from the phone call, and here are a few guidelines:

☐ 1. *Be a good listener.* You must remember that the guest has not called in order to offer you an opportunity to convince them that they are wrong, they called because they want to vent. Take the first few minutes of the call to let the guest explain what happened. Along the way be sure to ask them pertinent questions such as what day of the week they were in, who their server was, what they had to eat, did a manager stop by their table, and was there any attempt to make things right before they left. Take good notes when they are talking because you will want to review the incident with your management team. It is a good idea to have a standard form that leads you through all the questions you should ask so that you can document the conversation you have. Fill it out thoroughly and keep it filed when complete. You never know when you may need it again.

☐ 2. *Be sympathetic without sounding as though you are patronizing them.* Chances are that something wrong did happen to them and you must accept responsibility for the actions of your staff. Most guests who call you will more than likely be expecting you to defend your restaurant so you will win many points by admitting that you and your staff may very well have let this guest down.

☐ 3. *Do not let the guest off the telephone until you have gotten their work and home telephone numbers, and their home address.* If they were in with guests, make sure to get their guests' names and numbers as well. Any follow up that you choose should include the entire party that was affected by the negative experience.

☐ 4. *Solicit the guest's suggestion for how they would like the situation to be rectified.* Oftentimes, the guest has a solution in mind when they call and they will be impressed with you giving them an opportunity to be part of the solution. You may choose to offer your own suggestion but be sure to ask at the end "is my solution acceptable to you?"

(continued on next page)

How to Handle a Customer Complaint *(continued)*

☐ 5. *Never, ever hand off the follow up to an assistant or hourly employee.* These types of issues are yours to handle and you cannot delegate the handling of guest complaints to someone else.

☐ 6. *Whatever solution you collectively come to, there must be immediate action and follow up on your part.* If it involves writing an apology letter with a gift certificate included or if it involves an employee contacting the guest to apologize for an action they took, you should mark on your calendar to call the guest within a few days to be sure they are satisfied. Beyond that, it is also important to tell the guest to be sure to ask for you personally when they do come in again since it is imperative that you meet this person face-to-face to assure that your collective solution is satisfactory.

☐ 7. If you follow the guidelines set forth in steps 1–6, give yourself a pat on the back for turning a possible negative encounter into a positive experience!

Key Ingredients for Better Communication

Schedule and conduct regular meetings with employees. In this way, your people will get the message that you want to communicate with them, and are concerned about their well-being, as well as your own. Set up regular times for the meetings and establish in advance the length of the sessions. Be sure to start and end on time.

Next, prepare an agenda and set down the rules for the sessions. For example, your meetings might follow this sort of format:

- Each Monday at 2:30 P.M., schedule a meeting with all kitchen personnel

- Length of meeting is thirty minutes

- Ten minutes for review of previous week's business

- Ten minutes for any revisions to menu, for example, for current week

- Ten minutes for open discussion; each person limited to a total of three minutes

If items of business arise that require additional time, schedule a separate session with only the person or persons concerned. Don't forget to stick to *your* rules. Don't let any one person, including yourself, dominate the sessions. And be sure that you use the old ears. Listening to "them that does" can really pay off!

A bulletin board is another good way to communicate special messages, and will help to keep your employees better informed. For example, congratulating people on birthdays and special anniversary dates, or announcements of local social and sports events. Be sure, however, to place only current and meaningful notices on it. In addition, separate the official governmental or civic portion of the board from your own day-to-day operational postings. It is important to make sure that the bulletin board is worth the effort to read.

BETTER EMPLOYER–EMPLOYEE RELATIONS

Often managers fail to recognize the very important part that employees play in the success of a restaurant, and fail to communicate because they are either too busy or feel too important. This is one of the biggest mistakes a manager can make.

Fostering good employer–employee relationships is an ongoing management responsibility that holds true regardless of individual organizational structure. It doesn't matter if you own or manage a large or small restaurant, independent or chain operations, fast-food, or dinner house business—the relationship between boss and worker is still the same. This relationship also holds true in those organizations that are unionized. The contract does not supplant the need for management to relate to the workers on good terms.

What to Do If Your Restaurant Is Unionized

Although much has been written about unions and management–union relationships, the material deals mostly with preorganization matters. To our knowledge, there is a scarcity of information relating to actual management of the unionized organization.

When a contract between a union and your restaurant is being negotiated it is very important for you to carry on a continual dialogue with the attorney who is representing you. All contracts have a certain amount of boilerplate that is common to all contracts for a certain kind of business and the language is somewhat general in nature. There is a second portion of most contracts that will establish certain specific rules relating to your restaurant. It is extremely important for you to understand all parts of the contract and how they may impact on your business. Always keep firmly in mind that the union business agents that you will be dealing with have jobs with the union that they are proud of, and that they have a desire to keep their jobs. To keep these positions they must be knowledgeable about the contract and how to interpret its parts to the advantage of the employees. It is well for you to have equal knowledge of the contract and all its parts.

A major point to remember as far as unionization is concerned is that if it happens to your business, it will bring about a change in your style of management. Once a restaurant has been organized, the management and employees must begin to live with the contract negotiated between management and the union. When the contract is signed by both parties, it becomes a legal document, and management and employees become bound to abide by the terms.

When this happens, problems may develop because either side—management or employee—does not understand the terms or implications of the agreement.

Checklist of Steps Employees Should Take if the Power Goes Out in the Middle of a Shift

There are countless reasons why this may occur, but the important issue is not "why" it happened but what to do when it does happen. Here are the steps you should take and the order in which you should take them.

☐ 1. *Stay calm and don't panic.* Call your staff together and explain the steps you are going to take and how you would like them to help you.

☐ 2. *Turn off any gas flames that may be burning.* With your power off, your vent hoods will not be working and you don't want the heat to build up in the kitchen, especially if there is a chance that heat could trip your fire prevention system. Stop cooking and or preparing any foods in production.

☐ 3. *Call your local power company to report your outage.* Try to gather as much information as possible about the outage and ask for the person's name that you are speaking with so that if you call back you have a reference point. The power company should be able to tell you if it is a localized or widespread problem, or if it seems to be affecting only your building. Much of what you do next will depend on their information.

☐ 4. *Hand out flashlights to your staff and help them evacuate the building.* At the same time, your front of house staff should be informing your guests as to the information that you received from the power company. Be prepared to absorb the cost of all guest bills if the outage is for an extended period of time. Some guests may not want to leave and may opt to wait out the period of time it takes to restore power, and that is a decision that only you can make. It is never a good idea to have a building full of guests and no power, so the best advice is for you to calmly ask the guests to leave so that their safety is insured. Only in the event of a very short outage is it recommended that you even consider allowing guests to stay in the building. At the very least tell them that for insurance purposes you are requesting that they wait outside until power is restored. Be available to answer questions and have plenty of candles or flashlights available!

☐ 5. *Secure all your money in a safe or in a safe place.* We have known restaurateurs who have had their power restored only to find out that their money has disappeared.

☐ 6. *Be prepared to hand out certificates to your guests which invite them back for a free dinner.* Generally, you accept that an outage means lost dollars and you are in a position to ensure that it doesn't also mean lost guests. It's a good idea to look into business interruption insurance that can help lessen the sting of these types of unavoidable occurrences.

And these problems can result in misunderstandings and the filing of grievances that may require time and effort to settle. Too many grievances, although settled, tend to build adversarial relationships between management and employees to the detriment of the business.

If your business is organized, study the contract carefully. Have an attorney or labor relations expert explain any parts that you do not completely understand. Remember that the union has the mechanisms and talent available for administration of its contracts. You must do likewise.

Of major importance if you're unionized is a separate file for each employee in your restaurant. The file should contain the following documents:

- Application form

- Health card record

- Appraisal form

- Wage history

- Record of any and all meetings between you and the employee. (Contracts usually specify how meetings are to be conducted, and whether steward or committee person attendance is required. This sort of meeting normally refers to the handling of disciplinary measures.)

- Attendance records

- Record all actions taken that have an effect on the employee's job, wages, hours of work, etc.

The foregoing is a general list of items that are necessary for the administration of many contracts. Your own particular situation may be different and may require a different type of recordkeeping. The main point is that you must be as adept at contract administration as are the union representatives who service your employees. Otherwise, you may find yourself in costly and time-consuming grievance sessions, rather than spending it on better ways to run your restaurant.

HOW WELL-GROOMED AND SMARTLY ATTIRED PEOPLE CAN INCREASE SALES

If you want your restaurant to be a winner, you will have to make it look like one. Theme and concept seem to have become the number-one concern of investors, as each tries to outdo the other in pizzazz and glamour. At the same time, the simple basics of good grooming and smart attire for employees often get completely overlooked.

What to Do if a Sexual Harassment Claim Is Made Against an Employee

It is important to note the following is not intended to offer legal advice. Presented is a practical methodology in assessing the facts in the event of a claim. While this is a fairly new legal issue in the restaurant industry, it has been around for countless years as a concern for managers and owners alike. Given the fact that the restaurant industry employs so many young, single people and that there has always been a rather perceptible difference between front and back of the house employees, this issue of sexual harassment is capable of reaching epidemic-like proportions. And while many managers may not be aware of the potential problems that may be occurring in the restaurant, there is no denying the heightened awareness that employees and lawyers alike have about this topic. Ignoring your role in this issue can only mean big trouble for you in the future. Here are several suggestions:

☐ 1. If you don't have a copy of a sexual harassment policy posted in your restaurant, then post one immediately. You can write your own policy, with legal advice, or contact the National Restaurant Association to ask for sample policies. The first step in cracking down on the problem is to let all of your employees know that you have a very specific policy regarding an individual's rights in the workplace.

☐ 2. Have each of your managers take a short seminar or lesson (keep your eyes open for literature passed on by your state restaurant associations) on the issue of sexual harassment. Be sure that all managers have the same information and that you have a standard form or format for handling employee complaints.

☐ 3. When a claim is made by an employee against another employee or manager, do not jump to conclusions based on verbal claims. Become involved in the process of fact finding. Too often we see where an employee complaint is treated as if it were not valid and the issue ends up on the front page of some newspaper. Many claims can be defused quickly by taking the time to listen and getting to the root of the problem before more harm is done. A sincere approach is not only recommended but increasingly necessary.

☐ 4. Gather as much information as possible, including all employee names involved, extent of accusation, frequency of allegations, and witnesses to the behavior if available. Your stance must be that this is a valid complaint even if it has caught you completely off guard or if it involves an employee that is key to your operation. We have seen instances where a long-term employee of five or more years has been accused by an employee who has been on the job less than a month, with the charges being proven to be correct and the key

(continued on next page)

What to Do if a Sexual Harassment Claim Is Made *(continued)*

employee having his job terminated. Be prepared to have even your most loyal or trusted employee accused of sexual harassment because it may very well happen.

☐ 5. Once you have gathered all the information available, you must give the accused an opportunity to have his or her say about the accusation. If you are trying to resolve this issue without any legal help or outside counseling, be careful to not fan the fire by throwing around your own accusations. Your mission is to stay neutral in your fact finding and to not come to any conclusions until you feel you have enough information to make a decision on what to do. In the process of doing this, be careful to not have the accuser and accusee work the same shifts. Another reason why you want to handle this problem swiftly.

☐ 6. Be sure to document all of the information you gather because this could become an issue that is taken up outside of your restaurant and is eventually put in the hands of attorneys. If you feel it is an issue that can be handled with a sincere apology, then be sure both employees agree to not pursue the matter once an agreement is made. If, instead, you feel that the charges are serious enough to terminate or otherwise discipline an employee or group of employees, be sure that your decision has been well documented and investigated. This truly is a case where "more is better" and you want to be absolutely certain that you have been thorough. Either the accuser or the accusee could claim unfair treatment and each may seek legal counsel. At that point you really need to give your own attorney a complete file to work with. In the long run we do not recommend that you try to resolve every issue by yourself and to some degrees you must be able to determine the extent to which you may need some legal counsel to decide the best course of action.

During a visit to The Savoy Grill, a fine old restaurant in Kansas City, one of the first things noticeable was the appearance of its very efficient service staff. The dining room manager wore a dark suit, white shirt, and black tie. The waiters were in black slacks, white shirts, black ties, white jackets, and black shoes. The bus help were in black slacks, white high-neck jackets, and black shoes. The personal grooming of the employees complemented the sharpness of the uniforms. The jackets were clean, shoes shined, trousers creased, and everyone's hair was neatly trimmed. You may think that this was "before the action started." Not at all; it was well into the dinner hour and the restaurant was full.

The feeling one gets from a restaurant such as this one is that the management really does care about its customers. It says that the kitchen is clean and that the guest is in good hands. Evidently, it gives other people the same feeling, because the restaurant has been there since 1903. Mr. John Griffith is the general manager of this long-lived business. It still has the original décor; the uniforms for the staff are still the same and the white tablecloths and chair back dusters are similar to the original. It is the oldest restaurant in Kansas City and when asked how it has been so successful for all these years, Mr. Griffith stated that it is the excellence of the food and service provided.

How to Select Uniforms That Will Complement Your Restaurant

Before making your uniform selection, there are certain factors that you should consider. For one thing, you must be sure that the colors harmonize with the décor of your restaurant. They must also be colors that enhance and complement the food and service you offer. Aside from black and white uniforms, there are many color combinations that are very attractive.

A good way to select uniform colors is to seek the advice of people who are expert in that business. Certain colors tend to excite people and are attention getters (e.g., red and yellow) whereas others can be a turnoff (e.g., gray). Some colors are cool and relaxing, some are gay and cheerful, and others are somber and noncommittal. The uniforms in your restaurant can be a focal point and a very important sales tool for you.

After you have settled on color, you must give some thought to style, kind of material, initial cost, and maintenance. Consider the following when selecting uniforms:

1. Do the colors coordinate with your restaurant's décor? Be sure they liven up the food and service.

2. Will the style be complementary to all of the shapes and sizes of your employees? Arrange to see the uniforms modeled by a few people of different size and build.

3. Should you buy or rent your uniforms?

4. Is the replacement cost in line?

5. Can the uniforms be laundered? Are they colorfast? Or do they require dry cleaning?

6. Who will maintain the uniforms? Employees or the house?

7. Will you also specify accessories? What color and style of shoes will be worn?

8. Can you obtain samples?

9. Are aprons to be part of the uniform?

10. Will the uniforms readily show spots and stains? Can they be "spotted" for small stains, or must the entire garment be cleaned?

Key Point: **The "best" uniforms will look like the "worst" if they are not properly worn and maintained. So make sure your employees adhere to your expectations.**

How to Help Keep Your Employees Looking Sharp

Some people dress sharp and take care of their overall appearance, whereas others could not care less. This certainly includes your employees. Therefore, furnishing uniforms will not ensure that your employees are sharp and well groomed. If you want to have a good-looking staff, you'll have to work to get it—and work even harder to keep it. Here are some suggestions:

- Use some of your training time for modeling and demonstration.

- Do not use the best-looking employee as a model, but have an average, ordinary-looking employee model for the group.

- Check that everything is just right. Accessories, shoes, hair, uniform condition, tailoring, jewelry, hose, etc., should all be correct and in keeping with your own particular dress code.

- Talk to the group while the uniform is being modeled. Run your own little fashion show and sell the idea that careful dress "says" care and efficiency. Sell the group on the fact that neat dress and good grooming will earn more tips.

In addition, you can provide these aids for helping employees to look sharp and stay that way:

- Accidents will happen. Try to have clean aprons and some spare uniforms around, if needed.

- Some restaurants provide full-length mirrors with tips about grooming to the side. Employees should be encouraged to check their appearance periodically.

- You can obtain pictures that demonstrate proper attire. These can be posted where they will be noticed.

- You can use the old technique of an inspection before each shift. This is a very good practice if it is done in a professional and consistent manner. If you do this, make certain that each employee knows that he or she must be acceptable in appearance, or he or she will not work. This may seem a bit severe, but in the long run it will pay in dividends to you.

"Training for Profit" Programs

All of this business of grooming and manners can be very nicely incorporated in your "training for profit" programs. As stated previously, you should concentrate on short, meaningful subjects as topics for your sessions. You can handle the sessions yourself or call on various employees to participate. In addition, there are other business people who will probably be more than willing to give a talk on the subject. Here are a few ideas you might want to try:

- Ask a local hair stylist to give a short demonstration on hair care.

- There may be a shoe supplier who will demonstrate the proper methods of cleaning and caring for shoes for long and comfortable wear.

- The uniform people will very likely have someone who will demonstrate proper maintenance techniques.

- You may find a department store that is willing to furnish a cosmetician for a short demonstration on skin care and tips on applying makeup.

These are just a few suggestions. Undoubtedly, you'll come up with more. All of these "little" things will help to make your employees feel wanted and secure in their job—and you know what that means for you.

DEVELOPING A PERSONNEL POLICY MANUAL

Restaurant owners and managers are more the "action types" who enjoy the activity of a busy operation. It is difficult for these kinds of people to take the time to sit down and compose something like a policy manual. Consequently, lots of them turn out to be "hip shooters" who neglect to establish a written policy. This practice can only lead to inconsistent management and result in getting wrong answers. If you run your business like this, you risk having disgruntled employees and a high employee turnover rate. Better to plan carefully—and write it down.

Although the development of a personnel policy manual requires time to gather and compile the content, it will pay off big. You will need written guidelines that include the following:

- Rules to be followed by employees

- What actions can result from breaking these rules

- A complete breakdown of fringe benefits that are offered

- Government laws and regulations that must be adhered to

- Guidelines for recruiting, interviewing, and hiring of employees

- Payroll procedures to be followed

- Job specifications and descriptions, and the approved pay scale for the business

What to Do if You Suspect Employee Theft

One of the unfortunate realities of owning a business is that there will always be somebody who believes that he or she is entitled to more money than they have rightfully earned. In the restaurant business where cash flows pretty quickly and where so many people handle money and goods, there is ample opportunity for bad apples to practice their trade. While there are no entirely foolproof systems, here are a few pointers on addressing this problem.

☐ 1. The absolute best control available to you is the use of good supervision. You might argue that you can't afford to hire another manager, but did you know that it only takes two servers and one bartender stealing $30 a shift apiece, each working six shifts a week to total over $28,000 a year in theft? There simply is no better system of control than to have active and visual management presence on all shifts. The best deterrent to any thief is to know that someone may be watching.

☐ 2. There is very useful technology available to you that you should take advantage of in the fight against theft. Most point of sale equipment includes software that builds in checks and balances on all money transactions. Have your management team undergo a training session with your P.O.S. provider that specifically addresses the tricks used by "experienced" servers when attempting to manipulate the system. We promise you, they have seen all the tricks and can help you look for the signs. Most equipment can provide you with individual reports on all transactions by position at the touch of a button. Learn how to read these reports and put them to good use.

☐ 3. When indicated, use an occasional "shopper" service. There are companies that specifically train their staffs of "shoppers" to visit restaurants anonymously and, while under the guise of being a guest, watch closely for signs of employee theft. These companies can work with you to target suspected employees or simply schedule periodic random visits to observe your staff at work. Again, you might say you can't afford this type of service but you must think in terms of what you may save by using them. We don't endorse creating an atmosphere of suspicion in your restaurant, but we are less inclined to tell you to assume that everything is always on the up and up in your business.

☐ 4. Involve your accountant in the analysis of your records. Most accountants have a knack for knowing when numbers appear to be inconsistent. As an example, say you have sales of $10,000 on a weekend shift and you've served about 500 people. That would give you a check average of

(continued on next page)

What to Do if You Suspect Employee Theft *(continued)*

$20 a person ($10,000 divided by 500). Over time this should prove to be pretty consistent. What would you say if you found out that you continued to do sales of $10,000 but now it took about 580 people to reach that number? Divide $10,000 by 580 people and you now have a check average of $17.25. Something is obviously wrong and someone needs to be checking this type of statistics regularly. In all likelihood, you have someone pocketing cash sales and some further investigation needs to be done. A good restaurant accountant is trained to look for these types of inconsistencies and it is a good idea to utilize his or her services.

As stated, it is important for you to have made firm decisions on all these matters, and to have them in some kind of written form. Also, the form you elect to use must be such as to allow for changes, because very little or none of this type of material is cast in stone.

There are consultants who can do this work for you if you are unable or unwilling to do it yourself. As you shop around for this service, you will probably find a range of fees charged. Keep in mind, though, that you get what you pay for—no more or no less.

A Sample Personnel Policy Manual

The following outline can be used as a table of contents for your personnel policy manual. Each topic includes a short narrative relating to the subject, and some tips on gathering information and developing policy.

PERSONNEL POLICY MANUAL
"YOUR RESTAURANT"

I   Recruiting, Interviewing, Selecting, and Hiring Employees (This topic was covered earlier in this chapter.)

II   Orientation and Training of Workers (also discussed earlier)

III   Job Specifications and Descriptions

In this section, you will *specify* each different job in the restaurant, and the skills and requirements that are needed. Further, you will *describe* the duties, functions, and responsibilities that are part of each job. Here are a couple of examples to guide you. They are by no means complete, but should aid you in developing your own.

Job Specification	Waiter/Waitress
Age Requirements	Minimum twenty-one years
Experience	Not necessary, but one to two years preferred
Skills Required	Must have basic knowledge of food, and service of same
	Must have some knowledge of wines and alcoholic beverages
	Must possess basic arithmetic, reading, and writing skills
	Should be well groomed, friendly, and have a degree of self-confidence
	Must have ability to work well with other people
Job Description	Waiter/Waitress
Reports to	Hostess or manager (if no hostess is on duty)
Supervisory Tasks	None
Major Function	Sets up and assists in clearing tables. Performs side work as directed. Serves food and beverages to diners in a manner acceptable to management. Follows methods and procedures as established.
Responsibilities	Reports to work on time in a clean and proper uniform. Is alert, organized, and ready to provide cheerful and efficient service.
	Reviews and becomes familiar with the menu
	Assists in seating guests where needed
	Assists bus persons in clearing and setting tables as needed
	Takes orders from guests and provides service in a friendly and acceptable manner
	Prepares, presents, and processes guest checks

IV   Wage and Hour Policies and Benefits

This is a very important section that should contain information regarding federal and state labor laws that regulate your business. One such law is the Fair Labor Standards Act, which establishes a minimum wage rate for most businesses in the United States. There are various other state laws that regulate overtime work and payment for same. In addition there are the provisions relating to allowable credit for tips against minimum wage. You will also want to include policy information regarding uniforms and student employee wage rates, if allowed.

Of particular interest to the restaurant are the IRS provisions relating to tip reporting. The law is specific in how this matter is to be handled, and about the responsibilities of both employer and employees.

All necessary information relating to conformance with the tax law can be found in IRS Form 8027, *Employer's Annual Information Return of Tip Income and Allocated Tips.*

In brief, employers must report for the calendar year the:

- Total charged tips

- Total charged receipts on which there were charged tips

- Total amount of service charges of less than 10% paid as wages to employees

- Total tips reported by employees

- Gross receipts from fool or beverage operations, and

- Total allocated tips to employees if total amount of reported tips is less than 8% (or approved lower rate as explained in IRS Form 8027) of gross receipts.

It will be in your own best interest to do everything possible to ensure proper payment of taxes on tips by your employees. The payment of money due and the reporting of same is very important to you as an owner.

Other items you will want to detail in your manual:

- Any allowance for uniform maintenance

- Employee meal allowance

- Policy regarding minimum employee age

- How to use your own particular time record

- Pay periods and pay days

- How work schedule is prepared, and who is responsible for the preparation

- Your policies regarding sick leave, vacation, and holidays

- Life and health insurance

- Computation of bonus and profit sharing plans, if any

- Company policy on other items such as rest periods and parking privileges

Developing a Fringe Benefit Package

You must first determine how much money you can put aside to fund such a package. This can be decided after you figure your annual operating costs. Certain items such as overtime and premium pay may be fixed by law, or decided by various government agencies. But you can control the hours worked before the "OT" or premium pay is due.

Life and Health Insurance

These two items constitute a very worthy portion of any benefit package. How much you can offer will depend again on your financial situation. There are many insurance companies eager for your business, and they all have an ample supply of agents to serve you. Some points that you should consider before agreeing to institute an insurance program for your employees are the following:

1. Insurance is generally thought of as a very important item by people seeking employment. Your recruiting efforts will be enhanced if you are able to offer something, no matter how comprehensive the program.

2. Insurance programs are expensive. No matter how desirable, they are not recommended for businesses that can't afford to pay the premiums. You should of course investigate thoroughly before you make any announcements to your staff. Once you commit yourself to a life and/or health insurance program, you will have to see it through.

3. Decisions will have to be made as to the amount of coverage per employee. You will also have to decide if the house pays all premiums, or if the employee should be required to pay for all or a portion of the coverage.

Vacation Policy

Most businesses offer some sort of paid vacation to their employees—and most, if not all employees, will expect it. A typical policy is one week after the first full year of employment, and two weeks following the second year and thereafter. There are variations of these basic plans, including a two-week closing of the restaurant at which time all qualified employees receive vacation pay.

Bonus or Profit-Sharing Plans

Today, we are hearing more and more about stock ownership plans for employees. Most of these plans are found in large companies and have come about during recessionary times when the subject companies were faced with financial failure. In some of these companies, the best employees may really not be employees at all. They are actually minority stockholders in the business. This sort of arrangement is good theory as it relates to employee participation in the business. However, it may not be so good if the employees do not see any financial return on their ownership.

As a general rule, the plans related to bonus or profit sharing in our industry are for the benefit of management personnel. There are different forms of these plans, but they all relate to sales and profits. For example:

- Certain plans pay a bonus based only on sales increases over a base amount. These plans are rare.

- Other plans pay on sales, but only if costs and expenses are kept under base amounts.

- Still other plans pay a percentage of net profit from operations before occupancy costs and taxes.

If you feel that a bonus or profit-sharing plan is important to your business, you can construct one similar to any of these. When doing so, you should seek the advice of your accountant or an outside consultant for assistance. Any plan such as this must be equitable to all parties, or it can cause more harm than good. No manager will be enticed toward outstanding performance by financial goals that are unreachable. None of these plans should be instituted and ignored by the owners. There should be constant communication during the accounting period as to the present state of the plan and how the bonus can be maximized.

House Rules and Regulations

This section will reflect not only your own philosophy of business, but also will stipulate the rules that must be followed to conform with those agencies that safeguard the public welfare. Every restaurant is somewhat regulated by certain city codes regarding sanitation, fire prevention, and the overall safety of guests and employees. In addition, there are laws protecting minority groups from discriminatory job practices.

New laws and regulations are being enacted all the time, and we must keep alert for changes. Some restaurants will come under the provisions of the Occupational Safety and Health Act. There is legislation for prevention of sexual harassment on the job. All of the regulatory agencies that deal with these items have some form of enforcement machinery at their disposal. It is important that you contact your local restaurant association for information related to these items.

You will also want to include your own rules relating to conduct on the job. All prohibitions should be spelled out to prevent misunderstandings. Here are a few subjects for you to cover:

- Specify which persons are allowed access to the storage areas for food, liquor, and supplies. If you establish and stick to a policy, you will be sure to control pilferage better.

- Decide and stipulate whether employees are allowed to frequent the dining room or bar when off duty. A *not allowed* policy may help you control costs by preventing complimentary food and drink practices.

- Determine whether employees are allowed to eat at other than scheduled times and in predetermined places. Establishing and enforcing a firm policy in this matter will prevent constant snacking and will also save you money.

- Set up a policy relating to drinking alcoholic beverages on the job.

- Cheating on the time record. There should be a policy relating to employees handling their own time records that outlines the need for accuracy of time for starting and ending the work period.

There are lots of other rules that you may want to cover. The main point is you will run a better restaurant if you state the rules for *all to know.* Your policies should also clearly state what action will be taken when rules are broken. Last, but certainly not least, you must mean what you say and always act fairly, firmly, and consistently with everyone concerned.

There are sure to be other items that you will want to include in your manual. So be sure you make provision for change without having to redo major portions of the document. A loose-leaf notebook is probably the best form to use. If you are unsure as to how to construct a policy manual or if you don't have the time, you can, as mentioned, contract for the task. Some consulting firms offer this as a part of their overall service functions.

Chapter
6

---

*How to Get Service Help
to Do Such a Great Job
That Repeat Business Is Guaranteed*

Table of Contents

Chapter 6

How to Get Service Help to Do Such a Great Job That Repeat Business Is Guaranteed

You can make a lot of money in this business if you keep the notion of "repeat business" firmly in mind. It is essential that your customers not only return to your restaurant for more of your fine food and service, but that they also send their friends and neighbors too. When customers are treated to good food, served in a smooth and friendly manner, they are most apt to return.

HOW TO MAKE YOUR PLATES MORE ATTRACTIVE

It is said that people "eat with their eyes." There is no question that the appearance of food has much to do with how it tastes. And the technique that is used to make food more attractive to the eye is garnishing.

Garnish is a term in cookery that is often misused. Garnish is from the French word *garniture,* and in classical cookery means "to complete the dish as prepared." Properly used, it sets the mode and tells the diner what to expect. An example of this usage would be Veal Marsala, which would indicate that the entrée was sautéed and finished with marsala wine. In this case, the garnish is the sauce that is made with marsala wine. Other examples would be Forrestière, Newburg, à l'Orange, etc.

In addition, the term may describe the accompaniment, as in Veal Cutlets Provençale. Without going into detail, this description says the item, if properly prepared and served, will consist of sautéed veal cutlets garnished with a sauce containing madeira wine, tomatoes, and onions.

The common usage of the word "garnish" is quite different. To *many* people it means adding an item to a plate mainly for the purpose of providing color. We see examples of this in nearly all sorts of restaurants. They include sliced tomatoes, lemon wedges, and the most used (or overused) item, parsley.

When garnishing in this manner, you must make sure that the garnishes used are edible. Also, you should pay close attention to how the garnish will hold up in service. For example, not all garnishes will hold shape, color, or texture when subjected to heat, and therefore should not be used on heated plates. Similarly, it is very often improper to garnish a plate and then let it stand under a heat lamp. As a rule, the garnish should be added just before service, which means that the kitchen must be properly organized and supervised. The color of the garnish is also very important in that it should enhance the plate and complement the appearance of the entrée.

Selecting Garnishes That Will Complement Your Dishes

Because garnishes will be an important part of your plates, you must take a part in the selection of them. At those times when people are tired or busy, most anything may show up as a garnish—whether it fits the plate or not. And you don't want that to happen to you in your restaurant. Therefore, you should outline what garnishes you want with various types or kinds of entrée. This information is equally as important as the formulas and recipes in your preparation files. It must be readily accessible to the cooks and expediter, and more important, it must be used. It is easy to have rules and or policies that are easily ignored when supervision is either lax or nonexistent.

The following are some garnishes that will complement your menu offerings:

Rainbow Trout	Lemon Wedge/Green Onions
Red Snapper	Lemon Slice/Sprig of Dill Weed
Ocean Trout	Pat of Dill Butter
Sautéed Filet of Sole	Capers

(Most fish and shellfish items are enhanced with lemon. It can be served as a half or in wedges. Parsley is also widely used, and its green color is a nice contrast to most seafood dishes.)

Leg of Lamb	Most often served with mint jelly and a sauce made from the drippings.
Various Steaks	Pat of garlic butter, Mushroom caps
Pork Chops	Spiced whole apple or apple rings, Applesauce
Bratwurst	Sweet and sour red cabbage

(Fruit in season can provide a very nice touch to the finishing of a plate. These go especially well with cold or hot sandwich items, along with your own favorite pickles.)

Cold Sandwiches	
Ham and Swiss	Interchange depending on availability and cost—cantaloupe, honeydew or watermelon, blueberries, sliced apple
Corned Beef	
Pastrami	
Roast Beef	
Chicken Salad	

Hot Sandwiches	
Hamburgers	Use canned peach or pear slices or halves, cottage cheese, raw finger vegetables such as carrot or celery sticks, and french-fried zucchini.
Cheeseburgers	
Grilled Ham & Cheese	
Grilled Cheese	

We can all think of a particular meal in a restaurant that stands out above most others. One all-time favorite is simple yet outstanding in color, presentation, and overall enjoyment.

Surprisingly, a peanut butter and strawberry jam sandwich was offered on the luncheon menu at a very pleasant restaurant. The sandwich as served was excellent. It consisted of bread rounds, one with peanut butter and thinly sliced banana, and the other slice covered with strawberry jam. It was beautifully served with a garnish of assorted fresh fruit in a cast-iron ham and egg skillet. This particular item had everything—shape, color, texture, temperature, and contrast—all of the important factors in the presentation of food. Last, but certainly not least, it also tasted very good and gave the feeling that good value was received for the money spent.

Of course, garnishes will not overcome any deficiencies you might have with menu balance. You must be sure that each item on the plate, and those served on the side, is complementary to the others. Therefore, carefully study the appearance of each of your menu items and its appeal to the diner. Try for pleasing patterns in the shape and color of food served. And pay attention to visual values. In other words, every plate should be a "palette." All of this has to do with the menu and how skillfully it was crafted. Many liberties are taken with menu definitions and the wise operator will know how each item is prepared and how it should be served. These tasks are sometimes delegated to persons with insufficient skill or training necessary to produce the intended level of customer satisfaction. We all know the importance of training but we should never underestimate the necessity for consistent and ongoing supervision.

HOW TO ORGANIZE AN EFFICIENT SERVICE STAFF

The supervision of service starts in the kitchen. One of the most important jobs in a restaurant is that of the *expediter*. A brief description of an expediter's job would be liaison between preparation and service staffs.

An expediter is stationed in the kitchen and works in the prime areas to be supervised—the pickup stations for hot and cold foods. Part of this person's job is to insure that foods are dispatched as quickly after preparation as is possible. In other words, the expediter sees that diners receive their hot food hot and their cold food cold. Also, this person supervises the appearance of the finished plates for compliance with menu and garnish requirements. In addition, the expediter "keeps the peace" in the kitchen and makes sure the two departments—service and preparation—function in a smooth and efficient manner.

If you don't have an expediter, or don't have someone who could function in that capacity, consider getting one. The whole secret to profits lies in your ability to turn over your seats as often as possible. An expediter will help accomplish this, by keeping your customers happily returning to your restaurant.

How to Get Acceptable Employee Productivity

There is probably no such thing as a restaurant that has a complete staff of highly motivated and efficient people. Every restaurant seems to have some service stations where everything runs smoothly, and others that don't. Our business is described as a "people-intensive business," and therein lies the problem. Some of us are very good at our job, and some of us are not.

As outlined earlier in this guide, "turning seats" is the secret to profits in the restaurant business. A full restaurant with every seat taken is experiencing one turn. If a restaurant has 100 seats and serves 150 persons on a given night, we would say it had 1.5 turns. There are exceptions to this, such as those houses that serve a slow-paced gourmet menu with prices sufficiently structured. In these restaurants, one or two seatings for a given mealtime are sufficient to ensure proper sales and profits.

You can only produce satisfactory seat turnover with acceptable employee productivity. Therefore, it makes sense that you should provide as much supervision as possible—and it must be where it counts the most, in the kitchen. If the kitchen is not running smoothly, then neither will anything else.

Supervising the flow of orders in and out of the kitchen ensures that service persons and cooks work in unison with a first-in, first-out system. Such a system tends to force slower servers to pick up their orders on time. The total effect will be faster and smoother flow of service to the dining room, the turnover rate will increase, and all diners will receive the same smooth, efficient service.

SUREFIRE TECHNIQUES THAT TURN SERVERS INTO SELLERS

Servers must be sufficiently knowledgeable about the menu items to be able to guide diners intelligently toward selections. Therefore, they must know about ingredients, as well as preparation and service times. Furthermore, servers should be sales oriented. That is, they should approach the guest with a desire to sell; although a high-powered sales pitch should never be used.

How to Minimize the Problem of Starting a Shift Short Staffed

There might be no worse feeling that being a manager of a shift where two or three employees don't show for a scheduled shift. Ultimately, the people bound to suffer the most are your guests. Here are a few suggestions for minimizing the potential for being short staffed or recovering from a short staffed shift:

☐ 1. Each time you or your managers write a schedule, have the General Manager or the owner initial the schedule as a means of reviewing its accuracy. As a G.M. or owner, you should be able to spot potential problems and or weaknesses in the schedules and then you accept ultimate responsibility for the staffing. Oftentimes, short staffing occurs simply because the scheduler makes a mistake in scheduling and it is not caught until the shift occurs.

☐ 2. When sufficient help is available, always include at least one or two "on call" workers for your most important positions. One manager we know went so far as to tell his servers that they could come dressed for work on any shift that they were not scheduled for and could then pick up any short staffed shift or replace a server who might not want to work that shift. This kept him almost always fully staffed. Be sure to fairly rotate the "on call" shifts and check with your local labor laws to be sure that "on call" workers are not treated like scheduled workers. This can be a tricky situation to navigate and one that you must be sure is favorable to your operation.

☐ 3. Institute a very rigid policy about tardiness. If you relax your standards about starting your shifts, you may not know until it's too late if you're understaffed. When your employees know that you are serious about your schedules then they will respond accordingly. As always, **you** set the tone by your example and leadership.

☐ 4. Close a server station ʰ   ? you expand them. If your typical server station is four tables, then ʰ   about expanding the station size to six tables simply becaṵ   't show up. You may have a few servers who can haṛ   but automatically giving all servers more tᵃ   ntire dining room open should be avoided.

                              eefing up" on ancillary positions. If, for
                    in an extra bus person or two, or bring
                    roaming the dining room and helping
                    a station which is in a remote part
                    e tables together to make it look
                    v, never gets seated.

If done properly, everyone will benefit—the diner will probably try something new, the server will receive a larger tip, and the house will increase its sales.

The Approach

At all times, a server should approach a customer with a pleasant smile and a friendly greeting. A good morning or good evening greeting is always appropriate, but the server should not stop there. The following greetings will help make the diners feel welcome:

- Good morning. May I start your day with a cup of hot, fresh coffee?

- Good evening. We are pleased to have you as our guest tonight.

- Hello, I am (Mary, George), and I am here to help you enjoy your dinner with us tonight.

You should guard against the approaches becoming trite or insincere. When this occurs it can render good intentions worthless.

Suggestive Selling

Suggestion is probably the most important selling technique a server can learn how to use. When dining out, people are often preoccupied with business or personal matters, or are absorbed in conversations with companions. They may not want to take time to study the menu. Therefore, it makes sense for your servers to make suggestions, particularly if you offer daily specials. Here's how to do it:

When suggesting items for sale, it is wise to offer alternatives. This sort of selling makes a refusal more difficult. For example,

"May I serve you a manhattan or martini?" is better than "Would you care for a cocktail?" The first question tends to elicit a choice, whereas the second calls for a yes or no answer.

Offering a special that is properly described by the waiter will sometimes help a diner to decide. For example:

> "Good evening. Tonight our chef has prepared roast Leg of Lamb as a special item. He has seasoned it carefully. [You might want to mention the seasonings.] It is served with new potatoes and a choice of salad or the vegetable of the day. The special price this evening is $10.95."

You can also use suggestions when selling desserts:

> "Have you tried our pecan pie? No, then you have missed a taste treat. Would you like to try a piece with ice cream, or do you prefer it plain?"

The Premeal Briefing

The premeal briefing for your service staff should be done daily—even though your menu may not have undergone a recent change. During it, you can place emphasis on the items that you especially want to sell, including the specials of the day. The briefing should take the role of a sales meeting, providing information and answering any questions your service staff may have. It should also provide the impetus to "pump up" your servers, so that they go out and sell with zest.

The Tasting Session

A good technique for increasing sales is the use of a tasting session before the meal period. It is unfortunate, but true, that management and service staff in many restaurants never taste the food before serving it. In restaurants that carry a large staff, you may want to *limit* the taste session to only management and supervisory personnel. In smaller restaurants, however, the sessions should include the servers. In any event, such a program will ensure that the proper persons are acquainted with the products for sale. If the servers are not actually tasting the food, then they should at least be briefed by someone who has.

If you have a large restaurant and it is not feasible for the entire service staff to participate in a regular tasting session, you might try another plan. Select a person from the service staff as a participant in the regular daily taste session. Each day a different server would be selected, so that you would rotate the process throughout the entire group. That person could then conduct the menu briefing session under the supervision of management. Management could, for example, furnish reinforcement in sales technique. Such a program would effectively bring the entire group into the management process and aid greatly in the development of an esprit de corps and pleasant working conditions—all of which will translate into dollars for you.

The Bonus Plan

Because most of us want to make all the money we can, it follows that cash incentives are probably the best way to encourage employees to build sales. One such way is to pay a percentage of individual total sales during a given period as a bonus. This could serve two purposes: 1) it would reward the high achievers, and 2) it helps you to spotlight those servers who don't push for sales. However, this system will not work unless all servers have equal opportunity in desirability of assigned stations and fair placement of diners in the rooms. An alternative way to develop a bonus plan would be to select certain items, such as appetizers or desserts, and establish a bonus based on numbers sold over a given time period. There are certainly other methods you can devise to develop good sales habits, but the ones outlined above have worked extremely well.

In addition, it is your responsibility to provide training for your employees, as covered in Chapter Five. There are slide presentations available from some of your suppliers and also from the trade associations, such as the state and national restaurant associations. Role playing is another effective technique you can use in which some of your staff pretend to be customers, others serve, and the balance observes. During these sessions you can be suggesting and coaching in the proper service techniques that will build and sustain sales.

In addition, there are booklets available for outside reading. You also can post on the bulletin board tips on effective selling, service, etc.

HOW TO MARKET YOUR WINE FOR BIGGER PROFITS

The successful selling of wine is a specialty that can only be attained through proper training of your service staff. If your restaurant does not have a wine steward, and most restaurants do not, then you must be certain that your servers are fully informed about the wines you have for sale. In other words, they should be able to suggest a particular wine for a specific meal or occasion. This doesn't mean that the servers must become connoisseurs, but it does mean that they must have a general knowledge of what they are trying to sell.

You can include information on wine sales in your training programs. To encourage the selling effort, you can even offer a bonus to each server based on his or her own individual wine sales. In addition, remind everyone that every bottle or glass of wine sold means a bigger check and, most likely, a larger tip.

In the last several years wine sales have skyrocketed in the United States and there appears to be no indication that people are going to change their beverage preference. There are so many labels that most restaurant managers are hard pressed to decide what should be offered on their wine list. (The Bert Wheeler Beverage stores in Houston, Texas, have as many as 3,000 labels in their store inventories.) One way to research the market is to watch what is selling in the beverage stores and supermarkets for home consumption. If you will observe in those establishments where the type of diners who frequent your restaurant shop for the wine they prefer for their homes, it's a good chance these folks will also want to enjoy similar wines in your restaurant. There are several good small wineries that have limited production and the companies prefer to have their labels on hotel and restaurant wine lists. As a result, the wineries refrain from selling to the major retailers because these businesses would quickly deplete their inventories. Restaurants can profit from this trend by having some choice labels on their wine lists that are not sold in the retail stores. At the present time the construction of wine lists is difficult owing to the wide supply of labels, and we are seeing restaurants prepare their wine lists with computers rather than by printing the fancy and expensive lists that have been the policy in the past.

How to Prepare a Wine List

You, as owner or manager, must furnish strong support for your service staff if they are to be able to reach the full sales potential for you. This means developing a total sales support program. This program begins with the development of a wine list that fits the overall economic pattern of your business. For example, if you attract customers who traditionally spend in a moderate range (e.g., strong family trade including children), you will probably want to structure your wine list so as to merchandise the low- to medium-priced offerings. Conversely, if your menu, decor, etc. is pointed to the "carriage" grade, your wine list will reflect this by listing the more expensive labels. Above all, remember that the wine list is a catalog from which your guests will make their selections. You want the document to be clean and attractive to read. It must contain only those wines for which you have proper storage facilities designed to protect the quality of the products.

Proper preparation of a wine list will require that you start with some basic research on wines. There have been several books written on the subject. *Grossman's Guide to Wine, Spirits, and Beer* by Sherman and Sorer, Inc. and *The Management of Service for the Restaurant Manager* by Raymond J. Goodman Jr., William C. Brown Company, are two good sources of technical information. A trip to your local bookstore will undoubtedly turn up many more. Reading some of this material will help you greatly in establishing your wine sales program.

Another excellent source for information on wines and how to market them, including the preparation of wine lists, is your local wine distributor. Usually, he will be eager to help you and is well qualified to do so. The list on the next page is one that contains only some different types of wine that may appear on a wine list in any restaurant. They do not represent any kind of recommendation as to product or price. It is only a statement of several kinds of wine from which a person might make a choice and one way in which a list might be constructed.

Gathering the Necessary Information

Once you have acquired the necessary background knowledge, you should then begin to research the local market to determine:

1. What the big sellers are in similar restaurants to yours.

2. What wines are available on a consistent basis that "fit" your menu and your clientele.

3. What kind of prices you can realistically expect to sustain in your restaurant.

You will find some of the answers by visiting other restaurants similar to your own. As you make the rounds, you will want to study other wine lists and visit casually with service personnel and management. These trips will be most rewarding in that you will be able to gather considerable information on how to sell—and how not to sell—wine.

Here are a few items to consider when visiting other restaurants:

- Does the server present a wine list, or is the list a part of the table setting?

Wine List

California

Whites

Chardonnay

Chenin Blanc

Chablis

Reds

Cabernet Sauvignon

Zinfandel

French

White Burgundies

Puligny Montrachet

Chardonnay

Pouilly Fuissé

Red Burgundies

Chateauneuf du Pape

Beaujolais

Bordeaux

Chateau Lafite Rothschild, 1971

Chateau Margaux, 1978

Pauillac

Margaux

St. Julien

St. Emillion

Rosé

Rosé d'Anjou

German

Auslese

Bernkastler

Wehlener

Piesporter

Champagnes

California

French

Italian

- Does the restaurant and its service personnel actually try to sell, or is wine something that happens to be available if you ask for it?

- What wines appear to be big sellers? Bottles? Decanters? Red? White?

- Was a specific suggestion made as to label or type of wine?

- Are you able to estimate or ascertain a particular price range or level?

Making Your Wine Selection

Obtaining answers to the questions given above will be of great benefit to you when you begin the next phase of the program—selecting the wine. At that time, you will want to talk with reputable dealers regarding availability, prices, method of payment, and any requirements as to quantities to be purchased. Most dealers will be happy to assist you in the preparation of your wine list. You must be certain, however, that you have adequate storage and display areas to handle the volume that will be required to support your list. Often dealers can help you with merchandising the wines by furnishing table tents and menu clip-ons. Furthermore, most good distributors have sales literature, slide presentations, and film clips that can be used in your training programs.

Of major importance is, of course, your selection of the wines and the prices you want to sell them for. You must be particularly careful not to price yourself out of the market. Whereas liquors generally yield gross profit margins of 70 percent to 75 percent, wines will generally run from 60 percent to 70 percent. (For a menu-pricing formula refer back to Chapter Two.)

In pricing a carafe or decanter, you must first measure how many of *your* glasses are contained in each one. Once you determine that, you can then apply the formula to yield your own desired gross profit margin per glass. Remember, if your price is too high, you will not be fair to your customers, and your servers—regardless of their skill—will not be able to sell. Today, the general public is much more aware and sophisticated with respect to wine consumption, and will respond more favorably to the restaurateur who keeps this firmly in mind.

The decision whether to sell by the bottle, decanter, or glass may be determined by your customer's preferences. These preferences may be influenced by the general sales trend in your particular area. Your ability to alter these preferences can be accomplished through proper sales and merchandising techniques.

Your wine inventory should be large enough to satisfy the widest range of taste and price preference possible. It should therefore include an array of red, white, and rosé wines. In all probability, you will want to offer both imported and domestic wines, as well as house wine to be sold by either the glass or decanter. If your list is extensive and backed up by a good cellar, you might consider numbering the selections on the wine list. Storing the wines in a number sequence will then aid greatly in locating difficult-to-read labels, thereby facilitating and speeding service.

Checklist of Steps if You Misquote the Waiting Time for a Table

There simply is no avoiding the trap of under-quoting the wait for a table during very busy times. It happens in all restaurants at one point or another and is the source of great embarrassment and anxiety for hosts and hostesses. Sometimes the flow of guests simply defies prediction and a logjam occurs at the host stand. Many guests may wait quietly and pass the time talking amongst themselves, but more likely most guests will begin to get irritated when their time has been exceeded. Here's how you can handle this sticky situation:

☐ 1. It is imperative that a manager makes him or herself available to the wait area in order to absorb the inevitable criticism that results from extended waiting times. There is no avoiding the anger that guests will have and you should not have your host staff bear the brunt of the complaints. The manager should stay in this position until the situation returns to accurate wait times.

☐ 2. Have the kitchen prepare some type of appetizer plates that you can pass amongst the guests in the waiting area. We do not recommended buying alcoholic beverages for guests as a means of appeasing them and strongly recommend food instead. These appetizers should be passed out by a smiling and apologetic employee who also can verbalize that you are doing the best you can to rectify the situation.

☐ 3. Have the host or hostess make a note of the tables assigned to the guests that had to wait longer than their quoted time. Be sure that you or a manager go by each and every one of these tables to again apologize for the inconvenience, addressing the party by name and perhaps offering to buy the table a few desserts after they finish their meals.

☐ 4. Be sure to quote a range of time that tables may be ready. Instead of training your host staff to say "it looks to be about a 20 minute wait" have them say instead "it should take between 20 and 30 minutes to get you seated." If you are keeping a list which lists names and times quoted, be sure to have them write down 30 minutes, not 20 minutes, to give you that little extra cushion.

☐ 5. Alert your floor staff that you will need their assistance on turning tables more quickly. We do not suggest that you rush your guests out the door, but certainly your bus staff can pre-bus tables more thoroughly and your wait staff can be quicker to present checks and expedite payment procedures.

WHY GOOD SERVICE DOESN'T STOP WHEN THE MEAL DOES

After the meal, one type of surprise that diners don't want is to *find* out that only certain kinds of credit cards or no credit cards or personal checks are accepted for payment. So make sure that your guests know your payment policy in advance.

There are millions of people who buy solely on credit or personal check, and many of them carry little or no cash. For these people, credit card or check usage is a habit and they don't even consider that a busy restaurant might not honor them. If you surprise them after the fact, you may never see them again. But if you state your policy clearly—either with signs, a highly visible menu notation, in your advertising, or with table tents—you will probably win a new friend and a longtime customer. You might also consider telling your customers about your policy when they call for table reservations. Remember, it is very hard to repossess a consumed meal.

How Best to Present the Check

There are various ways of presenting the check to the guest. You may prefer to have the server give the guest the check. If so, then the check should be presented on a tip tray. Presentation should only be made after the server has ascertained—by offering additional service (e.g., an after-dinner drink, more coffee, etc.) that the diner has completed the meal.

It is important to have the check clearly written for easy readability. This can be done by hand or by a precheck machine or cash register. And keep the check simple. Some restaurants present two separate checks, and the final result only confuses the guest.

Following presentation, the server should complete the transaction as smoothly as possible. The process should not be hurried, but at the same time the guest should not be made to wait an unnecessary amount of time. Some restaurants do very well as far as serving the food and beverage, but break down completely after the meal, by either not presenting the check shortly after the meal, or by taking an interminable amount of time to return with the change or charge ticket. When this happens, all the goodwill created during the meal is lost—and the diner remembers only the poor service after the meal.

If you prefer that guests pay a cashier direct, then you should take steps to inform them as to the procedure. Such steps could include a notice on the guest check and also a verbal reminder by the server, for example, "You may pay the cashier when ready" or "When you are ready, I will take the check to the cashier for you."

Some restaurants add a percentage (usually 15 percent) of the raw sale price before tax as a service charge. This is certainly an acceptable practice that ensures tips for your servers. Once again, clear communication with the diners as to your policy is very important. If you have such a policy and also honor credit cards, be sure that the entire transaction is entered on the charge ticket with tax and gratuity clearly indicated.

Regardless of the cash control method used, bright smiles and pleasant thank-yous by the servers will please your guests and bring bigger and better tips for them, and higher profits for you! Sometimes servers can develop habits that are well meaning on their part but that could be viewed as annoyances by your guests:

Touching or hugging

Removing the plate from one diner before others have finished

Visiting for too long a time at one table

Management can also develop habits that are annoying to guests:

Never leaving the office or kitchen long enough to recognize the guests and observe the food that was served.

Having music so loud that guests are unable to visit with each other.

The above lists are a sampling of situations that can develop in a restaurant and that can be damaging to the business. It must be assumed that these situations are not common, but they do happen in some places. Don't let them happen in your restaurant.

Chapter
7

Hidden Gold in Your Cocktail Lounge

Table of Contents

Chapter 7

Hidden Gold in Your Cocktail Lounge

The next best thing to a gold mine or a producing oil well may be a busy, well-managed cocktail lounge. Today, busy lounges deliver a gross profit margin on sales ranging from 70 percent to 80 percent. That means that a lounge selling $500,000 in beverages annually can produce a gross profit of $350,000 to $400,000. In addition, this figure is highlighted by the low supporting expenses needed for the operation. Labor and operating costs will of course vary with labor rates and other expense items such as entertainment. But if you run your lounge properly, it should return 50 percent or more on the bottom line. Those dollars will in turn aid in offsetting the higher costs of your restaurant operation.

THREE IMPORTANT ASPECTS OF INTERNAL CONTROL

Internal control throughout your restaurant operation is a management function that must be performed by you. This goes double for the bar, because the drainage expense there can have a disastrous effect on the profit line. Although the profit margin on alcoholic beverages is great, so too are the cracks through which those profits can slip. Here are some of the loopholes through which those profits can disappear:

- drinks disappear free to employees, including management personnel

- "complimentary" drinks given to "good" customers in the interest of sales promotion, but done mostly for the devious purpose of increasing tip revenue for lounge personnel

- failure to record sales—pocketing cash

- bar personnel actually selling their *own* merchandise on the house bar

- collusion between bar and table service personnel to accomplish any of the foregoing

- overpouring of liquor for "stiff" drinks—again, in the interest of increasing tips

- failure to empty liquor bottles completely before discarding

Remember, every drop of alcoholic beverage, every slice of fruit, every drop of soft beverage, each and every container of beer and wine represents a unit of cost. Each unit lost—no matter how you lose it—will reflect as lost revenue and profit to you.

How to Set Up a Cost Control System

Cost control starts with the price range of the beverages that you are going to offer. The hard liquors—whiskey, gin, rum, etc.—come in many shapes and sizes, and in a wide range of prices. What you buy will depend on the quality you are able to sell in your own particular location.

Generally speaking, hard beverages are classified by operators as "bar" or "well" liquor and "call brands." The bar or well liquors are used when a patron orders a drink without requesting a particular brand. Call brands refer to just that. They are kept on inventory for the patron who specifies the brand of liquor when ordering his or her drink. The bar or well brands used by most operators are usually lower-cost brands that are judged to be acceptable by the house. This does not mean that only cheap liquor is sold as bar or well stock, but it usually means that it is less expensive than a majority of the call stock. Wine sold as "house" wine by the glass or carafe is usually a less expensive brand than that sold in a bottle.

Here are a couple of comparisons from the Houston, Texas, area between high- and low-priced brands of liquor. They readily demonstrate the difference in gross profit per drink for the house.

Brand	Cost/Btl*	#1-1/4 oz. Drinks	Sell Price	Gross Profit
Call Brands—Scotch Whiskey				
Chivas-Regal	18.80	26	3.00	$59.20—76.0%
J & B	12.85	26	3.00	65.15—84.0%
Bar Brand—Scotch Whiskey				
	7.01	26	2.50	57.99—89.0%
Call Brand—Bourbon				
Wild Turkey	12.84	26	3.00	65.16—84.0%
Bar Brand—Bourbon				
Evan William's	4.79	26	2.50	60.21–93.0%

As you can see, the call brands that sell for $0.50 per drink more than the bar brands actually deliver a lower margin of gross profit per bottle.

If you used the following call brands as bar whiskies, the margin would be even less:

Brand	Cost/Btl.	Yield	Sell Price	Gross Profit
J & B	12.85	26	2.50	$52.15—80.0%
Wild Turkey	12.84	26	2.50	52.16—80.0%

How to Avoid Overbuying

Once you have made your decision as to quality and price range, your next move is to research the market for the brands of beverage that will fit into your overall sales philosophy. This will mean checking out prices and probably doing some sampling. You will also want to investigate other bars catering to your type of customers. Such trips will provide the information relative to brands that will sell or not sell.

After going through this exercise, you will be able to order intelligently and will be much less apt to buy brands that don't move. There are many bars that have gotten stuck with inventory items they can't even give away. This is usually a result of not knowing what to buy, overreacting to a sales pitch, or letting some unqualified person do the buying for you.

Common mistakes made by operators are overbuying different brands in stock and stocking too high an inventory. This can be controlled by carefully forecasting sales, as outlined in Chapter Four. To sum up: Don't overbuy! There are an untold number of different brands of each beverage category, and it is impossible to stock them all. Without a doubt, you will have isolated requests for a certain kind of beverage, but unless there is a strong identifiable demand, you will probably be wise not to carry it.

Remember, excess inventory requires cash outlays that may be better used in other ways. (In your own pocket, for one!) You will no doubt hear about promotions that will earn you big bucks. Maybe some of them will, but be sure you study each individual case thoroughly as it relates to your own clientele and your own sales capability.

Check Your Order Carefully

Be very sure that what you buy is what you get! Before signing for or paying for merchandise, check it thoroughly. Because beverages are generally purchased in case lots, the chances of losing individual containers through breakage or pilferage are high. The following case study shows how this can happen:

> An acquaintance was at one time responsible for the convenience store operations in a large midwestern city. In several locations, he was experiencing a high loss of soft drinks. He was unable to stem the losses. So the company decided to assign a troubleshooter, who quickly identified the problem.

It seemed as though certain drivers were delivering full cases of beverage, which they unloaded and stacked in the storerooms. At the same time, they would remove the empty cases. However, the stacks of empties they removed had also contained full cases. In addition, the stacks of full cases being stored contained empty cases that had just been removed.

Result: The company not only was being shorted of merchandise, but was also being double-charged for the deposit fee on the full and empty bottles.

KEY WAYS TO KEEP TRACK OF YOUR INVENTORY

The next step is the control of your inventory after you receive it. This is best accomplished by storing it under lock and key, and providing very limited access to persons other than trusted management personnel. Your storeroom should be spacious enough to accommodate your stock, and the goods should be stored in a manner that facilitates quick and easy physical inventory. If you have a storeroom that is too "small," take a long hard look at your purchasing procedure and sales records along with vendor delivery schedules, to see if you really need as much inventory as you are actually carrying.

Where restaurants are having cost problems, in almost every case, the problem is either with overbuying or with little or no inventory control—and often it is a combination of both. You cannot remain competitive in this business while absorbing losses of this kind! Restaurants losing money through pilferage must raise their prices to cover their losses—and that practice soon results in lost sales.

There are two basic bar control methods used throughout the industry: a physical inventory and an operating statement. Although somewhat different, they are similar in one respect.

The Physical Inventory

Any system of internal control requires a periodic physical inventory of goods on hand, and this "counting" of the stock must be done on a consistent basis. The inventory must coincide with the closing of the fiscal period for control, and if accuracy is to be maintained, it cannot be postponed or rescheduled for any reason.

If, for example, you opt for a monthly operating period and decide to close your operating books after the close of business on the last day of a calendar month, you must take a physical inventory before opening for business on the first day of the following month. It doesn't matter whether the first of the month falls on Sunday (the day you're closed, and when the fish are biting); inventory must be taken before you open for business on Monday.

Consistency is the key to good recordkeeping. It is the ingredient that provides valid comparisons of operating results from one period to another. In addition, it provides records that coincide exactly with your budgets. Probably the most basic reason of all for taking a physical inventory is to verify that you *have* on hand what you are *supposed* to have. In this case, the "eyes" have it! The most sophisticated control system in the world will not *verify* the physical presence of items on hand.

The Operating Statement

Probably the simplest control system is the preparation of an operating statement that includes a verification of goods on hand by physical inventory. This system requires that purchases be recorded during a fiscal period. The value of the purchases is added to the value of a beginning inventory (the ending inventory from the previous period). Finally, the value of the ending inventory for the current period is subtracted from that total, to arrive at the dollar cost of goods sold. Control is exercised by dividing the cost by the net sales (after taxes, etc.), to arrive at a ratio of cost of sales. This ratio is then compared with the previous period ratio and also with the budget.

This system is considered the simplest, because it does not require daily recordkeeping in the form of issues from storeroom to bar. It is probably the best system for a low-volume operation, because it reduces the amount of paperwork necessary for the maintenance of other systems. The problems with it are as follows:

1. There is no way to discover cost distortion, either up or down, until the operating period is closed.

2. The owner/manager must be ever vigilant during operating hours. This means watching the bar closely at all times for such loopholes as were mentioned earlier in this chapter.

Establishing a Par Stock

Another method of control is one in which a par stock is established for the bar. This means that all brands of alcoholic beverage available for sale are kept at a predetermined level. These levels are known as pars, and each brand has a par. If you have a storeroom from which you issue to one or more bars via a written requisition, you would establish a par for each brand on each bar.

In addition, to ensure that you keep your inventory at the lowest possible level, you would establish a set of pars for your storeroom. This means that there would be a reorder point at which time you would buy more of a brand, trying not to exceed par. What happens here is that you establish a minimum and a maximum amount for each brand of beverage to be on hand. When a particular brand reaches a minimum amount (reorder point), you buy more—trying not to exceed the maximum (par) amount. This system has definite advantages, as follows:

- It controls inventory both in the storeroom and on the bar by avoiding overages and shortages.

- It keeps management well informed as to the popular and unpopular sale brands.

- If invoices are tabulated for cost each day, it provides a daily cost of sales figure that is a good indication of how current costs are running.

The one disadvantage this system may have is the amount of paperwork that is involved. Each brand of liquor must have an individual record of receipts and issues, and these records (bin cards) must be kept up-to-date in a consistent manner. If you have people to handle chores such as these, then you should by all means install such a system. If, however, you have a small restaurant and have to tend to most of the administrative details yourself, then it may be difficult to take on a system such as this. If it is not maintained consistently and accurately, it is worthless.

Automatic Beverage Metering Systems

Automatic beverage metering systems use a storage for open bottles that are each locked in place. Each bottle has a draw-off valve that can be preset to deliver the desired quantity per drink. It eliminates the free-pour system on most brands and ensures accuracy as to quantity per drink sold. The system also uses a metering device that counts the number of drinks dispensed from each bottle. These systems are widely used in hotels and large, high-volume restaurants.

ESTABLISHING THE RIGHT PRICES

Beverage prices are arrived at in the same manner as are prices for cooked foods. Full containers such as beer present no problem other than marking up in price to return the desired gross profit per unit. However, opened containers (e.g., bottled goods sold by the drink or in combination as mixed drinks) present a more complex problem for control.

Before you can price beverage by the drink, you must first decide on the yield or how many drinks you want to get from a bottle. This, of course, will vary with the size of the drink served and also with the size of the bottle. Until recently, liquor was sold in bottles containing 0.80 of a quart, 1 quart, and 0.5 gallon. Since the inception of metric usage in the United States, that has all changed. We now find liquor being sold in bottles as follows:

1.75 Liter = 59.2 fluid oz.

1 L = 33.8 fl. oz.

750 mL = 25.4 fl. oz.

500 mL = 16.9 fl. oz.

200 mL = 6.8 fl. oz.

In the last several years there has been talk of changing the method of liquid measurement in our country to the metric system. In addition, we can find many brands of bottled goods, especially wine in bottles, that use the metric measurement systems. It is possible that someday there will be a change to a system in glassware for drinks and measuring equipment such as jiggers. Should this take place there will be a lot of equipment that could become difficult to use without some guidelines for their usage. The following gives examples using both English and metric measures.

Easy Ways to Use the Metric System

It is almost an impossibility to realize a 100 percent yield from a bottle of liquor that is sold by the drink. Because of this fact, an allowance to account for spillage, waste, etc. is established as a deduction from the total amount available for sale. As an example in which we use milliliters converted to ounces, let's assume that we are using the 760-mL bottle, which contains 25.4 fluid ounces. If we allow 1.4 ounces per bottle for waste, we will have a net salable bottle containing 24 ounces (for purposes of analysis). If we pour a 1.5-ounce drink, we should then realize a sale of sixteen drinks from the bottle:

750 mL	= 25.4 oz.
25.4 oz. − 1.4 oz.	= 24 oz.
24 oz. ÷ 1.5 oz.	= 16 drinks at 1.5 oz. each

Using the same loss ratio per bottle, but analyzing by milliliters, will produce the following:

1.4 oz. (waste) ÷ 25.4 oz.	= 5.5 percent loss
750 mL × 5.5 percent	= 41.25 mL waste per 750 mL bottle
750 mL − 41.25 mL	= 708.75 net salable quantity

(1 oz. = 29.5730 mL)
29.5730 mL x 1.5 = 44.595 mL per each 1.5–oz. drink

708.75 net ÷ 44.595 mL/drink = 15.89 per bottle

(The above analysis has been simplified for illustrative purposes only. Actually, 1.4 oz. waste per bottle is too high. Waste shouldn't be more than one-half of that amount.)

If you are using the 1-liter bottles on your bar, you can analyze in the same manner as the foregoing, except that you must decide how much waste and spillage you are willing to allow.

How to Arrive at a Selling Price

To arrive at a selling price, you must first decide what gross margin on sales you want to realize. Once decided, the rest is relatively simple. For example:

> 1 — 750 mL bottle of Scotch
> Cost — $10.00
> $10.00 ÷ 16 net drinks/bottle = $0.625/drink

Let's suppose you need to realize 75 percent gross profit from each drink as highball or straight up. (For this example we will ignore the cost of mixers and deal with that later.) You would use the following formula for this calculation:

> Cost ÷ (100 percent — Gross Profit) = Selling Price
> $.63 ÷ (100 percent — 75 percent) = $2.52 Selling Price

The foregoing represents what you must do to arrive at unit selling prices that will yield the profits you want. As for beer and wine, you follow the same procedure:

1. Determine the quantity to be sold (e.g., a full bottle or a glass holding a certain number of ounces or milliliters).

2. Determine the cost of each salable unit.

3. Calculate the selling price with the aforementioned formula.

There are many different types of handheld calculators on the market that will save you a great deal of time in figuring costs, in addition to preventing errors. When making calculations like these, it is always good to prove the answers to prevent errors in final pricing.

It is also possible to arrive at reciprocals to apply on certain kinds of liquor to cost out mixed drinks. These calculations are more complex and too time consuming for the average restaurateur—unless he or she has a controller on the payroll. Don't forget the importance of monitoring the cost of mixers, fruit and other supplies in dollars of cost and ratio to total beverage sales. Such diligence will yield additional profits for you.

HOW TO SET UP HOUSE RULES FOR EMPLOYEES AND PATRONS

There are certain "house rules" for employees and patrons that should be instituted and adhered to.

Guidelines for Employees

1. It should be strictly forbidden for employees and supervisory personnel to consume any alcoholic beverage during their working hours, or after closing. Serve coffee or soft drinks only.

2. Employees should be discouraged from frequenting the restaurant while off duty. This will help to avoid disruptions, such as socializing, in the other employees' workday.

Guidelines for Protecting Your Patrons

The house must be considerate and protective of *all* of its patrons. Your customers will expect a reasonable amount of peace and privacy, and there are certain things you can do to ensure this.

One of the things you will have to consider is the fact that some people don't like a noisy restaurant, whereas others can't abide a quiet place. Some people can be loud and boisterous in a nonoffending way. They are often entertaining to others around them, and usually do not present a problem for you. However, this is not true of everyone. Sometimes this boisterousness is not entertaining to others. Such a situation arises when a guest decides to table-hop around the room. Another potential problem can develop with people who are loud, and especially if they are using off-color or foul language.

These kinds of situations can only be handled by a firm and consistently enforced house policy against such behavior. You must move quickly and diplomatically to "nip these problems in the bud." Be sure to smoothly, yet firmly, let the people involved know that they are most welcome in your place, but that they must also be considerate of other guests. If situations become very bad and you must threaten to force them to leave the premises, *don't back off.* Only threaten action when you are fully prepared to carry that action all the way.

There are the smokers and nonsmokers. Usually, the nonsmokers are very vocal in their objections to smoke. And there is the further complication of the cigar and pipe smokers, against whom the antismokers are particularly hostile. In an effort to satisfy both groups, many restaurants have divided their public rooms into smoking and nonsmoking areas.

Today the matter of who can smoke and where is largely taken out of the hands of the restaurant owner by government restrictions and demanding customers. One or the other of these groups will probably decide what you can or cannot do in your own restaurant. What is especially interesting to owners today is the change that has taken place in the smoking of cigars. We are now seeing cigar-smoking rooms being established in many restaurants, and they have gained greatly in popularity. This trend has helped the bottom line in many restaurants that have opened a facility such as a "martini bar" where cigar smokers can get together with other smokers over a friendly martini or other libation of their choice. We also notice the selling of cigars in many department stores along with humidors and other paraphernalia. In addition, there is a great amount of advertising now dedicated to the selling of cigars that is directed at both men and women. This is another example of how change can affect your business and how you must adapt to take advantage of it.

In addition, when you sell liquor you always run the risk of someone becoming intoxicated in your establishment. This situation is something that all good restaurateurs seek to avoid at all times for the following reasons:

1. Intoxicated persons are difficult to handle and are often offensive to other customers.

2. Drunk driving has become a great concern in many communities. Of course, none of us wants to contribute to that problem. We must also consider the surge of DWI legislation, much of which seems to be pointed at the lounge and restaurant owners. Good business sense plus the protective feeling we have for our customers tells us that letting patrons become intoxicated is bad business. And that holds true whether they are driving or afoot.

You must always be on the alert—watching out for those persons who seem to be spending a long period of time drinking and not eating. In addition, you should take special care in training your employees (bartenders, servers of both food and drinks) to be watchful and to alert management when a person seems to be drinking too heavily. Signs to watch out for are an unsteady walk, slurred speech, loose tongue, and an unsteady head.

Even if you and your people watch carefully, you will probably still encounter the occasion when a guest has "had too much." Here are some tips on how to handle that situation:

- Most intoxicated persons will not be belligerent unless someone—a bartender, waiter, manager—makes them that way. Usually, you can reason with them if they sense that you are really on their side, and only want to help them enjoy their stay in your place.

- If the guest has not eaten, try to get him or her to do so. Try to seat the person in an area that is as remote from others as possible. In the process, don't try walking him or her through the entire restaurant.

- Don't assume, because the person has eaten or consumed some coffee, that he is sober. Actually, this person may now be nothing more than a "fully satiated drunk."

- Don't force intoxicated persons to leave your premises without being in the care of others who are sober. This may mean calling a taxi or even the police. Regardless of what action you must take, it is in the best interest of your guest, and he or she will certainly appreciate it. (If not, you really don't need that sort of guest in the future anyway.)

Your biggest problem requires experience and good judgment to assess state of intoxication in a person. It also requires tact and diplomacy to refuse to sell, especially when dealing with good "steady" customers. In any event, when you are in the business of selling alcoholic beverage, you should always maintain high ethical standards, along with a sense of responsibility for the health and welfare of your patrons.

CONTROLLING CASH AND CHARGE SALES

Whether or not your restaurant has a liquor business, it is vulnerable to drainage expense through waste, neglect, and pilferage. Gaining and retaining the profits to which you are entitled requires diligent management by you. Up to now, we have discussed control of bar cost and the importance of purchasing and receiving. Of equal importance is the control of cash and charge sales dollars.

Direct Sales at the Bar

Most well-operated bars use modern, well-designed cash registers on which sales checks can be documented. The style or brand of register you use is of course a matter of individual preference. (Chapter 1 includes a discussion of cash control systems that are available at this time.) However, you must always remember that the systems selected, no matter how sophisticated, will not supplant the need for diligence and consistent management on your part.

All sales should be recorded on a bar check, and the recording should be done at the time of sale. Each patron or party seated at the bar should have a check on which the price of each drink or round of drinks purchased has been entered. It is not a good practice to serve several customers and then go back and ring up the different sales at one time. Bar employees will sometimes argue that ringing up each sale takes too much time. However, this method will help to prevent lost profits through uncollected sales.

A policy of recording at the time of sale will greatly aid observation and inspection of your business. Some businesses use spotter service companies to identify wasteful or dishonest employees. These people frequent a subject lounge as patrons for the purpose of observing employees at work. Reports are filed following the visits, with any discrepancies so noted.

How to Handle Complimentary Drinks

You should prohibit the giving of complimentary drinks by anyone other than management. It is probable that you will want to "buy" for certain patrons at certain times.

When such occasions arise, be very sure that a check is properly filled out and recorded. Adjustment to your promotion expense account can be made later by your bookkeeper. This is important because:

- It establishes your internal control by strictly accounting for every unit of cost in your inventory.

- It tells your employees that you are in fact controlling your inventory, and any shortages will be quickly noted and appropriately dealt with.

Controlling Table Service

Once the merchandise (liquor) leaves the relative confines of the bar proper, extensions of control become necessary. Again, it becomes absolutely necessary to have all sales recorded when picked up from the bar. This recording of sales can take place either at the bar or at a checker/cashier station, remote from the bar. In any event, no matter which system you elect to use for recording, that recording must take place before any drinks are served anywhere.

Generally speaking, liquor will be served at tables both in the cocktail lounge and in the dining room. This kind of sales activity presents some unique problems for the restaurant. When only drinks are purchased, tabulation and collection of guest checks are simplified because there is only one point of sale, namely, the bar.

A further complication to all of this arises when a guest begins with a drink in the bar, and then moves into the dining room without paying for drinks consumed in the bar. Some restaurants require that drinks consumed in the bar be paid for before moving into the dining room. Such a system will work, but it is sometimes annoying to the guests. Your guests will be happier if you allow bar checks to follow them into the dining room.

Each restaurant will need specific solutions to these problems because of the various interior layouts, equipment being used or contemplated, and the methods used for control of food checks. If you have problems such as these, they can best be addressed by conferring with an outside consultant or a representative of the company that furnished your cash control system.

A very simple yet effective control of sales at tables in the cocktail lounge is to have the serving persons pay for the drinks in cash when they are picked up at the bar. This puts the responsibility for collection on the server. A problem could be created when payment at the table is by a credit card, but there are ways that this situation can be dealt with by refunding the server in cash. However, the matter of house charge to the restaurant by the credit car issuer would have to be accounted for by some sort of adjustment and this could become annoying. If this situation develops you should confer with your bookkeeper or accountant for advice on how to best handle this kind of payment.

INVENTORY CONTROL

The frequency of inventory control should be identical to that for food. You probably can't afford to go any longer than one week between inventory and preparation of operating statements. If "leaks" in your system continue to eat into profits for longer than that, a great amount of money will be lost in the process. Some places can afford the type of system that renders full accounting on a daily basis; however, if you are not able to do that, you must personally look at your inventory, because no automatic or electronic system will tell you when an item has been physically removed. Further, records can be "doctored" and mistakes will always be made. No system has yet supplanted the need for lock and key and periodic physical counts.

Most of the big hotels and restaurants make an effort to identify their own bottles as they leave storage. Such a system aids in the inspection of bar merchandise and helps to prevent employees selling stock they have brought from outside. Such a practice is not uncommon in this business and can be very costly to the house.

How to Take Bar Inventory

Bar inventory is best taken by estimating or measuring the fractional parts of opened bottles along with full bottles. Full bottles present no problem and are merely carried at their cost price. Opened bottles may be inventoried in any fractional amount you desire; however, most businesses do their accounting in one-eighth parts. For example, we can use the same bottle of scotch that originally cost $10.00. It has now been opened and all but four-eights or one-half is gone. To arrive at our cost for inventory purposes, we merely multiply the total cost by 4/8, and we have the fractional cost of the bottles:

$10 × 4/8 = $5—cost for inventory purposes

The retail value of the opened bottle is now reduced by one-half or eight drinks that have been sold:

16 drinks (original amount) × 4/8 × 2.52 (retail price per drink) = $20.16 retail value—remainder of bottle

The financial importance of inventory control is monumental. If you lose a bottle of liquor, you not only lose the cost, but you also lose the profit from the sale that will never happen.

Drainage is an expense that is caused by different factors (e.g., pilferage of money or product, unauthorized complimentary drinks, etc.), any of which will have the effect of reducing your profits. This type of expense will show up as an increase in cost of sales and drop right to the bottom line.

If you have costs that are higher than they should be, you will have that much less profit for your business. For example, if your restaurant budgeted sales of $90,000 for a given period and cost of sales at $22,500, you would be planning on a gross profit of $67,500 or 75 percent of sales. Now look at the following example showing $100,000 in sales for an increase of $10,000 over budget. Unfortunately, the cost of sales is 3 percent higher because of drainage. Although your sales increased and the dollars of gross profits are over budget, you have lost a total of 3 percent and your gross profit is 3 percent lower than it should be. Although you received 10 percent more in sales, you realized 3 percent or $3,000 less in gross profit for those increased sales. All of which means that you did not have that extra $3,000 to put toward your direct operating expense.

	Budget		Actual	
	$	**%**	**$**	**%**
Sales	90,000	100.0	100,000	100.0
Cost of Sales	22,500	25.0	28,000	28.0
Gross Profit	67,500	75.0	72,000	72.0

Chapter
8

Internal Control: How to Keep Track of All Your Money

Table of Contents

Chapter 8

Internal Control: How to Keep Track of All Your Money

The restaurant industry can be interesting and rewarding if you take the necessary steps to survive and make it so. This chapter discusses the need for an Internal Control System (not to be confused with accounting) and how to put one in place.

The purpose of a restaurant's Internal Control System is to keep track of whether you are operating at a profit or loss. (Such items as debt service, rent, real estate taxes, and other unforeseen expenses such as landlord applied assessments for property upkeep or legal action are not included.)

Although some tasks can be assigned to an outside bookkeeper, the restaurant owner or manager must perform much of this work. For example, you must monitor your inventory for pilfering. In addition, the only sensible way to buy food and supplies is with a sound knowledge of what is on hand in kitchen and storeroom and with a record of usage.

KEEPING GOOD RECORDS

You must keep appropriate and timely operating statements, whether you prepare them yourself or have someone else prepare them. Most businesses, however, employ bookkeepers or bookkeeping firms for ongoing services. In addition, certified accounting firms are used for tax work. To get the most from these services, the records prepared must meet certain conditions:

- Operating statements must be prepared and given to you as quickly as possible following the close of the financial period. For example, if your restaurant operates on a monthly period, you should receive those statements during the week following the close of the month. If you don't, you could be looking at statements showing costs that may have been incurred seven or eight weeks earlier.

- If you install an internal control system in your restaurant and use it consistently, you will have a set of quickly accessible internal statements that will show how your business is doing financially. This chapter will show you, step by step, how to put this system in place.

- An internal control system consists of inventory control methods, purchasing techniques, sales statistics, and budget preparation. Once you have developed this kind of system, you can use statements prepared by an outside firm to measure your internal system to see how well you are doing at keeping control over your business.

- Your financial statements should be put on a special type of chart of accounts widely used by restaurants. You can procure such a chart from the National Restaurant Association, 1200 17th Street NW, Washington, DC 20036–3097. It is in book form entitled *Uniform System of Accounts for Restaurants,* see Appendix, beginning page 201.

- You may elect to have your accountant furnish you with the Charte of Accounts that he or she is using or in the case of a new business, intends to use for keeping the records for your restaurant. Just be sure that the chart will furnish the data needed for comparison with restaurant industry statistics that are published by the various restaurant associations throughout the United States.

There are three main reasons why you must have a tight control over incoming dollars from sales as well as outgoing dollars for cost and expense:

1. It will ensure that *you* receive all the money spent by the customers in your restaurant.
2. It will allow you to *meet* your financial obligations.
3. It will *provide* you with the sales and income statistics that are needed for your operating statements, and the basis on which to forecast future income levels.

What Daily Sales Records Can Do for You

A daily sales record is the document on which you record all of your income each day. If you use a cash register, it should provide you with all the information needed for the report. The daily sales report should tell you things such as the following:

- The total volume of business for the day, and a breakdown of cash and charge sales

- Information about the day (e.g., the weather and any special events including holidays)

- What items or categories of items were actually sold. This sort of information is easy to obtain with the kind of cash register systems that are on the market today.

- The volume of sales per individual waiter or waitress, and whether or not all guest checks are accounted for

- How many diners were served. What the average sale per guest was

- The amount of your bank deposit for the day, and net amounts after taxes

- The opening and closing cash register readings, and a cash over or short report

There may be other kinds of information you may wish to include, but recording the foregoing items will surely help to put additional profits in your pocket.

Figure 8.1 is an example of a daily sales report that will help you to manage your restaurant properly. It is particularly handy in that it consolidates all the information on one sheet of paper. In addition, you might find that having this form printed on an 8 1/2 x 11 or legal size envelope would comprise a good filing device. The outside of the envelope would be used for recording, with all supporting documents such as cash register tapes or charge sale invoices contained within.

How to Turn Your Daily Sales Record into Profits

Here's what you can do to make your daily sales record into a profit source:

- Compare your cash sales with your charge sales. You must determine if your net sales (after credit account charges) are sufficient to meet your needs, or if adjustments to prices are necessary.

- Make certain adjustments for seasons, holiday, etc. These are generally necessary when forecasting sales for the future.

- Analyze your sales against your menu and continually adjust to eliminate poor sellers and unnecessary, low-profit items.

- Monitor your salespeople to see how each of them is doing. In that way, you can help the poor performers to improve.

- Watch the average sale per guest to rate your menu as to efficiency of sales mix. Also, the average sale statistics tell you how well your sales force, in total, is actually doing. Whenever there is movement either up or down in this

Figure 8.1

DAILY SALES REPORT

Date 1/12/98

Day of Week Monday
Weather Warm/Cloudy
Spec Events Convention in town

Meal & Reg. No.		Register Reading	Register Reading Diff.	Cash	Over (Short)	Charge	Sales Tax	Tips	Net Sales
L	E	7805	310	135.-	(1.25)	930.-	10.14	93.00	826.86
	B	7495							
D	E	7920	115	210.-	.60	1470.-	16.04	147.-	1306.96
	B	7805							
	E								
	B								
	E								
	B								
Day Totals			425	345	(.65)	2400.-	26.18	240.-	2133.82

Comments: Convention helped sales & weather was good for walking

Bank Deposit $ 2133.82

Statistics

Check Numbers Issued	645	thru	1175
Check Numbers Returned	1100	thru	1175
Check Numbers Missing	None		
Action Taken	None		

Number of Diners Served

Meal	No./Diners	Sales	Sales/Diner
Lunch	163	1065	6.54
Dinner	128	1680	13.13

Waiter/Waitress Individual Sales

	Luncheon	Dinner
#1	205	310
2	210	315
3	195	290
4	225	340
5	230	425

statistic, it should be compared with the individual sales figures per server. If, for example, the general trend overall is down, it may be the fault of less spending by all diners, or a failure to sell or provide good service by one or more of your staff. If the condition is less spending by everyone, it is time to examine your operation in depth. Here are some questions to ask yourself:

—Should my menu be overhauled with an eye toward better merchandising?

—Should I add or delete certain items?

—Do the specials have a desired good effect? Or are they encouraging less spending with no increase in traffic?

—Am I providing the training that is needed to encourage employees to adopt and use good sales techniques? Are my training sessions consistent?

—Has the "shine" gone from the decor? Do the guests now find my place uninteresting?

—Has the quality of my food and service begun to slip? If so, is it the fault of all the menu items or just certain ones, such as appetizers or desserts?

• Keep accurate and consistent records so that the information that is transmitted for statement purposes is clear and easy to get. This will save you a lot of time.

HOW TO DEVELOP AN OPERATING BUDGET

Management, as noted earlier, consists of four key functions: planning, organizing, directing, and controlling. A budget has both a *planning* and a *control* function, and is essential for the profitable operation of your business.

The first step necessary in the development of a budget is the determination of a plan that incorporates the goals that you want to achieve during the upcoming fiscal period. For example, the following might be the way the ABC Restaurant would approach its planning for the new year.

If you will pay close attention to the forecasting of associations such as the National Restaurant Association and the Texas Restaurant Association as well as those from various U.S. government departments, you will be able to anticipate surpluses or shortages of certain food items in the next year. For instance, there might be a forecast of a shortage of beef, which probably means that beef prices to your restaurant will increase. These increases must either be absorbed or passed on to your customers. To avoid any increases in menu prices, we will try to offset these price increases. Although we know that we must continue to serve beef due to customer demand, we will make every attempt to offset the higher cost by selling more pork, poultry, and fish items. We plan to accomplish this task in the following way:

• By featuring lunch specials consisting of nonbeef items.

- When we reprint our menu, we will highlight nonbeef items and play down the beef.

- We will place a strong emphasis on the sale of nonbeef items during our regular waiter/waitress training programs during the year.

- We will aggressively seek out and buy beef products from those sources that furnish the best price while satisfying our requirements for quality and service.

Once a plan such as this has been established, you are ready to begin forecasting your sales and expenses. Of course, there could be much more involved than the foregoing example, such as changes in operating hours, search for new markets, upgrading of personnel, and upgrading of salary structure, and so on. The important point to remember is that goal setting is the first and most vital step in the planning process for a viable budget.

Of equal importance are the matters of internal control and the preparation of accounting statements, analyses, and projection of future trends. These procedures and documents constitute the fiscal record of the past that is necessary to the forecast of the future.

Once all these factors are in place, the actual construction of a budget can be started.

Forecasting Sales and Other Revenue

Most forecasters take sales history and add a percentage factor to account for growth, expansion, and inflation (if necessary). Few businesses, if any, stand still or regress and still remain in business for long. Taking a sales history is relatively simple to accomplish once the percentage factor has been determined. It involves "looking down the road" and deciding how the business will be affected by any and all of the factors you have taken into account.

The following reminder checklist will help you to identify these factors—events and demographic developments—that may have some impact on your business.

- Population changes by total city or area of the city, either up or down

- Planned changes to your area that would have an effect on traffic patterns that in turn could affect your sales (e.g., street repairs, sewer repairs)

- New industry or activity coming into your area (e.g., new plant or office building)

- Changes in laws or ordinances that might mean cause for certain adjustments to operating policies and procedures (e.g., legal age for alcohol consumption)

- Ethnic or economic changes in your immediate market area that could cause sales fluctuations (e.g., aging neighborhood with an increase in senior citizens)

- Expected shortage of certain commodities that are big sellers for you (e.g., Texas ban on commercial fishing for redfish)

- Major conventions, meetings, or shows that could bring business (e.g., site of the Republican or Democratic National Convention)

Many of these developments will be reported in your local newspaper. Therefore it is important that you read it every day. Other places where information can be gathered is from your local, state, and national restaurant association, city planning and traffic departments, state highway department, Chamber of Commerce, and trade publications. You probably will be able to think of many other happenings that could affect your sales—and the more you can identify the better. As for the mechanics of the forecast, it's quite easy and you can become very good at it with study and practice.

An Action Example of How to Forecast Sales

Suppose there is a new factory coming into your area with a workforce of 2,500 persons. A little checking should disclose how many people will go out for lunch or dinner. You can probably attract a good many of these.

You can translate these figures into economic data by estimating how many of these folks you are apt to attract to your restaurant. You then multiply this amount by your check average and the number of days a week that the factory is open. This computation will yield a dollar figure that can be used in your forecast of income.

There are many sources that forecast inflation figures, and that figure (in percentage) should also be included in the total sales picture.

Here's how one such forecast might look:

Last Year		
Food Sales		$ 800,000
Beverage Sales		250,000
Total Sales		$1,050,000
New business coming into area:		
Food	$ 100,000	
Beverage	25,000	
Inflation @ 8 percent—		
1,050,000 × .08=	84,000	
Total estimated increase	$ 209,000	
Next year forecasted sales		$1,259,000
Total estimated increase		$ 209,000
Breakdown		
Food Sales	75%	$ 944,250
Beverage Sales	25%	314,750

(The luncheon and dinner percentage breakdown would come from your own past years' sales records.)

Forecasting Costs and Expenses

The same basic rules apply to the forecasting of cost and expense items as for sales forecasting. You must search out and identify those areas where change may occur and adjust your forecast accordingly. For instance, in the example of the impending high beef prices, mentioned earlier, you would want to adjust your food cost to show the increased cost of beef in the next year. The forecasting of cost and expense can be made a lot easier by the way you and your accountant keep records of *actual* cost and expense of operations.

Earlier in this chapter, you learned about the importance of good recordkeeping and the Chart of Accounts published by the National Restaurant Association. It is at this time that such records take on added importance. Compared with many other types of businesses, the restaurant business is a comparatively low-volume operation that is made up of thousands of small details. Consequently, the recordkeeping must be such that it keeps track of all of these small details, and of the thousands of dollars that go through the register.

A Model Statement of Costs

All restaurant accounting systems should break down the various income, cost, and expense categories so that control is facilitated. Such a breakdown might be similar to the following sample statement:

Revenue	$	%
Food Sales	480,000	80.0
Beverage Sales	120,000	20.0
Other Income	—	—
Total Revenue	600,000	100.0
Cost of Goods Sold	**$**	**%**
Food Cost:		
Meat	54,000	9.0
Seafood	66,000	11.0
Dairy	18,000	3.0
Produce	12,000	2.0
Groceries	36,000	6.0
Bakery	6,000	1.0
Total Food Cost	192,000	32.0
Beverage Cost	48,000	8.0
Total Cost of Goods Sold	240,000	40.0

Controllable Expense	$	%
Payroll	162,000	27.0
Taxes & Fringe Benefits	24,000	4.0
Employee Meals	—	—
Direct Operating Expense	12,000	2.0
Advertising & Promotion	12,000	2.0
Utilities	18,000	3.0
Administrative & General	24,000	4.0
Repairs & Maintenance	6,000	1.0
Rent	42,000	7.0
Profit Before Depreciation and Interest	60,000	10.0
Depreciation	12,000	2.0
Interest	6,000	1.0
Profit (Loss) before Income Tax	42,000	7.0
Net Profit	—	—

The foregoing is a standard type of statement that furnishes the information necessary for good, tight internal control, and the facts needed for accurate forecasting. The numbers used in this operating statement and in any other financial statements are hypothetical and have no real relationship with your or any other restaurant. They are included in these statements as examples of how statements may be constructed depending on the individual owners, managers, and accountants' individual desires. None of these categories appear automatically. Rather, they are derived from the proper classification and handling of all documents including sales reports, inventory records, invoice files and records, and payroll registers.

You can record food cost by category if you start with a purchase/invoice record and post all invoices in the proper category. For example you might purchase different kinds of food from a single vendor. The invoice for that purchase must be broken down into the categories that fit your records. The invoice might include meat, frozen fruit, and vegetables. Each of these items must be properly posted. Figure 8.2 is an illustration of an invoice record that you might use. As discussed in Chapter Four, you must set up your storeroom in a way that will facilitate the taking of inventory. Then you can construct your inventory record to fit the physical layout. The next step is to develop the invoice record as described in Figure 8.2.

Food cost is then calculated as follows:

BEGINNING INVENTORY + PURCHASES – ENDING INVENTORY = FOOD COST (IN TOTAL AND BY CATEGORY).

Construction of forms and the keeping of internal control records such as these can be facilitated by using your computer. All of this work can be accomplished with standard word processing and spreadsheet software.

Figure 8.2

	A	B	C	D	E	F	G	H	I
1									
2				INVOICE RECORD					
3				Meat, fish & poultry	Produce	Frozen fruits & veg	Groceries	Dairy/eggs	Other
4									
5									
6	Supplier	Inv Amt/							
7									
8	Jacks eggs	85						85	
9	Carsons	458		225		100	133		
10	Mountain Dairy	155						155	
11	Variety, Inc.	300							300
12	Gardens, Inc.	300			300				
13	Deep Water Co.	150		150					
14	Marios Melon	75			75				
15	Fresher/Fresh	125			125				
16	Carsons Turkey	360		360					
17	Variety, Inc.	150							150
18	Downhome Dairy	125						125	
19									
20									
21	Total purchases	2,283		735	500	100	133	365	450
22									
23									
24									

How to Budget Food Costs

When your records show a breakdown of cost by category (e.g., Meat, Seafood, Groceries, etc.), you can structure your budget in the same manner. Here is how to do it:

Your Operating Statements

Last Year

Food Sales	$800,000	
Food Cost	280,000	35.0%

Breakdown of Cost by $ and % of Sales

Meat	$ 78,400	9.9
Seafood	78,400	9.9
Dairy	36,400	4.6
Produce	28,000	3.5
Groceries	42,000	5.4
Bakery	5,600	0.7
Beverage	11,200	1.4
Total	$280,000	35.0%

The above breakdown will come from the statements that are being prepared at the end of each operating period. The process of budgeting now becomes one of applying these percentages to next year's forecast of food sales.

Food Sales (Forecast)	$944,250	
Food Cost	330,490	35.0%
Meat	93,480	9.9
Seafood	93,480	9.9
Eggs & Cheese	45,320	4.6
Produce	33,050	3.5
Groceries	50,990	5.4
Bakery	6,610	0.7
Beverage	13,220	1.4

The above would represent the food cost portion of the budget for the new year. To arrive at other expense amounts, the same type of calculations would be used. For instance, if direct expense were 10 percent last year, then you would forecast 10 percent of $944,250, or $94,425, in direct expense for next year. This budget assumes no increase or decrease in any individual category. If that were the case, then the particular category or categories would be adjusted accordingly. For example, if beef cost were forecast to be higher, you would have two options:

1. Raise prices to deliver the same percentage cost.

2. Adjust budgeted cost category for meat upward, which in turn would raise food cost and lower net profit.

How Budgeting Gives You the Opportunity to Evaluate Your Past Performance

Budgeting gives you the opportunity to study your past performance carefully. During this process, you should examine every item on your statement to see where improvements can be made. Once done, you then construct your budget by building in sensible and realistic goals that will keep your restaurant moving forward. Here are some examples this process would reveal, and the solutions for them:

- An examination of sales—along with an assessment of your in-house training—discloses some slippage in wine sales and several canceled training sessions.

  Remedy: Conduct consistent training with an emphasis on wine. Make a practical forecast for wine sales in the new year.

- Investigation of rising utility costs discloses that a further steep increase will occur in the new year.

  Remedy: Have a comprehensive energy audit performed, and incorporate those recommendations for improvements that are possible for you to make. Even though you may have forecast a higher utility cost in the new year, make it a realistic one that requires everyone paying attention to cost.

- Examination of supply cost reveals a high cost for paper products:

  Remedy: Examine storage and handling procedures and implement improvements. Forecast a lower percentage cost in the new year—and keep to it.

ANALYZING SALES AND COSTS

Your operating statements should reflect sales and costs for the current period, as well as the previous period. These figures will tell you whether your business is improving or falling behind. Operating statements should also reveal the performance of the business as compared with the goals you have set in your budget. These comparisons may not appear on any one statement, but they all are important to you. Several statements, then, may be necessary.

How to Use Statistical Tables to Compare Your Operating Results

There are several sources for operating statistics that relate to the restaurant industry. Some of these cover operating results in a particular city or state; others relate to the United States as a whole. Most of the magazines and trade papers will print some form of operating results that will be helpful to your own restaurant.

One example of a statistical source is as follows:

> National Restaurant Association
> 311 First Street NW
> Washington, DC 20001
> (Annual publication in cooperation with
> Deloitte and Touchellp)
> Title: *Restaurant Industry Operations Report*
> (year of study)

Using these statistics to compare with your own operating results can bring big dollar rewards to you. What you must recognize when dealing with them is that they are usually a compilation of historical data that may be one or more years old. The important point to note is the *trend* of business and how it affects you at any particular time.

Following is a report of Restaurant Industry Operations during 1997 (Fig. 8.3). These pages are excerpted from *1997 Restaurant Industry Operations Report* and are reprinted here with the permission of the National Restaurant Association. The report is full of some very meaningful facts about the industry across the United States. There is no need to repeat these facts but a few comments about how they can be helpful to you in your restaurant is in order.

- Note the change in total sales between 1996 and 1997.

- Did your restaurant have a similar increase? Did the restaurants in your area have an increase? Why? Do you expect an increase next year?

- Note the change in consumer statistics as regards age and why people feel that restaurants fill a niche in peoples' lives.

- It is interesting to note how entertainment plays a significant role in restaurant sales. Some folks enjoy entertaining guests or relatives at the local restaurant, and they get great satisfaction from being recognized by owners and employees. Are you able to recognize your customers on sight? A friendly atmosphere adds to dining pleasure. Do you circulate through the restaurant and make the diners feel "at home"? Different styles of service can draw new customers. Note how buffets have been gaining in popularity and why. Will that have any effect on your restaurant in the future?

THE RESTAURANT INDUSTRY

The restaurant industry is a large and diverse business:

- Industry sales will reach $320 billion in 1997 and account for over 4% of the U.S. Gross Domestic Product (in current dollars).
- There are almost 787,000 locations offering foodservice in the United States.
- 43% of the consumer's food dollar goes to meals and snacks away from home, up from 25% in 1955.
- More than nine million people are employed in the foodservice industry with employment projected to reach 11 million by the year 2005.
- The restaurant industry continues to be mostly small businesses. Average unit sales in 1992 were $501,000 at table-service restaurants and $473,000 at fast food restaurants.
- Almost one-half of all adults are food-service patrons on a typical day.

THE INDUSTRY IN 1997

The restaurant industry has become firmly entrenched in the fabric of daily life in the United States. Consider the following statistics, based on recent National Restaurant Association research:

- The typical person (8 years old and over) consumed an average of 4.1 commercially prepared meals per week in 1996, up from 3.8 just five years earlier.
- Three out of four adults agree that they have a larger selection of restaurants available to them today than they did two years ago.

- Almost one-half of all adults (47 percent) agree that they are cooking fewer meals at home than they did two years ago.
- Almost two out of every five consumers (38 percent) consider meals prepared at a restaurant or fast food place essential to the way they live.
- Two out of three adults agree that their favorite restaurant's food provides flavor and taste sensations that they can not easily duplicate in their home kitchen.
- Roughly three out of 10 adults indicate they are not eating on premises at eating places or purchasing takeout/delivery foods as often as they would like.

It is in this climate that the restaurant industry should post real sales growth of 1.4 percent in 1997. New Association research offers some key insights into the how and why consumers choose to purchase freshly prepared food. This research indicates that when they want fresh food that they don't prepare themselves, consumers try to balance three different and distinct goals:

1) social pleasure or " togetherness"
2) eating pleasure
3) lifestyle support or "convenience."

Depending on specific circumstances, such as the time of day, the day of the week or party composition, consumers will attempt to balance those three goals differently.

Why is it important for operators to take note of consumers' goals and need states regarding the purchase of freshly prepared food? Because the restaurant industry is a very competitive arena. And,

with the proliferation of options consumers can choose today, if one operator doesn't meet their needs, diners know that another operator across the street or down the block will. Consumers are quite cognizant that their restaurant choices have expanded in the last two years— three out of four agree that dining options have increased. Among individuals age 45 to 64, a prime target of casual-dining operators, a higher four out of five feel they have more restaurants to choose from than they did two years ago. Operators, too, are well aware of the increased competition. Indeed, when tableservice operators were questioned about their top challenges in 1997, competition ranked first, edging out labor concerns.

Still, despite intense competition, the 1997 *Restaurant Industry Forecast* calls for continued but somewhat more moderate growth, with ample opportunities for operators and their suppliers. Food-and-drink sales in the Commercial Restaurant Services Group are projected to show the strongest industry gains, advancing 4.3 percent to $288.9 billion and accounting for 90.1 percent of total industry sales. Within the eating-place category of the Commercial Group, food-and-drink sales in 1997 at fast-food restaurants and social caterers are expected to outpace the industry's overall real growth. Within the food contractor category, the highest real sales growth in 1997 should occur in educational markets, manufacturing/industrial plants and hospitals/nursing homes.

The rapid growth of establishments in certain niches, however, has contributed to a shakeout, which will probably result in lower than expected menu price growth. In 1997, menu prices are projected to advance a modest 2.7 percent, on the heels of a 2.4 percent gain in 1996. Menu-price inflation in the 1990s has remained low, reflecting competitive pressures, a more modest economic environment and price-sensitive consumers.

RESTAURANTS SERVE UP SOCIABILITY

Mealtime has always been a social time. From ancient tribal gatherings around the fire to modern meetings at the mall,

RESTAURANT INDUSTRY SALES—1996 AND 1997 ($000)

	1996	1997
Total Restaurant Industry	$ 307,627,410	$ 320,447,103
Commercial Restaurant Services	276,830,630	288,871,295
Eating Places	207,872,743	217,434,889
Fullservice restaurants	100,255,612	104,366,092
Limited-Service (Fast Food) Restaurants	98,396,743	103,530,904
Institutional Restaurant Services	29,712,154	30,480,695
Military Restaurant Services	1,084,626	1,095,113

Note: 1996 and 1997 figures are projected.
Source: National Restaurant Association.

family and friends have come together to share food, drink and sociability.

Consumers' search for comfortable social environments outside of the home has helped fuel sales at fullservice restaurants. Food-and-drink sales at fullservice restaurants are projected to exceed $104 billion in 1997—up 4.1 percent over 1996, or a 1.3 percent advance in real terms.

Fullservice restaurants, the largest segment in the eating-place category, should account for 32.6 percent of total restaurant industry sales and 48.0 percent of total eating-place sales in 1997.

Although still popular gathering spots, bars and taverns can expect to see a decline of 4.6 percent in real sales in 1997, mainly because of regulatory constraints and societal pressures regarding alcohol consumption. Bars with an entertainment concept, such as sports bars, will probably fare better than other establishments in this category. Brewpubs should continue to do well, but the most successful of these operations will have a strong food component.

BEYOND SOCIABILITY

When dining out for social pleasure, consumers have a number of expectations beyond simply a comfortable place to socialize. The Association's *Dinner Decision Making—1996* reveals a number of characteristics that consumers associate with a great place to eat: a sit-down meal, including tasty food, fresh ingredients, a comfortable atmosphere, a good reputation and friendly service. Many consumers also expect large portions, a variety of menu choices, knowledgeable servers, and unique food.

Quality service goes a long way toward ensuring that a restaurant meal is a pleasant occasion. A 1996 Association consumer survey shows that after good food, service is the most important component of a pleasant dining experience.

Generally, waitstaff seem to be doing a good job of pleasing the consumer. More than 80 percent of consumers feel that waitstaff are good or excellent at providing friendly service, answering questions about the menu items and delivering an accurately totaled check.

Unfortunately, top-notch service is not always as easy to achieve as top-notch

food. Today's operators deal with a labor pool they believe to be less-qualified, which makes good service even more difficult to provide. To meet customers' high service expectations, about three out of four tableservice operators state that they have improved training for hourly employees in the past year. In addition, incentive-and-recognition programs have gained prominence at tableservice establishments. In fact, almost two-thirds of tableservice operators offer such programs to improve morale in the workplace.

More operators are also implementing technologies such as POS systems, hand-held ordering terminals and seating-management software to meet customers' needs. For example, in 1990, fewer than two out of five tableservice operators used a POS system, but today that proportion has increased to roughly three out of five. These technologies improve the ability of service staff to present tableservice customers with an accurately totaled check and help to expedite the protocol associated with placing orders. Such technology should continue to heighten productivity and service into the coming century.

FUN FOR THE WHOLE FAMILY

Patrons are seeking a refuge from their hectic lives at home and at work. This is particularly true of families with children. As more households depend on dual incomes, the need for easy, fun and flavorful fare for the whole family served in relaxing environments has become more pronounced. Taking children to a fullservice restaurant was once reserved for very special occasions, but restaurant time has become family time. According to *Dinner Decision Making—1996,* almost 30 percent of dinner parties for on-premises occasions include children.

As a result of the baby-boomer "echo," children under the age of 19 are one of the fastest growing population segments. Tableservice operators today recognize the importance of catering to this growing market and understand that families often desire a change of pace from fast food.

Pleasing children can be more difficult at tableservice restaurants than at fast-food establishments, however. Meals usually take longer to prepare, and children are seldom patient. But those pint-size patrons can be won over. Providing a varied menu that tempts tiny taste buds is one way to keep tots happy at the table.

According to the Association's *Menu Analysis—1995,* four out of five restaurants with check sizes from $8 to $24.99 provide special children's items on the menu. Offerings often go way beyond the ubiquitous hot dog or hamburger and chips; on average, tableservice establishments offer five different entrees for children, and as many as 13 different entrees are available at some establishments.

DISHING UP A SIDESHOW

Entertainment can also add to the overall dining experience and increase social pleasure for children and adults alike. Many tableservice establishments offer entertainment to help pass the time while food is being prepared and throughout the dining experience. According to *Dinner Decision Making—1996,* consumers have higher expectations of some type of entertainment at restaurants with check sizes of more than $20; such expectations decline as check size declines.

Entertainment can include anything from live music or a comedy show to a display kitchen where meals are prepared within the patrons' view. According to the 1996 Tableservice Operator Survey, roughly three out of 10 tableservice operators offer live music or live entertainment, approximately two out of 10 offer display kitchens or ovens, 16 percent provide video or board games, and 7 percent offer cigar rooms. Live music, live entertainment and cigar rooms are offered more frequently at higher per person check establishments ($15 or more), whereas video or board games tend to be on the menu at lower average per person check establishments (less than $8). At many entertainment-based concepts the ambiance and decor of the restaurants themselves serve as the entertainment. Visual sensations of any type—ranging from fish tanks to walls of video screens—can help hook consumers searching for a stimulating and lively environment.

TEMPTED BY TASTE

Just as mealtime has always been a social time, eating has always been a pleasurable activity. American tastes, however, are constantly evolving. As cultural forces shape consumers' taste for ethnic foods, diners' palates have become more sophisticated and worldly. At the same time, Americans have also held onto a core of "family" foods—the mild, nostalgic, comforting foods of yesteryear—and pursued lighter, nutritious options. The result is the gradual transformation of "American" cuisine into a melting pot of healthy foods, ethnic foods and comfort foods.

Having grown weary of hearing what's good for them- and more often what's not- and tired of self-denial, Americans are indulging in eating pleasure once again. According to the National Restaurant Association's *Dinner Decision Making—1996,* 57 percent of on-premises dinner patrons are seeking to satisfy a craving for a particular type of food or seeking a replacement for the "home-cooked" meal they don't want to prepare themselves.

INDULGENT IMPULSES
Twenty-eight percent of on-premises dinner occasions are motivated by a craving for a particular type of food, according to *Dinner Decision Making—1996.* When consumers satisfy a craving, they are driven by taste and not as concerned about the food's nutritional value. These consumers have relatively high expectations in terms of their restaurant-dining experiences, including great-tasting food and fresh ingredients, a variety of menu choices, and unique or original food.

According to *Dinner Decision Making-1996,* Oriental restaurants and pizza places are the leading restaurant types chosen to satisfy a craving. Consequently, it's no surprise that Italian, Chinese and Mexican restaurants account for one-quarter of all establishments, according

to the 1992 Census of Retail Trade. Also, those three "mainstream" ethnic cuisines have become so ingrained in American culture that consumers no longer need to seek out exclusively Italian, Chinese or Mexican restaurants, since those cuisines are now embedded in all sorts of restaurant menus throughout the country.

Restaurant menus are also featuring a greater number of spicy and highly seasoned dishes, as operators continue to experiment with herbs and spices to boost flavor and generate excitement. Nearly nine out 10 menus identified an herb, a spice or other seasoning in at least one appetizer or entree selection, according to the National Restaurant Association's *Menu Analysis—1995.*

FREEDOM OF CHOICE
The popularity of buffets, cafeterias, and self-service salad or food bars in restaurants and grocery stores suggests that today's consumers derive pleasure from choosing from a selection of food and assembling a plate for themselves.

Many restaurateurs have installed self-service salad or food bars in their operations to satisfy a range of tastes—particularly at lower-check-size establishments. According to the Association's 1996 Tableservice Operator Survey, more than two out of five tableservice operators with average checks of less than $8 and one-third of

operators with checks between $8 and $14.99 report offering salad or food bars, compared with roughly one out of five operators with higher average checks.

The buffet boom also reflects a trend toward satisfying appetites of different sizes, since patrons may take as much or as little as they desire from the dishes offered. Tableservice restaurants also continue to accommodate varied appetites by offering half portions. More than one-half of all tableservice operators serve half-size portions, according to the 1996 Tableservice Operator Survey. Those petite plates are likely to become increasingly important as older patrons demand smaller portions and healthy alternatives.

FOOD AS A COMPETITIVE POINT OF DIFFERENCE
As consumers dine out more frequently, they become more knowledgeable about a wide variety of foods and cuisines, yet they don't know how to prepare them. A 1996 Association consumer survey reveals that two-thirds of adults agree that their favorite restaurant foods provide flavor and taste sensations which they cannot easily duplicate at home. Young respondents (those between the ages of 18 and 34) are most likely to agree with that statement. The product of households where working mothers never found the time to pass on cooking skills, many young people do not have the time or motivation to learn the

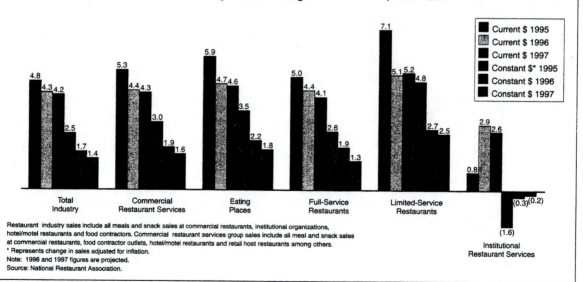

Restaurant Industry Percent Change in Dollar Sales, 1995–1997

Legend:
- Current $ 1995
- Current $ 1996
- Current $ 1997
- Constant $* 1995
- Constant $ 1996
- Constant $ 1997

Total Industry: 4.8, 4.3, 4.2, 2.5, 1.7, 1.4
Commercial Restaurant Services: 5.3, 4.4, 4.3, 3.0, 1.9, 1.6
Eating Places: 5.9, 4.7, 4.6, 3.5, 2.2, 1.8
Full-Service Restaurants: 5.0, 4.4, 4.1, 2.6, 1.9, 1.3
Limited-Service Restaurants: 7.1, 5.1, 5.2, 4.8, 2.7, 2.5
Institutional Restaurant Services: 0.8, 2.9, 2.6, (0.3), (0.2), (1.6)

Restaurant industry sales include all meals and snack sales at commercial restaurants, institutional organizations, hotel/motel restaurants and food contractors. Commercial restaurant services group sales include all meal and snack sales at commercial restaurants, food contractor outlets, hotel/motel restaurants and retail host restaurants among others.
* Represents change in sales adjusted for inflation.
Note: 1996 and 1997 figures are projected.
Source: National Restaurant Association.

cooking skills required to prepare those foods themselves. So they seek satisfaction at restaurants.

Operators agree that their most popular entree can not be easily duplicated at home, particularly those at higher check establishments. According to the Association's 1996 Tableservice Operator Survey, nine out of 10 tableservice operators with per person average checks over $15 agree that their most popular entrees provide flavor and taste sensations that can not be easily replicated in home kitchens, while about eight out of 10 operators with checks between $8 and $14.99 (83 percent) and roughly seven out of 10 operators with lower average checks (72 percent) agree with the statement.

So what sets restaurant foods apart? To offer superior food, operators are using top quality and fresh ingredients, hiring trained and highly skilled chefs, and equipping facilities with premium kitchen equipment.

And what are the most popular entrees that customers cannot duplicate at home? Ethnic entrees rank highest overall. According to a 1996 Association consumer study, 45 percent of respondents who say they cannot easily duplicate their favorite restaurant foods at home cite Oriental food, Mexican food and other ethnic cuisines. Consumers also feel seafood, poultry and steak entrees are difficult to duplicate in the home kitchen.

LIFESTYLE SUPPORT
According to a 1996 Association consumer survey, meals prepared at a restaurant or a fast-food place are essential to almost 40 percent of American adults. Consequently, convenience is a major factor in dinner decision making. Fifty-seven percent of carry-out occasions today occur when consumers are either pressed for time or have no energy to cook, according to *Dinner Decision Making—1996*. Association research indicates that speed of service and location are the two most important attributes in choosing an establishment that offers carryout.

With limited time, and unlimited choices, choosing the most expedient alternative for getting the best taste in the most sociable and comfortable environment is hardly easy. But when time is of the essence, fast food is one way to go, whether it be via carryout, delivery or dining on premises.

Consumers' need for speed translates into healthy growth in the fast-food segment. In 1997, sales at limited-service restaurants are projected to rise to $103.5 billion, up 2.5 percent in real terms. Limited-service restaurants should account for 47.6 percent of eating-place sales in 1997, up from 43.8 percent a decade earlier.

DEMOGRAPHICS

BABY BOOMERS TURN 50
The aging of the baby-boom generation (the population born between 1946 and 1964) has been one of the most significant demographic forces shaping U.S. society and will continue to be, well into the 21st century. According to the Census Bureau, more than 40 percent of the nation's households are headed by people aged 30 to 49—almost all of them baby-boomers. As boomers move up the age ladder, their influence—on restaurants and on the overall marketplace—will continue to be felt.

The first boomers turned 50 in 1996, a milestone that could mean big business for restaurants. Historically, households headed by people aged 45 to 54 have the highest incomes and are the biggest spenders, because they are in their peak earning years. Hence, these households are a prime target market for restaurants. In 1994, this group accounted for 24 percent of the all expenditures on food away from home, despite comprising only 17 percent of all households. The ranks of 45-to-54-year-olds will continue to swell in the coming years, as more and more of the baby-boom generation moves into middle age.

BOOMER "ECHO" HAS STRONG VOICE
Children aged 5 to 15 are one of the fastest-growing segments of the American population. After several years of decline during the "baby bust" of the late-'60s and '70s, the teen population began to rebound in 1991, thanks to the baby boomer "echo." By the end of the current decade, the teen population will have increased by 5.1 million.

The growth of this large demographic group has many implications for restaurant operators. First, teens have a significant influence on their parents' decisions about dining out. Second, this group is the labor pool of the future, and the current tight labor supply situation among

16-to-24-year-olds—a traditional source of labor for restaurants—should receive relief in the years ahead. Third, these individuals are the restaurant customers of the future. Their exposure to restaurant options today will influence both their palates and their proclivity to dine out in the future.

WOMEN IN THE WORKFORCE
The importance of women in the workforce cannot be overstated. When women began entering the workforce in record numbers, the face of the economy—and consumers' lifestyles—changed immeasurably. Working women have had a pronounced impact on the restaurant industry in two ways: they have created a higher demand for meals prepared outside the home, because no one is home to cook, and they generate additional household income that can be used to purchase food prepared away from home.

In 1993, the wife was the sole worker for only 5 percent of married couples, but in more than half of married couples (54 percent), both spouses worked. Today, the highest proportion of those two-income couples is found among older boomers, where 72 percent of couples in their 40s are dual-earners. Those households have traditionally been the restaurant industry's best target market, and the proportion of married couples earning two paychecks is expected to continue to grow through the end of the century for all but the oldest workers. Projections made by the Conference Board show that 64 percent of all married couples should be dual-earner households by 2000, and 80 percent of households headed by individuals aged 25 to 44 are likely to have two incomes.

IMMIGRANT POPULATION INCREASING
The Asian and Hispanic populations in the United States are growing at a greater rate than the U.S. population in general. According to the Census Bureau, the Asian population grew from 4.9 million in 1984 to 8.9 million in 1994—an increase of almost 80 percent. The Hispanic population grew at a similar rate, increasing from 17.6 million in 1984 to 27.9 million in 1994—a 58 percent increase.

The flavorful cookery practiced by many of the immigrating cultures has become a mainstay of the American diet. Southwestern cooking, Pacific Rim dishes, Cajun/Creole cuisine, and Caribbean and Mexican preparation methods all conjure up images of hot-and-spicy fare. Many restaurants popularizing the terms "Pacific Rim" and "Tastes of Asia" offer a menu that includes dishes from parts of Korea, Taiwan, Thailand, Vietnam, Burma, Malaysia, the Philippines, and Indonesia, as well as India, Japan, and the various regions of China.

Cantonese, Mexican and Italian cooking are the most popular ethnic cuisines, according to the Association's study *Ethnic Cuisines—A Profile.* More than 95 percent of consumers report familiarity with these three cuisines, and more than 90 percent of consumers have tried these types of cooking.

OPERATIONAL TRENDS

Increased competition and labor concerns should keep restaurateurs on their toes in 1997. Continued consumer resistance to menu-price increases will probably once again require operators to manage their businesses extremely efficiently. The bottom line: restaurateurs who do not take advantage of technology, diligently train their staffs and tightly monitor their costs are likely to be at a competitive disadvantage.

LABOR-POOL PROBLEMS INCREASE PRESSURES
The primary foodservice labor pool—traditionally 16-to-24-years-olds—has been shrinking for the past several years. At the same time, the demand for workers in that age group has been intensifying, as both the foodservice and the retail industries expand.

Predictions of a tightening labor market in the short term should not come as a surprise to operators. A majority of respondents to the Association's 1996 Tableservice Operator Survey report a decreasing pool of applicants for both salaried and hourly positions, especially at multi-unit organizations and establishments with check sizes of less than $8.

Fortunately, the shrinking labor pool should soon start filling up again. The dearth of 16- to 24-year-olds is expected to come to an end within the next decade, as the children of the baby-boom generation expand the pool of teenagers and young adults to healthy numbers by 2005. Until that time, however, foodser-

vice employers will be likely to expand their recruitment of alternative labor pools, such as the elderly and the growing immigrant population.

TRAINING IS CRITICAL
Not only has the number of applicants for foodservice positions decreased, but the quality of applicants has declined as well. According to roughly half of the tableservice operators surveyed, the qualifications of hourly employees have decreased over the past few years, and roughly one-third of operators report a decrease in the qualifications of salaried applicants.

In addition, operators have become more choosy in their selection processes. Around one-third of operators claim to have more stringent selection criteria today for both salaried and hourly employees than they did a few years ago. This juxtaposition can be explained partially by consumers' demand for improved service: Although there is a dwindling supply of labor, the consumer increasingly expects better service, and better service requires better employees.

As the need for superior productivity, efficiency and service become paramount, proper and thorough training is even more important. And operators are responding to increased demands for training. Analysis of the 1996 Tableservice Operator Survey shows that approximately three-fourths of respondents have improved their staff-training programs in the last year, up from two-thirds in 1992. Improved staff training programs are more common among restaurants with higher check sizes, but growth in the number of training programs has risen sharply at lower and mid-priced establishments.

AUTOMATION IMPROVES PRODUCTIVITY
Technology can also help operators untangle the troubles produced by a shrinking labor pool, by improving consistency and productivity. According to Association research, more tableservice operators are using computers and other automation technologies each year. In 1990, only about one out of six tableservice operators used computer systems, compared with more than eight out of 10 operators in 1996. This increase in usage is especially apparent at lower-check-size operations, as the decreasing cost of computer technology has made both hardware and software more accessible

to smaller establishments. As both software and hardware systems become less expensive and more sophisticated, both should become even more prevalent at restaurants in all check-size categories.

ENTER THE INTERNET
Use of the Internet has exploded in the past few years. According to the Association's 1996 Tableservice Operator Survey, roughly two out of five operators report jumping onto the information superhighway. The uses for this communication vehicle are as limitless as the information it offers. Information is available on virtually every topic of interest to foodservice operators, from the latest restaurant-design trends and recipe-costing techniques to listings for industry suppliers and food distributors. Consumers, too, are increasingly surfing the Net seeking dining information.

Consequently, the growth of on-line advertising is also exploding. In the '70s and '80s restaurateurs used radios and newspapers as their primary advertising platform; today, operators are making wider use of the Internet and its graphic capabilities to reach connected consumers. This advanced advertising can convey all sorts of information about restaurants to consumers. Floor plans, photos, menus, phone numbers and credit-card acceptance for restaurants—around the corner or across the country—can be accessed with a simple click of the mouse or touch of a button.

MAKING CUSTOMERS FEEL SAFE AND SECURE
One reason customers cocooned in the early 1990s was a heightened awareness of crime and a general feeling of insecurity. Households purchased home surveillance equipment, car alarms, and guard dogs in record numbers, and people stayed home where they felt safe. As people become more inclined to socialize outside the home again, security must be provided in their new environments. Operators are aware of that. In fact, about two out of five tableservice operators indicate that they made security improvements to their establishment within the past year. The most prevalent security measures taken by restaurateurs include the installation of an alarm or a security system and the installation of video cameras.

National Restaurant Association
Research Division

HIGHLIGHTS FROM THE RESTAURANT INDUSTRY DOLLAR

- Full service establishments with average check under $10 reported income before taxes of 3.6% of total sales, while full service restaurants with average checks of $10 or greater reported income of 3.5% of total sales.

- Limited service fast food restaurants had income before income taxes of 9.5% of total sales. The payroll and employee benefits costs for limited service fast food establishments were a combined 27.9% of total sales, the lowest among the three restaurant categories.

- At full service restaurants (average check per person under $10) direct operating expenses were 7.0% of total sales, the highest of the three categories.

The Restaurant Industry Dollar*

	Full Service Restaurants (Average Check Per Person Under $10)	Full Service Restaurants (Average Check Per Person $10 And Over)	Limited Service Fast Food Restaurants
Where It Came From			
Food Sales	89.6 %	76.0 %	95.7 %
Beverage Sales (alcoholic)	10.4	24.0	4.3
Where It Went**			
Cost of Food Sold	32.2	30.0	28.4
Cost of Beverages Sold	3.2	7.8	1.2
Salaries and Wages	28.0	26.9	24.2
Employee Benefits	3.9	4.2	3.7
Direct Operating Expenses	7.0	6.5	6.7
Music and Entertainment	0.2	0.9	0.1
Marketing	2.3	2.5	5.7
Utility Services	3.2	2.3	2.8
Restaurant Occupancy Costs	5.2	5.3	7.4
Repairs and Maintenance	1.7	1.6	2.0
Depreciation	2.3	1.8	3.1
Other Operating Expense/(Income)	0.3	0.2	(0.4)
General and Administrative	3.2	4.2	3.7
Corporate Overhead	2.7	1.4	0.8
Interest	0.8	0.6	0.8
Other	0.2	0.3	0.3
Income Before Income Tax	3.6 %	3.5 %	9.5 %

*All figures are weighted averages based on 1996 data.
**All amounts are reflected as a percentage of total sales.

- There is strong growth in immigrant populations throughout the country. How has it affected the industry in your area and your restaurant specifically? There is no doubt that American tastes have changed with the introduction of flavorful cooking and seasonings by immigrant cooks.

- Labor continues to be a problem as the market for qualified food service personnel shrinks. This heightens the need for selective hiring and training programs and consistent supervision by you and other staff members in your restaurant.

- A study of the table "Highlights from the Restaurant Dollar" will provide information about how your restaurant compares in the areas of cost and expense. The format for the statement will also provide a guide for the construction of operating statements for your restaurant. It is important to produce statements of this type to make comparisons between your restaurant and such statistical data as shown in Figure 8.3.

How to Manage Sales and Costs with Good Budgets

If the ABC Restaurant has constructed a budget that is meaningful and practical in 1999 for 2000, you can next analyze actual results versus budget. Your budget represents your goal or target and is a necessary ingredient for any business. It should set the goals to be met for sales, cost, and expense that are necessary to pay for the fixed cost and debt of the business (minimum payroll, utilities necessary to "open the door" each day, rent or mortgage, depreciation, and interest). In addition, because you want to make a profit, that amount must also be recognized in your budget.

ABC RESTAURANT

Profit & Loss Statement

(2000)

	Actual $	%	Year-to-Date Budget $	%	Variance $
Sales					
Food	600,000	80.7	575,000	79.3	+25,000
Beverage	144,000	19.3	150,000	20.7	−6,000
Total Sales	744,000	100.0	725,000	100.0	+19,000
Cost of Sales					
Food	192,000	32.0	184,000	32.0	+8,000
Beverage	30,240	21.0	36,000	24.0	−5,760
Total Cost of Sales	222,240	30.0	220,000	30.0	+2,240
Expenses					
Payroll	200,800	27.0	188,300	26.0	+12,380

Taxes & Fringes	37,498	5.0	35,525	4.9	+1,973
Utilities	14,880	2.0	15,225	2.1	−345
Advertising	18,600	2.5	14,500	2.0	+4,100
Direct Op'n Ex	71,424	9.5	72,500	10.0	−1,076
Total Expenses	343,282	46.0	326,250	45.0	+17,032

You should budget for each item in your operating statement. This would include each of the sales, cost, and expense categories. Studying the foregoing shows a rather healthy experience in sales that are increasing over budget, as well as cost of sales which are either right on target or better.

The same, however, is not true in the expense category. Payroll has increased in both dollars and percentage. This is also true for taxes and fringes and for advertising expense. Such a condition would call for an analysis of labor like the one in Figure 8.4, and a hard look at your advertising program. The same sort of analysis should always be made for every item on the Profit and Loss Statement on both a monthly and year-to-date basis. Consistent bookkeeping and analyses of this kind will certainly bring maximum dollar profits to you.

There is a tendency on the part of most persons, whether owners or managers, to "blue sky" sales figures to "fit" expense items into a budget or a pro forma statement in which those items are causing the profit line to show less than acceptable results. This may be the result of dealing with percentages that are easy to adjust when forecasting. There is a method to check one's own work by dealing with expense and cost dollars only and then comparing the result with sales dollars calculated using statistical means. It requires being honest with yourself when preparing a schedule of cost and expense estimates in dollar amounts. The following calculations illustrate how to accomplish this comparison:

PROPOSED BUDGET
Based on past history and market research

Your research has indicated there is a potential market of 750 persons in the area of your business, and you estimate that you can capture a minimum of 30 percent of that number as restaurant customers. You have prepared your menu and are estimating a daily check average of $7.00 per day per seat for lunch and $18.00 per day for dinner. The restaurant has 110 seats and you expect to turn them over as follows:

LUNCH—110 seats (customers) × 2.0 turns × 6 days per week × 50 weeks = 66,000
Customers at $7.00 per seat = $462,000.

DINNER—110 seats × 0.5 turns × 6 days × 50 weeks = 16,500 dinner customers
at an average of $18.00 per seat = $297,000.

TOTAL ESTIMATED SALES—$759,000.

Figure 8.4
Weekly Labor Analysis

	A	B	C	D	E	F	G	H	I	J	K	L	M	N	O	P	Q	R	S	T	U	V
1							HOURS OF OPERATION							PM								TOTAL
2	AM	5	6	7	8	9	10	11	12	1	2	3	4	5	6	7	8	9	10	RATE	HRS	
3	TITLE																			*		*
4	CHEF																					
5	COOK																			15.00	40	600.-
6	COOK																			15.00	40	600.-
7	COOK																			15.00	40	600.-
8	PREP																			6.00	40	240.-
9	PREP																			6.00	40	240.-
10	SAN																			5.50	40	220.-
11	SAN																			5.50	40	220.-
12	SAN																			5.50	40	220.-
13	SAN																			5.50	40	220.-
14																						
15	CASH																			8.00	30	240.-
16	CASH																			8.00	30	240.-
17																						
18	BAR																			10.00	40	400
19	BAR																			8.00	30	240
20																						
21	SERV																			2.13	25	53.25
22	SERV																			2.13	25	53.25
23	SERV																			2.13	25	53.25
24	SERV																			2.13	30	63.90
25	SERV																			2.13	25	53.25
26	SERV																			2.13	25	53.25
27	SERV																			2.13	25	53.25
28																						
29	BUS																			5.50	25	137.50
30	BUS																			5.50	30	165.-
31																						
32	SAN																			6.00	40	240.-
33																						
34	TOTAL PAYROLL																					5205.90
35																						
36																						

SALES REQUIREMENT

To cover estimated dollar cost and expense plus needed profit.

	$	%
Sales		
Cost of Sales	——	35.0
Gross Profit	——	——
Operating Expense:		
Payroll and Benefits	5,000	
Automobile	500	
Telephone	150	
Advertising and Promotion	700	
Rent	1,500	
Utilities	1,200	
Total Operating Expense	9,050	
Before Tax Profit Need	——	10.0

Method:

Assume sales to be 100.0% of total. Assume cost of sales to be 35.0% of total.

100% − (10% + 35%) = 55%

$9,050 ÷ 0.55 = $16,455

$16,455 × 50 weeks = $825,000 (Estimate based on cost & expense)

$759,000 (Estimate based on history and market statistics)

$66,000 - Possible shortfall in sales

Case Study

Case 1

Sales—Based on history and market	$759,000	100.0%
Cost of sales	265,650	35.0%
Gross profit	493,350	65.0%
Operating expense	432,500	57.0%
Net profit	60,850	8.0%

Case 2

Sales—based on cost and expense	$825,000	100.0%
Cost of sales	288,750	35.0%
Gross profit	536,250	65.0%
Operating expense	453,750	55.0%
Net profit	82,500	10.0%

Summary

It's obvious these results call for further study. If after study the numbers appear to be substantially correct, then some action regarding a reduction in cost and expense might be in order. Or there might be some way to increase sales (e.g., menu changes, hours of operation, increased training of staff, etc.).

The most important point in this scenario is to remind you to think hard and plan carefully. In the above example it is assumed that management salaries are included in payroll cost. However, there is no provision for taxes or for any debt service, and there are probably few businesses that have no debt.

Checklist

✔ Can the menu be revised to increase sales?

✔ Can we add more specials?

✔ Is the speed of service including check presentation adequate for turning seats fast enough?

✔ Are the food and wine menus easy to read?

✔ Is the lighting right or is it difficult to read?

ANALYZING LABOR COSTS

Because restaurant conditions are subject to constant changes, you as owner or manager should always be aware of all the costs required to produce the quality of food, beverage, and service needed to sustain your business.

Among the cost items you'll need to keep track of are the introduction of convenience foods and labor-saving devices. If such implementations take place, and menus and service are not extended to capture additional sales, then there may be decreasing profit margins. Frequently, labor-saving improvements are "absorbed" into the system, resulting in higher food cost (convenience item) or added capitalization (new equipment) without any increase in revenue.

How to Do a Labor Analysis

There are different ways to do a labor analysis. In general, a detailed study of movements (i.e., hand, feet, etc.) against a stopwatch is unnecessary. Instead, an analysis of the total staff work routines in one-half or full-hour increments over the workday is done. There are many possible variations of charts on which you may plot duties and shifts. One such chart is included here for illustrative purposes (see Fig. 8.4). Regardless of the form used, to be useful, the chart must include the following:

- Title of jobs to be analyzed. Names of persons on the workforce should not be substituted for job titles. Such a practice only leads to bias, which, in turn, invalidates the analysis. A good analysis should include only those jobs necessary to run the restaurant efficiently and economically. Once this is accomplished, then the names of those best qualified are slotted into the schedule.

- Hours of work and task assignments.

- Hours of operation for the restaurant. These may vary from day to day. For example, Friday and Saturday may be longer operating days than the other days of the week.

Developing Work Schedules from the Labor Analysis

Employee work schedules should be developed from your labor analysis. It is easy to schedule additional time, if needed. The sample labor analysis chart can be used with an actual or projected operation to

1. Estimate labor requirements when a restaurant is in the planning stage.

2. Analyze labor usage in an existing restaurant operation.

The technique required for preparing such an analysis is simple. It consists of charting the work hours from the beginning to the end of each shift for each person. If certain days of the work week differ from others, two separate charts may be needed.

For example, you may need a chart for Monday through Thursday, and separate ones for Friday and the weekend. Furthermore, instead of using arrows to schedule the various tasks, as shown in Fig. 8.4, you can color-code the chart. To do this, you would use different colors to indicate the blocks of time for prepreparation, dining room setup, preparation, meal serving, and cleanup.

Important: Make sure that you stick to the schedule you draw up. If a job can be accomplished in seven hours, schedule it to be completed in that length of time. Remember, each one of those extra hours costs you in lost profits.

For example, if your restaurant "loses" only eight hours a week at $4.50 per hour, and you have a 17 percent tax and fringe benefit cost, your yearly loss for fifty-two weeks is more than $2,190.

Put another way, if you had paid attention to your labor cost, you could have realized an additional $2,190 in pretax profit!

Appendix

Sample Chart of Accounts Based on
Uniform System of Accounts for Restaurants

The chart of accounts is a numbering system for the income and expense classifications conforming to the *Uniform System of Accounts for Restaurants.* The codes used here are not the only method for classifying the accounts; however, this is an acceptable standard grouping used by many restaurants.

The illustrated code-numbering system is designed to be flexible and to be added to or reduced to fit the requirements of the individual restaurant owner. Modern restaurant accounting methods dictate that some type of account code-numbering system be used.

Chart of Accounts

Account Number	Account Name
	ASSETS (1000)
1100	Cash
1110	Change funds
1120	Cash on deposit
1200	Accounts receivable
1210	Customers
1220	Credit card accounts
1230	Other
1240	Employees' loans and advances
1250	Provision for doubtful accounts
1300	Inventories
1310	Food
1320	Beverages
1330	Supplies
1340	Other
1400	Prepaid expenses
1410	Insurance
1420	Deposits
1430	Taxes
1440	Licenses
1500	Fixed assets
1510	Land
1520	Building
1530	Accumulated depreciation
1540	Leasehold improvements
1550	Amortization of improvements
1560	Furniture, fixtures and equipment
1570	Accumulated depreciation
1580	Automobiles
1590	Accumulated depreciation
1595	Operating equipment
1600	Deferred charges
1610	Marketing program prepaid
1620	Pre-Opening Expenses
	LIABILITIES (2000)
2100	Payables
2110	Notes payable
2120	Accounts payable
2200	Taxes withheld and accrued

2210	Income Tax
2220	FICA
2230	Federal unemployment tax
2240	State unemployment tax
2250	Sales tax
2260	Employer's share of payroll taxes
2270	Provision for income taxes

2300	Accrued expenses
2310	Rent
2320	Payroll
2330	Interest
2340	Water
2350	Gas
2360	Electricity
2370	Personal property taxes
2380	Other

2400	Long-term debt

SHAREHOLDERS' EQUITY (3000)

3100	Common stock
3200	Capital in excess of par
3300	Retained earnings

REVENUE (4000)

4100	Food
4200	Beverages

COST OF SALES (5000)

5100	Cost of sales—food
5200	Cost of sales—beverages

OTHER INCOME (6000)

6100	Cover charges and minimums
6200	Commissions
6210	Gift shop operation—net
6220	Telephone and coin box commissions
6230	Concessions
6300	Salvage and waste sales
6400	Cash discounts
6900	Miscellaneous

CONTROLLABLE EXPENSES (7000)

7100	Salaries and wages
7105	Service
7110	Preparation
7115	Sanitation
7120	Beverages
7125	Administrative

7130	Purchasing and storing
7135	Other
7200	Employee benefits
7205	FICA
7210	Federal unemployment tax
7215	State unemployment tax
7220	Workmen's compensation
7225	Group insurance
7230	State health insurance tax
7235	Welfare plan payments
7240	Pension plan payments
7245	Accident and health insurance premiums
7250	Hospitalization, Blue Cross, Blue Shield
7255	Employee meals
7260	Employee instruction and education expenses
7265	Employee Christmas and other parties
7270	Employee sports activities
7275	Medical expenses
7280	Credit Union
7285	Awards and prizes
7290	Transportation and housing
7400	Direct operating expenses
7402	Uniforms
7404	Laundry and dry cleaning
7406	Linen rental
7408	Linen
7410	China and glassware
7412	Silverware
7414	Kitchen utensils
7416	Kitchen fuel
7418	Cleaning supplies
7420	Paper supplies
7422	Guest supplies
7424	Bar supplies
7426	Menus and wine lists
7428	Contract cleaning
7430	Exterminating
7432	Flowers and decorations
7434	Auto and truck expense
7436	Parking lot expenses
7438	Licenses and permits
7440	Banquet expenses

7498	Other operating expenses
7500	Music and entertainment
7505	Orchestras and musicians
7510	Professional entertainers
7520	Mechanical music
7525	Contracted wire services
7530	Piano rental and tuning
7535	Films, records, tapes, and sheet music
7540	Programs
7550	Royalties to ASCAP, BMI, and SESAC
7555	Booking agents fees
7560	Meals served to musicians
7600	Marketing
7601	Selling and promotion
7602	Sales representative service
7603	Travel expense on solicitation
7604	Direct mail
7605	Telephone and telegraph used for advertising and promotion
7606	Entertainment cost in promotion of business (including gratis meals to customers)
7607	Postage
7610	Advertising
7611	Newspaper
7612	Magazines and trade journals
7613	Circulars, brochures, postal cards, and other mailing pieces
7614	Outdoor signs
7615	Radio and television
7616	Programs, directories, and guides
7617	Preparation of copy, photographs, etc.
7620	Public relations and publicity
7621	Civic and community projects
7622	Donations
7623	Souvenirs, favors, treasure chest items
7630	Fees and commissions
7631	Advertising or promotional agency fees
7632	Franchise fees
7640	Research
7641	Travel in connection with research
7642	Outside research agency

7643	Product testing
7700	Utilities
7705	Electric current
7710	Electric bulbs
7715	Water
7720	Removal of waste
7725	Fuel
7730	Engineer's Supplies
7795	Ice
7800	Administrative and general expenses
7805	Office stationery printing, and supplies
7810	Data processing costs
7815	Postage
8920	Telegrams and telephone
7823	Management fees
7825	Dues and subscriptions
7828	Executive office expense
7830	Traveling expenses
7835	Insurance—general
7840	Commissions on credit card charges
7845	Provision for doubtful accounts
7850	Cash over or (short)
7855	Professional fees
7858	Directors or Trustees Fees
7860	Protective and bank pick-up services
7865	Bank charges
7870	Miscellaneous
7900	Repairs and maintenance
7902	Furniture and fixtures
7904	Kitchen equipment
7906	Office equipment
7908	Refrigeration
7910	Air conditioning
7912	Plumbing and heating
7915	Electrical and mechanical
7916	Floors and carpets
7918	Buildings
7920	Parking lot
7922	Gardening and grounds maintenance
7924	Building alterations
7928	Painting, plastering, and decoration
7990	Maintenance contracts—elevators

7992	Maintenance contracts—signs
7994	Maintenance contracts—office machinery
7996	Autos and trucks
7998	Other equipment and supplies

RENT AND OTHER OCCUPATION COSTS, INTEREST AND DEPRECIATION (8000)

8100	Rent and other occupation costs, interest, and depreciation
8105	Rent—minimum or fixed
8110	Percentage rent
8115	Ground rental
8120	Equipment rental
8125	Real estate taxes
8130	Personal property taxes
8135	Other municipal taxes
8140	Franchise tax
8145	Capital stock tax
8150	Partnership or corporation license fees
8160	Insurance on building and contents
8200	Interest
8205	Notes payable
8210	Long term debt
8215	Other
8300	Depreciation
8305	Buildings
8310	Amortization of leasehold
8315	Amortization of leasehold improvements
8320	Furniture, fixtures, and equipment
9000	Income Taxes
9010	Federal
9020	State

Chapter 9

How to Increase Your Profits by Staying on Top of Changes in the Marketplace

Table of Contents

Chapter 9

How to Increase Your Profits by Staying on Top of Changes in the Marketplace

Staying abreast of the constant changes that can affect the restaurant business is one of the most important things you, as owner or manager, can do. One good way to stay alert to impending changes in the community that could influence your profits is to spend the maximum time possible in your restaurant's dining room talking with your guests. Your customers represent an excellent source of information about many different subjects, including local happenings.

HOW TO TURN NEGATIVE CHANGES INTO POSITIVE ONES

Changes in the community can affect your business by causing changes in your market that can be either beneficial or disruptive. Often, seemingly disruptive changes can have a positive effect if you are alert and imaginative enough to turn negative situations into positive ones.

For example, suppose you hear from a steady customer that a new building will be going up near your restaurant, and that your driveway is going to be partially blocked for some time because of the need to extend or modify utility lines. This may at first appear to be disastrous for you. However, after checking to see if this information is factual, here is what you can do to turn this into a benefit and come out a winner.

You find additional parking space within easy walking distance of your restaurant for which you are able to negotiate a short-term lease. You then use table tents, signs, and your regular method of advertising to inform your customers of the temporary inconvenience to them. At the same time, you emphasize that the food and service will still be the same fine quality they have enjoyed in the past.

Next, realizing that you might still lose some regular business because of this inconvenience, you take your miniature sample menus and personally visit other businesses, institutions, etc., within walking distance, inviting folks to try your restaurant. To help this program along, you hand out some coupons that offer discounts on your daily specials.

Results:

- You have shown your regular customers that you care enough to alleviate the inconveniences.

- You have opened new markets and secured some new customers.

In other words, you have turned a negative into a positive.

Changes in the marketplace that could hurt your business can also have a disastrous effect on your employees. For example, service people may lose tips and want to seek other employment. Or production people may have to face the possibility of layoffs due to poor sales. In both cases, you may suffer the loss of good employees who will have to be replaced later.

Employees are often a good source of grapevine information. Therefore, by keeping open the lines of communication, they may alert you to troublesome events. In addition, ongoing communication may help to forestall future employee dissatisfaction.

WHERE TO FIND OUT ABOUT CHANGES

There are many different sources from which information is available about events that could affect your business. The most common and obtainable are television, radio, and your daily newspaper. By watching the news or listening to at least one newscast each day on the radio, you will keep yourself informed of national and state news, as well as certain important community items. In addition, your local newspaper should be read daily because it is full of tidbits about what is going on around town.

When you read the paper, you should pay particular attention to the following:

1. *The Business Section*—for events related to companies and institutions in your town; for news about companies moving in and out of the area; for personnel and executive changes within various organizations; for real estate development.

When you hear of new companies coming into the area, you may want to establish contact by presenting sample menus, welcome letter, and other materials. Personnel or executive changes may call for your contacting secretaries to suggest your restaurant for congratulatory parties or get-togethers. Such events as birthdays, christenings, and wedding announcements would also invite some action on your part.

2. *City/County Government Section*—for happenings at city council meetings; planning related to street or sewer construction; any contemplated changes in tax laws or rates of assessments

You should be aware of what is happening in city government to be forewarned of events that could either help or hurt you.

3. *Sports Page*—for what's happening on the local sports scene
Watching the local sports scene could offer opportunities for award banquets, luncheons, etc. If you are able to pick up only ten banquets in one year for fifty persons at $18.00 per person, you will bring in a nice extra $9,000. Not only that, you will probably make a minimum of $3,150 in operating profits from just those few parties.

Trade Periodicals: Another Excellent Source of Information

Trade periodicals are publications that relate to a specific industry. In addition to these are business periodicals, which report on business conditions and happenings to industries and governments. Both of these are informative. But of special interest to you are those periodicals that report on the food service industry.

The following is a partial listing of some of the various restaurant publications, and what they cover:

- **Restaurant Association Publications**

  For example, the Texas Restaurant Association publishes a monthly magazine entitled *Texas Food and Service*. It contains articles written by many different people in the industry, covering all facets of restaurant operations. Included in it are such items as menu construction, marketing and sales, employee training, labor relations, and the latest information on present and proposed legislation that will affect the restaurant industry. Each state has an association, and each tries to keep its membership informed as best it can.

- **Nation's Restaurant News**
  Published by Lebhar-Friedman, Inc. 425 Park Avenue, New York, NY 10022.

  This paper is published biweekly, every other Monday. It contains over 150 pages and covers current events in the restaurant industry throughout the country. In it you will find articles dealing with current and proposed laws; what is happening with various companies and independent restaurants; sales and earnings statistics; editorial comments about the industry; and reports on past, current, and future meetings, conventions, and events.

- **Restaurant Hospitality**
  Published monthly at 1111 Chester Avenue, Cleveland, OH 44114.

  In it you'll find articles about different restaurant operations around the country. Usually it has at least one story related to restaurant design. Each month there are comments from various writers covering a wide expanse of topics.

- **Restaurants and Institutions**
  A Cahners publication, 1350 Touhy Avenue, Des Plaines, IL 60018.

  This magazine is published twice a month. It contains statistics of interest to the industry, including current restaurant industry sales and forecasts for the future. Products—both new and established—are reported, and there are the usual stories about specific companies. Included are menus and recipes from restaurants, and a classified section containing information on personnel recruiting, real estate, and franchise opportunities.

- **Food Service Equipment Specialist**
  Published monthly by Cahners Publishing Company, Five South Wabash Avenue, Chicago, IL 60603.

  This publication is a sourcebook for virtually every type of equipment used in a food service operation of any kind. If you are looking for a certain product or products, try this magazine. It also carries a listing of industry manufacturers and associations.

- **Restaurant Design**
  Published quarterly by Restaurant Business, Inc. 633 Third Avenue, New York, NY 10017.

  This magazine is all about restaurant interior design and facility planning. It has feature articles on specific installations and includes pictures and diagrams. If you are going to build a new facility or remodel an existing one, you may get some very valuable ideas from this periodical.

- **Food Service Marketing**
  Published monthly. 5325 Sheridan Drive, P.O. Box 1160, Williamsville, NY 14231–1160.

  Includes statistics on dining out in various market segments of the industry. This magazine offers information on marketing techniques through merchandising of menu and interior design. You will also find results of research into pricing of products, energy, standardization of menu items, and more. There are also articles by contributing editors on a variety of subjects ranging from personnel problems to facilities planning.

- **Restaurant Business**
Published monthly (except semimonthly in March, May, and September) by Restaurant Business Magazine, 633 Third Avenue, New York, NY 10017.

Includes many different articles about various market segments and companies in the industry. Also has a good coverage of statistical data related to the economics of our business.

- **Bon Appetit**
P.O. Box 10747, Des Moines, IA 50347–0747

- **Cornell Quarterly**
Cornell Hotel and Restaurant Administration
Subscription Office
Madison Square Station
P.O. Box 882
New York, NY 10160

- **Food Net**
An internet publication

- **Food Service and Hospitality**
101-23 Lesmill Road
Don Mills, ON M3B 3PG
Canada

- **National Restaurant Association**

The National Restaurant Association has several publications directed to the restaurant business. For example, *The Survival Guide,* National Restaurant Association, 1200 17th Street, Washington, DC 20036–3097, includes several different topics: industry studies (business, accounting and promotion), legal and social issues, management information and training, and operations (purchasing, preparation, handling, and nutrition).

The following is a listing of some of the general business periodicals:

- **The Wall Street Journal**

Published Monday through Friday. This is a regional paper that you can probably find on your favorite newsstand. The paper covers all aspects of current happenings throughout the country. For the most part, it is dedicated to business news, but it also carries articles on subjects of general interest.

- **State Business Publications**
  In Texas, we have a magazine entitled *Texas Business* published monthly by Commerce Publishing Corporation, 5757 Alpha Road, Suite 400, Dallas, TX 75240.

  This magazine specializes in the reporting of business news around the state. In addition, it reports on economic statistics and news on legislation having an effect on business in the state. There are probably journals such as this in your state, and any good newsstand or bookstore usually carries them.

- **The Kiplinger Washington Letter**
  Published weekly at 1729 H Street, NW, Washington, DC 20006.

  This publication consists of a capsulized version of current happenings in Washington and on the national scene. It is short, easy to read, and quite informative.

You should decide how much time you can give to this particular activity, and then select those publications that you personally enjoy and that will fit into your busy schedule. Obviously you can't read everything that is written on the subject, but you should certainly try your best to read some.

An Example of How You Can "Lose Your Shirt" by Not Keeping Informed

Although there are always exceptions to any rule, a good and accessible location is of prime importance to the success of a restaurant. Of course, the surrounding traffic situation is one of the factors to be considered (Chapter Ten discusses site selection in detail), as is the residential and commercial development in the surrounding neighborhood. However, no matter how judicious you are in your original choice, unfortunately, nothing stays unchanged.

Let's take a look at the disastrous results that can happen when the changes come unexpectedly.

Herman's restaurant is located on the east side of E Street in a nice, relatively stable town of 100,000 population. E Street is a moderately busy street running north and south between the suburbs on the south side, and the downtown area to the north.

Herman's restaurant does an excellent breakfast business that begins at about 6:30 A.M. and lasts until 9:00 A.M. In fact, Herman is so busy cooking that he doesn't hear about the new thirty-five-story office building that will be constructed just up the street from the restaurant. And by the time he gets the news, plans have been finalized and the city is getting ready to close down the east side of E Street to widen the street and install new sewer and water lines. This means that northbound traffic will be routed one block to the east, and E Street will become one way for southbound traffic during the construction period.

Herman obviously has a big problem. Now he will really have to scramble to protect his business. And before he gets reorganized, he will probably have lost many of his steady customers because of the inconvenience.

Earlier in this chapter, you saw how just such a situation as this could be handled. The key, of course, is to stay alert and become aware of the impending change long before it happens. If you are an alert manager, you will be able to make plans that may get you through such a crisis, even though you suffer some loss of business.

Keeping Track of Events That Affect Supply and Demand

The last several years have seen the restaurant industry move toward specialization in menu offerings. One is hard pressed to find a dinner or family-style restaurant that offers a wide variety of foods over a three-meal period. Restaurants now tend to specialize in specific foods such as steak, barbecue, seafood, health food, etc. Much of this specialization is seen in the fast-food restaurants. A big factor in the success of these types of restaurants is their ability to purchase competitively so that they can sell at competitive prices.

You can "stay ahead of the pack" if you watch for any sort of disruption to the future supply of any of the food on your menus. A very good example of this is produce, which fluctuates wildly in price owing to long or short supplies. These overages or shortages can occur through changes in weather conditions (e.g., killing frost; long dry, hot spells; floods; etc.) or through such things as labor strife, insect infestation, or import–export law. Therefore, by watching for events that will affect supply and demand, and price (either up or down), you will be able to feature the items that will be most profitable for you.

Where to Find Out about Important Legislative Changes

Your State and National Restaurant Association bulletins will keep you apprised of the latest legislative changes you will need to know about. So it is important that you belong to an association, receive its bulletin, and read what you receive.

In the last few years, the restaurant industry has absorbed some steep increases in the minimum wage, and increased costs from changes in work rules related to overtime hours. Another change that has occurred is the method by which tips to service personnel are reported. When changes such as these appear on the horizon, they usually mean that some adjustment—either to prices or to staff—may be necessary. Therefore, the sooner you know about them, the quicker you can formulate plans—and the smoother will be the result.

There is nothing more unsettling to most people than change. But because it is inevitable and occurring rapidly these days, your success as an entrepreneur could be related directly to your ability to handle it. One sure way is to stay alert and learn as much as possible about disturbing events before they occur.

HOW TO CASH IN ON CHANGES

Construction in your neighborhood can mean a boom in your business. When new buildings are being remodeled, there is always an influx of people into the area. These include the various construction trades and labor, as well as engineers, architects, administrators, and inspectors. All of these people mean potential business for you. However, when opportunities present themselves they sometimes are accompanied by problems that have to be dealt with.

For example, in the case of construction, this can mean carpeting ruined by the muddy and dirty boots of the workers from the construction site. One way to handle this problem—while capitalizing on the opportunity for extra business—would be to take a tip from the New Orleans hotels. During Mardi Gras, they cover the lobby floors with plastic to protect the carpeting from any damage by revelers. There is no reason a restaurant couldn't do the same thing. Or you could let your imagination run wild and temporarily open "The Japan Room" with a checking arrangement for shoes and boots at the door. That might be fun, and could even bring you free coverage in the local news media. Once again, be alert to change so that you have time to plan, adapt, and execute for profit!

How Best to Deal with Changes That May Occur in Shopping Centers

Because there are many restaurants located in strip and major shopping centers, there are many events that may have an influence on them. A restaurant located in a strip center usually relies heavily on auto traffic for its business. And if street traffic patterns change, its business may experience beneficial or harmful effects.

For example, a strip center could be located on a major thoroughfare that carries a steady, moving flow of traffic. As activity increases, the flow of cars could reach the point where a left turn to enter the center would become so difficult that people would pass by the restaurant. Thus, most of its business would come largely from one side of the street. Such a situation could be disastrous for a restaurant in that kind of location.

How do you deal with such a problem? You will need to work closely with the local business association to bring about additional control with traffic signal lights.

Major shopping mall restaurants present a somewhat different situation, in that they depend largely on foot traffic. When a mall adds stores, it often alters traffic patterns that could affect a restaurant. For instance, a "hot" location can become "cold" if new stores, more competitive than your immediate neighbors, move in at the other end of the mall. Such a problem might require a change in advertising techniques, strategic placement of signs, or in a very extreme situation, actually moving to a new location.

Changes That Might Influence Your Business: A Checklist

- *A new hotel opens close by.* Be sure that the workers, auto valet, bellmen, and front desk personnel know about your restaurant. You will want them to refer hotel guests to you. You may also be able to place advertising in the guest rooms.

- *A new factory with high employment opens within easy driving distance of your restaurant.* Pay a personal call to as many of the executive offices as possible. Also, be sure you introduce yourself to the secretaries. Ask them to remember your restaurant when they are making lunch or dinner reservations, or when booking special parties.

- *The city plans to build a new convention center.* This could well mean an increase in business for you. To make sure those who attend the convention will know about your restaurant, make contact with people in the convention bureau.

- *New senior citizen apartments are going up.* Gear your menus toward offering specials at reduced prices, and with smaller portions. Contact any formal social organizations for the elderly, and try to attract them as customers.

- *You notice a decline in the average check.* Do additional research to determine what specifically is causing the decline. Look toward a change in menu, addition of specials, increased advertising budget, or stepped-up sales training of your staff.

- *Fall off in liquor sales.* Find out why. Maybe it is part of a national trend related to drunk driving campaigns. If so, look toward picking up the lost sales with increased emphasis on your food sales. If it is a condition related only to your restaurant, look for a letdown in service or pilferage.

- *An increase in theft of automobiles and auto accessories in your neighborhood.* Take on some sort of private security. Consider valet parking. Examine your parking areas for lighting and accessibility to your restaurant.

- *There is construction on the building housing your restaurant that has blocked your sign and has partly concealed your restaurant.* Try to have a temporary sign placed on the scaffolding that is responsible for screening your restaurant.

- *A new restaurant plans to open on your block.* Keep a close watch and be ready with promotional and sales planning in the event that it turns out to be strong competition.

- *There is a change in economic conditions, and a sudden surge in unemployment in your town.* This condition will hurt business whether the newly unemployed are your customers or not. During times such as these, everyone cuts back on spending. To help ease the cutbacks, you can run special promotions, especially tied to the family theme. Or you can offer reduced prices, all-you-can-eat deals, or coupons for discount. It is also very important to look for those areas where you can cut back on spending to be able to absorb the increases in food cost.

Remember, a change can mean new, fresh ideas that will open the way to expanded and original opportunities—even though they may be temporarily unsettling. You can profit from change if you look for the bright side. Be optimistic, and above all, keep that good old imagination working overtime!

Chapter 10

How to Simplify Remodeling or Expansion Plans Including Franchises as a Strategy for Future Development

Table of Contents

Chapter 10

How to Simplify Remodeling or Expansion Plans Including Franchises as a Strategy for Future Development

We all tend to equate success with size—the bigger, the better. Although this is often true, it is not always the case. For some restaurant operations, expansion of present facilities or relocation has meant disaster. Your success, therefore, will depend largely on whether you have thoroughly examined and prepared yourself for this undertaking.

The following is a series of questions to ask yourself before you actually make the move toward expansion. The rest of this chapter deals with the steps you should take if "go and grow" is the right decision.

A PREEXPANSION CHECKLIST

☐ Is my system for counting customers and tabulating sales accurate? Do I know when peak customer hours are? How many are served during those hours? Are the peak loads long enough and often enough to justify expansion?

☐ Is parking a problem that can only be solved by expansion? Are there other parking facilities available for lease or purchase around?

☐ Is the kitchen really worn out, or is it only in need of some overlooked repair? Will a larger kitchen produce more meals, or will it only require more labor for staffing, and consequently, greater operating expense?

☐ Do I have the management expertise and capability to operate either a larger restaurant or additional restaurants? Have I worked up some preliminary financial plans relative to expansion?

☐ Will the expansion mean a sufficient increase in profits to justify the additional work that I will have to do?

☐ Has the market changed? Is it likely to change in the future?

STAY ON TOP OF CHANGES

The need to be aware of changes is of utmost importance when considering expansion. For example, if you are located in a big city and you are weighing the probable success or failure of a lounge and restaurant in a downtown location, you must consider present and future energy costs, and their impact on individual driving habits.

An investment like this will rely mostly on the 4:00 P.M. to 7:00 P.M. cocktail-hour trade. Therefore, you must first determine what the market is. For instance, you may find out that the movement toward car and van pooling has "softened" the market. If this is the case, there may still be a strong and viable market available, but you may have to alter your thinking as to a restaurant concept to capture it.

DEVELOPING FINANCIAL DATA ON THE PROFITABILITY OF A NEW RESTAURANT

After asking yourself all of the questions in the preexpansion checklist, you must develop some financial data before going ahead to expand or remodel your restaurant, or open a second one. The data developed will eventually result in a pro forma statement, which will indicate to you whether the investment will be feasible.

This information will also indicate to your investor—a bank or individual— whether the plan is economically sound. Inasmuch as an investor will base his decision on the evidence you present in this statement, you would do well to consider having the document drawn up by a professional consultant. (The hiring of a consultant is covered in detail later in this chapter.)

The pro forma statement should contain both sales and expense projections. These figures will come from different record keeping sources. For example, if you are contemplating expansion of an *existing facility,* the past financial results of the business will be used. In addition, other economic data relating to increased sales potential must be assembled.

The following illustration shows how to use the information on these records to prepare a pro forma statement.

How to Prepare a Pro Forma Statement

Let's say that ABC restaurant is five years old and is located in an expanding area of a rapidly growing city. It is a table service restaurant with 100 seats for dining, and it offers a moderately priced menu. In addition to the dining room, it also has a small cocktail lounge with fifteen seats. Although alcoholic beverage sales are good, most of the revenue is derived from the dining room rather than the lounge.

An examination of the operating statements for the past three years indicates that sales have risen as follows:

Year	Food Sales	Bev. Sales	Total
3	$450,000	$150,000	$600,000
	75%	25%	100%
4	$475,000	$160,000	$635,000
	75%	25%	100%
5	$510,000	$170,000	$680,000
	75%	25%	100%

(For simplification, all number amounts have been rounded off.)

Calculating percentage increases from year to year yields the following:

Year	Sales	$	% Increase
3	Food	450,000	
	Beverage	150,000	
	Total	600,000	
4	Food	475,000	5.6
	Beverage	160,000	6.7
	Total	635,000	5.8
5	Food	510,000	7.4
	Beverage	170,000	6.3
	Total	680,000	7.1

To simplify this example, let's assume that the increased sales were the result of menu price increases. Consequently, we can assume that, because ABC is considering expansion, the restaurant is operating at capacity. In other words, it is unable to accommodate any increase in patrons, and diners must regretfully be turned away at very busy times.

The next step is to break the sales down by seat. Because food is also served in the lounge, let's say that this restaurant has a total of 115 seats:

	$Sales	Per Seat
Year #3: Food	$510,000	$4,435
Beverage	170,000	1,480
Total	$680,000	$5,915

Assuming that there is space available for thirty additional seats with remodeling, and further assuming a 3 percent increase in dollar sales per seat to correct for expected price increases, we could project sales upon completion of the project as follows:

Food Sales:	145 seats × $4,568.05 = $662,367
Beverage Sales:	145 seats × $1,524.40 = $221,038
Total Projected Sales:	$883,405
Proof:	$5,915 × 3% increase = $6,092.45 per seat
	$6,092.45 × 145 seats = $883,405

Obviously this is an oversimplification, but it is one way to arrive at the necessary financial data you will need. When you contemplate expansion, there are factors other than past history that you must also consider. Later in the chapter, you will see how to forecast sales using economic statistical data, which can be applied as a check on the accuracy of a forecast from historical data.

How to Forecast Costs and Expenses

Estimating these items, as shown in Figure 10.1, will require the use of a slightly different technique from the one outlined above. Here are some key points to keep in mind:

Cost of Sales. These should remain constant with the addition of a new facility. For example, if food cost was 35 percent and beverage cost 22 percent, then you should be forecasting at the same percentage cost. In actuality, the costs may drop with the increase in volume. However, you would probably have a reasonable forecast by using the same ratios as before the remodeling.

Labor Cost. For the purpose of forecasting, many people would apply a similar percentage cost before remodeling to the increased sales volume. However, a more accurate way—and considering that the increased size may result in some un-knowns—would be to analyze the labor requirement in the same manner as you would for any facility with which you have had little or no previous experience (see Chapter Eight).

Other Operating Expenses. Here again, you can apply the same percentage of expenses that you have been experiencing before renovation to the increased sales figures. Employing this technique will probably yield an acceptable fore-cast for the expanded facility. However, this is a time of change, and it is an opportunity for you to examine closely each and every item to effect economies wherever possible.

For example, during remodeling, you may find that a new style of broiler will allow for faster cooking at reduced energy cost. Further, you may feel the need to

Typical Income and Expense Statement Before and After Renovation

	Before	%	After	%
Revenue:				
Food Sales	$510,000	75.0	$662,367	75.0
Beverage Sales	170,000	25.0	221,038	25.0
Total Revenue	$680,000	100.0	$883,405	100.0
Cost of Sales:				
Food	$178,500	35.0	$231,828	35.0
Beverage	37,400	22.0	48,627	22.0
Total COS	$215,900	31.7	$280,455	31.7
Operating Expense:				
Labor	$193,800	28.5	$238,520	27.0
Employee Benefits	27,200	4.0	35,335	4.0
Direct Op'n. Exp.	47,600	7.0	61,840	7.0
Entertainment	5,440	0.8	7,065	0.8
Adv. & Promotion	13,600	2.0	22,085	2.5
Utilities	20,400	3.0	26,500	3.0
Adm. & General	34,000	5.0	44,170	5.0
Rep. & Maint.	10,200	1.5	13,250	1.5
Total Op'n. Exp.	$352,240	51.8	$448,765	50.8
Profit from Op'ns.	$111,860	16.5	$154,185	17.5
Other Costs:				
Rent, Insurance	$ 34,000	5.0	$ 44,170	5.0
Depreciation	17,000	2.5	20,320	2.3
Interest	13,600	2.0	22,085	2.5
Restaurant Profit	$ 47,260	7.0	$ 67,610	7.7

increase your advertising and promotion budget to realize the full potential of the new facility. Each of these items should then be adjusted accordingly. Keep in mind that a 1 percent savings in any cost or expense items in our example will yield an increase of $8,834 in profit before taxes. You, too, can have a similar pleasant experience in your own restaurant.

Multi-Unit Operations. We all look toward the day when we can consider ourselves "captains of industry." It fits nicely with our capitalistic system and provides the often-needed incentive to "get out of bed and go to work." But like all dreams and goals, there is also a catch in this one.

Obviously, managing one restaurant is vastly different from managing two—as the complexities of running two restaurants often multiply at a rate much faster than the rate of growth. Business activities that are confined to one location can be supervised efficiently by one person. Multi-unit operations must also be organized in such a way as to provide the same sound management and control on a *consistent* basis.

Therefore, if you are contemplating opening a second restaurant, there are certain important facts you should keep in mind. Consider the following:

1. Many diners will return to a restaurant business because they enjoy the personal attention a manager or owner gives to them. There is an element of prestige or price for patrons when recognized in front of their guests or companions by the "person in charge." You will want to continue this same personalized attention.

2. Diners want to feel confident that the food they are eating has been properly handled by kitchen and service personnel. The presence of caring management conveys that message.

3. A major task that will confront you will be the problem of finding management people who will conscientiously watch your money for you. Once you have opened the new facility, you will find it necessary to spread yourself between the two. Because it is impossible to be in two places during the same mealtime hours, it follows that you will need some good and loyal people to assist you.

WHERE TO FIND GOOD MANAGEMENT PEOPLE TO STAFF AN ADDITIONAL RESTAURANT

Finding some good management people can be a difficult job. However, there are many sources from which you can draw people—some of which may require you to spend some money for them. The following are a few of the sources available to you:

- *Executive Search Firms.* These companies specialize in finding people for their clients. Some of them specialize in certain industries (e.g., energy or manufacturing). Other firms are more generalist in nature and deal with a broad range of companies across industry lines.

- If you are considering retaining such a firm as an aid in your search for people, try to find one that has some contact with the food service industry. In addition, because these firms charge for their services, be sure you know what you are getting before your sign your agreement.

- *Colleges/Universities Having Courses in Hotel and Restaurant Management.* Some of the larger and better-known schools that offer these courses and that have placement services are Michigan State University, Cornell University, University of Houston, Oklahoma State University, Florida International University, and the University of Nevada at Las Vegas. There are also many smaller colleges and vocational schools that have programs in food service skills that can be drawn on.

- To reap the most benefit from these placement services, you should contact the person who is directly responsible for this job. In addition, prepare a well-organized and well-written presentation about the job or jobs that you are trying to fill. On it, include information about salary range, benefits, and the reasons why working for your company would be beneficial.

- *The Open Market.* Through well-written newspaper advertisements and by "keeping an ear to the ground," you will be able to find many capable people for the job.

- *"Grow" Your Own Management.* A good organization, complete with advancement opportunity through training and exposure, will yield people who are ready to move "up the ladder." If you have developed such an organization in your present restaurant, you'll no doubt be able to select from a few likely candidates.

To sum up, the actual needs for your business will be determined by your organization plan and by the limits of your financial resources. The pro forma will give you a good indication of what you can afford. If you are honest with yourself during the process of projecting revenue and expense in the new business, you will have a guide that will warn you before overcommitting for an expense during preopening or in the early growth stages.

Your actual management needs will be largely determined by the following:

- The revenue volume in each of the restaurants

- The strength and quality of the production and service staffs

- The operating schedules in hours and days that will determine the amount of coverage needed

HOW TO SUCCEED AND EXPAND AS AN ABSENTEE OWNER

To establish controls for an absentee-owned business, you must be willing to delegate responsibility to those who will actually be running the restaurant on a day-to-day basis. Before the delegation is assigned, however, adequate control procedures in the form of overall supervision of operations and fiscal accountability must be established. As pointed out earlier in this *Guide,* internal control and accounting are two different functions—each one is necessary to the balance and control of the other.

For a multi-unit operation to attain a high degree of success, it is necessary to develop and hold a competent and loyal management group. This can be accomplished in a number of ways, such as with monetary incentives in the form of bonuses, profit-sharing plans, or by building a high standard of pride in the management group.

Every manager of a successful business, along with others on the staff, should have the opportunity to share in the proceeds derived from their efforts. Smart absentee owners know this. They also know that money paid out of profits works very much like seeding and fertilizing a garden—and just as a garden must be hoed and kept free of weeds, so too must a business be constantly tended and cared for.

To sum up, establishing control for absentee ownership is developed in three basic steps:

1. Establishing the management needs by development of concise plans, including monetary needs

2. Proving the ability of the business to provide the funds to support the plans

3. Setting in place the operational and fiscal controls, including necessary incentives, to ensure profitability of the business

HOW TO GET STARTED ON AN ACTUAL EXPANSION PROGRAM

Before discussing the specific topic of site selection, it is necessary to define the difference between market research and site selection. For our purposes, the following definitions will suffice.

Market Research. The purpose of market research is to characterize a particular area or segment of the population with regard to such criteria as size, income, spending habits, etc. It is on this analysis that you base your decision as to the feasibility of making an investment (e.g., opening a restaurant).

Site Selection. Refers to the selection of a specific site or sites within a pretested market area. The site must conform to the parameters established as necessary to the success of the business.

When you research a market before deciding to invest in a restaurant, you will be able to obtain important information from the research findings from ongoing studies done by associations, agencies, and governing bodies. These results are available in books, papers, and reports, and are found in office libraries and on newsstands. Additional information is also available from the professionals that did the original research.

If you retain a consultant to do the job for you, it may save you time and money in the long run. Consultants have the expertise to find the needed information quickly, and usually have extensive files containing necessary updated information. A consultant will be able to relate the economic potential of a market area in terms of population and spending habits to the intended project.

Selecting a Site

Once you identify a general market area, you can undertake the search for a site. The particular concept or theme you have in mind for your restaurant will dictate the needs for the site. The location of potential sites is a job for real estate people, who should be given the necessary research data to make preliminary decisions. In turn, they will find and suggest to you a number of alternate locations, together with land or leasehold prices. Once this is done, you can evaluate and select the best location. You can also decide whether leasing a facility or buying land and building is best for you.

Your decision regarding the potential value of a particular site requires verifying the economic value in terms of your need for an acceptable location in the identified market area. In determining site value, many factors must be considered such as the following:

Sales Generators. These are activities carried out by people that bring about sales activity in a certain area. For example, a location surrounded by office buildings will surely generate a luncheon business. However, the same location may have nothing else in the area that will produce dinner or weekend business. Another similar location may have an office population as well as a nearby theater district. This particular site may offer opportunities for both lunch and dinner business, as well as the much-needed weekend activity.

Population. Simply because an area is heavily populated does not necessarily mean it is a good prospect. Much will depend on the restaurant concept plus the income level and spending habits of the area's residents. For example, an expensive restaurant may not survive in a low-income area any more than an inexpensive concept will make it in an affluent area. The age of the population is also a factor. To be successful, businesses must plan for the long run; thus, ascertaining the ongoing trends is very important.

Traffic Volume. This poses a difficult dilemma because heavy automobile traffic can be a help or a hindrance. Much depends on the specific location and such factors as kind of street (e.g., two-lane, four-lane, or boulevard). You must know if the site is on the proper side of the street to make ingress and egress easily accessible. If, for example, you are on a four-lane street and dependent on an early cocktail-hour business, your restaurant must be on the same side as the evening traffic flow. Traffic counts and patterns must be studied very carefully for direction at various times of the day and night, and for speed limits and total volume. Other considerations relate to curb cuts and growth trends within the city generally. Of course, the parking situation is of utmost importance.

Travel Distance. Depending on the type of restaurant, the prime market area is considered to be within a one- to three-mile radius. The secondary market may extend over a distance of five miles. Fast-food establishments generally cater to a market area of one to two miles, whereas a specialty dinner house attracts people from much greater distances. The fast-food restaurant will look at the potential in volume at moderate and competitive price levels. The specialty house will offer much more in the way of service and menu, and necessarily charge much higher prices. The specialty house will require a wide market area, whereas the fast-food restaurant will operate in a rather narrow one.

Competition. You must survey the competition in any new area; you will see firsthand which kinds of restaurants are already there and, more important, which types are successful. You will also learn the price range being charged. This information will tell you whether your concept will be readily acceptable.

To present your request to a lending institution in the best possible light, it may be wise to consult a professional. In most—if not all—cases, lending institutions will require outside consulting reports with all loan requests. Obviously, this is because they don't want to make bad or questionable loans.

Many small businesses today, including restaurants, are facing greater difficulties in trying to qualify for loans. Hopefully, this situation will soften because the small business is a very important part of our economy. Nonetheless, you can help by being thoroughly prepared before requesting a loan. Thoroughly prepared means a complete package professionally prepared—whether you prepare it yourself or have a professional do it.

HOW TO ANALYZE THE FRANCHISE ALTERNATIVE

There is an alternative to the expansion of your own particular restaurant plan into a second or third location. The purchase of a franchise would provide such a plan for you. There are many restaurant owners who have different types of restaurants. These situations probably result from the desire by owners to provide a hedge against future revenue slippage due to changing conditions that would affect an original investment.

Simply stated, a franchise is an established business or "brand" that can be purchased by an individual or company who wishes to operate that brand in a specific location or territory. In the restaurant industry there are more than fifty national companies that offer franchise opportunities ranging from full-service restaurants like T.G.I. Fridays and Chili's to limited-service providers like delivery pizza (Papa John's and Domino's) and frozen yogurt or ice cream (TCBY or Baskin Robbins). In addition, many cities or states have local concepts that can be franchised on a smaller scale. Essentially, franchising is a strategy that companies use to expand their coverage, sales, and reputation.

It has become a popular form of expansion for much the same reason in the restaurant industry as it has in other industries. In the best of cases it brings together people who have money and interest, but not a strong inventive or creative touch, with people who have proven concepts and a will to expand and grow more rapidly than they may be able to without external financing. Some companies may grow through franchising primarily, owning as little as 10 percent or less of the total store network; other companies may prefer to grow franchising more conservatively, having as few as 10 percent to 20 percent franchise-owned stores. The following section explains why strategies differ and provides guidelines so that you can consider whether this is a viable option for you. Please remember, the most important aspect of franchising is that if you choose to franchise, you do not own a brand or concept, you own the rights to operate a brand or concept in a very specific area under specific guidelines.

Determining Whom You Can Buy a Franchise From

You can buy a franchise from anyone willing to sell you one. In some cases, that "anyone" can be a small, independent operator of one or two restaurants, or it can be a multimillion-dollar restaurant company operating hundreds of restaurants nationally and internationally. The opportunity to buy a franchise may cost you, depending on the type of franchise, as little as a few thousand dollars, to as much as $100,000, merely to buy the franchise name. You will then have to absorb all or almost all the normal costs of building your business. As an individual, you will have limitations. For instance, the larger companies are not in the market to sell individual units to individual people; they generally want a growth partner financially capable of operating multiple units within a designated area. You could not, as an example, buy a one-unit franchise of Chili's or Applebee's restaurants because typically they set up franchise opportunities with companies prepared to operate multi-units. It would be unrealistic for a larger corporation to try to grow with individuals; there simply would be too much time and energy spent for the potential return. On the other hand, small or emerging companies are better equipped and more motivated to grow through franchising because it allows them to grow more quickly and they generally have more time to spend with franchisees. This, however, does not mean it is a better scenario for you. Often, smaller companies cannot or do not offer the technical and professional support you would need to operate your franchise. In either instance, the most important homework you can do is thoroughly study the brand you wish to franchise *before* you buy.

There are franchising magazines and industry journals constantly updating the franchise market. In addition, there are organizations like the I.F.A. (International Franchising Association), which are great resources for information on this aspect of our industry. Also, you can attend one of hundreds of franchise shows held nationally that allow you to meet the people and companies that have franchise opportunities available.

You should try to look at only the franchises that you or your group are truly interested in operating and stay away from investing in something that merely sounds like a "money maker." In the long run, you will only be successful with a franchise if it, like any other business, is something you truly enjoy doing!

What It Means to Buy a Franchise

Buying a franchise, whether it be a one-unit or a multi-unit and area opportunity, basically means that you are entering into a partnership relationship with another individual or company. And like any partnership, there are advantages and disadvantages to this decision. Mr. Ted Leovich, director of franchise operations for Brinker International, tells what the franchisor provides the franchisee and vice versa. (Brinker International franchises several of its nationally and internationally known restaurant concepts including Chili's Grill and Bar, Romano's Macaroni Grill, and On the Border Mexican restaurants.) The following is a listing of benefits provided by the franchisor to the operator:

1. *Brand Identity.* When you enter into a franchise relationship, you are in effect purchasing an already proven brand. Your guests will recognize the restaurant name and may have already become brand loyalists. In this regard, a franchisor does not have to live through much of the growing pains associated with new restaurants.

2. *Operating Systems.* The franchisor generally provides excellent organizational, administrative, and financial reporting systems, which they help install. Proven methods for cost controls, sales tracking, and daily operational management come with the franchise package. In addition, although not physically provided, franchisors give excellent feedback on point-of-sale systems and information technology that many franchisees find very useful in setting up their reporting systems.

3. *Tracking Support.* This occurs at three levels in most cases. The franchisee's principals or owners get excellent brand orientation; the management teams undergo a thorough management training program—the same one generally used by the franchisor's managers, and hourly level hired employees are supported by the franchisor's training team during the new unit opening(s). Each of these levels of franchisee training and orientation support is provided at the franchisee's expense, but in the long run, the franchisee is left with all the training programs and systems used by the franchisor.

4. *Brand Development.* As the franchisor evolves, so too does the franchisee. New menu items, new building designs, updated training and development techniques, and marketing and advertising innovations all are provided for franchisee support.

5. *Investment Protection.* The franchisor provides the franchisee with a specific contact for all issue follow-ups and logo registration protection, and quality assurance through regular franchise visits and meetings. Communication in the partnership is a critical component to ongoing success.

In return for these benefits, the franchisee is asked to bring some support and strength to the partnership. Often, franchisees allow the franchisor to grow and evolve in ways outside the franchisor's capabilities. Included in the resources provided by the franchisee are the following:

1. *Local Real Estate Expertise.* Although most or all franchisor companies have site selection departments, often the franchisees have more "local knowledge"

and expertise in their specific geographic area. Teamed with a franchisor's demographic models, the local knowledge helps provide a hedge against poor location choices.

2. *Brand Growth through Franchise Investments.* Because the franchisees are fronting the money for restaurant development, the franchisors expand their brand without capital investment.

3. *Idea Source for Brand Development.* Often, franchisees play a role in the evolution of the brand. New ideas are not limited to those innovated by the franchisor's company-owned units. Although the franchisor does not require (or in some case even want) the franchisee to provide creative input, many franchisees help keep the brand "fresh" with new ideas.

4. *Revenue Source Helps Overall Growth.* The fee paid to the franchisor by the franchisee helps fuel the growth for the entire company, which is a win-win situation. The fee paid by the franchisee is extremely variable from company to company but can range from 3 percent to 7 percent of sales depending on marketing support. The franchisor has few expenses against this fee income, so the franchisee is an excellent source of income for the franchisor.

As with any partnership, the relationship between the franchisor and franchisee will dictate the potential success of this option. Knowing that buying a franchise is no guarantee of success may sound like an oversimplification of fact, but many people have failed when buying a franchise because they underestimated the importance of this simple factor.

Franchise Resources

There are a number of resources from which to draw when exploring franchise opportunities. The most direct way is to contact the corporate office of the company you want to franchise from directly. Generally, someone there will tell you whether they franchise their concept. The larger companies who do franchise are required to provide potential franchisees information about their franchise system that answers most questions to help make an informed decision about this option. The franchisor-provided report, titled the Uniform Franchise Offering Circular (UFOC), can be obtained from any franchisor.

You may also want to contact your local convention and visitors' bureau to get a list of conventions and trade shows coming your way. On that list, often there will be at least one large franchise opportunity show. At these shows, franchisors set up exhibitions and booths describing their concepts and share a wealth of information to help sort out opportunities. One of the best shows annually is the National Restaurant Association show held in Chicago in May. And though this show is a massive exhibition of products and services available to restaurateurs, it also features booths and exhibits from large to small companies where information can be sought and shared.

Other sources of franchise information can be found in industry trade journals, magazines, and newsletters appearing in bookstores and libraries. Again, the National Restaurant Association, based in Washington, D.C., is a great source for helping to set you in the right direction.

Gauging When to Purchase a Franchise

It is often the best decision to franchise when you want to reduce your risk of failure and increase your chance of success. The price you pay for this is the additional expense of the franchisor's fees. If a typical restaurant, without franchise affiliation, can return between 12 percent and 20 percent net profit, then a typical franchisee restaurant operating with the same efficiencies will return perhaps 1 percent to 14 percent new profit once fees are paid to the franchisor. To some, this might sound reasonable, to others outrageous. It all depends primarily on your risk and security nature. Risk takers and creative types generally discount the franchise option because they feel that they can get better rates of return; more cautious types with lower return expectations and diversification strategies may see the franchisor fee as a small price to pay for the anticipated security of franchise protection.

The real benefit of having franchising as an option is that it allows you to enter this industry even if you don't have a great concept or idea in mind. The wonderful irony of franchise opportunities is that they wouldn't exist if somewhere in time in their history a founding father or group of individuals had not taken the risk to start the concept. All franchise companies started the same way: a risk taker took a great leap of faith and somehow succeeded. You can attempt to hitch your wagon to that success train or you can attempt to try to become one of the innovators. It's your choice and that's a great option to have!

Common Reasons Why Franchise Relationships Fail or Succeed

After more than five years of managing franchisor–franchisee relationships, Mr. Leovich states the reasons why franchisees may fail:

1. *Changing the Brand.* Before seeing how well the brand works, franchisees may "tinker" too much with the system by using unapproved products, changing operating systems, abandoning proven daily controls, or getting away from valuable information technology support.

2. *Focusing on Cutting Expenses, Not Increasing Sales.* In an effort to try to "recoup" the franchisor fee, franchisees may look to cut other expenses to help the bottom line improve. But the key to improvement in profit is concentrating on increasing sales.

3. *Losing Track of the Importance of Repeat Clientele.* The franchisor cannot guarantee return business simply by providing a proven brand. The franchisee must ensure business volumes by taking care of the guest.

4. *Not Continuing or Not Updating Training Programs.* The investment in training is ongoing, and many franchises lose sight of the importance of training once the new business opens.

5. *Poor Management Selection.* Bad or incompetent managers hire bad staffs or drive away good staffs. Without great staffs, guests get mediocre or poor service and business never has a chance.

6. *Poor Communication with Franchisor.* Although this is a two-way street, the franchisee must accept the responsibility to communicate the business development progress. Franchisors can only help solve problems if they are made aware of them in time.

And although it can be argued that the ball is in the franchisee's court, the franchisor must also avoid some common pitfalls in setting the franchisee up for success. The franchisor must play a major role in the successful partnership by avoiding the following:

1. *Selecting the Wrong Partners.* Many potential franchisees may be undercapitalized, have little or no track record in the restaurant or food business, or simply have a radically different culture or business philosophy.

2. *Franchisors Must Be Open Minded.* There may be a better way out there to do business, and a franchisor must be smart enough to recognize when a franchisee can actually help the entire company.

3. *Make Sweeping Brand Decisions without Considering the Impact on Franchisees.* If, for instance, a franchisee is located in a very competitive price market, a franchisor would negatively affect the franchisee if it forced the franchisee to install a marketing program that drives prices higher. Changing the brand must consider the impact on franchisees.

4. *Focusing on Franchisee Fee Exclusively.* The franchisor must not look at the franchisee as merely a revenue source, it must treat the franchisee as a true partner and provide the support it would to any partner.

5. *Poor Communication Skills.* The investment that a franchisee makes in a franchise, and its quarterly fee payment, requires the franchisor to be an excellent communicator. There can be no "dialing out" simply because the franchisee owns the business. Communication support is often the franchisee's lifeline and is expected in this relationship.

A Final Word on the Franchise Option

There is no right or wrong answer to the question "Should I choose a franchise?" In essence, you have to ask yourself the same questions you would if you are trying to decide on designing your menu. What are your expectations? What image do you want to present to your guests? What type of return on investment are you looking for? Buying a franchise is no guarantee that you will succeed in the restaurant industry. You may reduce your chance of failure by franchising but only if you choose the right company. And, as in the case with any product or service, the best advice is "buyer beware."

Anyone thinking about buying a franchise must look very carefully at the franchisor. Keep in mind that the franchisor is selling and you are buying. You must know what you are buying in terms of your expenditure versus the kind of return you can expect. You must do your own business plan and not rely on the "canned" PR form that is part of the franchisor sales package. There is nothing wrong with franchising. Quite the opposite—it can be a very profitable way to build a business. But it is not a way to avoid intense critical investigation and the hard work necessary to succeed in any business.

THE ADVANTAGES OF CONSULTING PROFESSIONALS

The importance of using competent consultants during the planning stage of a new business cannot be overemphasized. Such a person will either confirm or discount the opinion of an operator or potential investor regarding an intended new business.

Consultants are trained in research techniques and will search out and identify any positive or negative factors that may influence the business. In addition, a second opinion is particularly valuable because it is a neutral source outside the business.

The time when a person has become flushed with the success of one business and is casting about for a second can be a dangerous period. At a time such as this, people can become overwhelmed with their success and overlook the pitfalls in another venture. Good research, done by competent, neutral consultants, may turn up information that is very valuable to the intended project. Investing in a new restaurant is a big step that can mean huge success or dismal failure. The money spent in planning and researching such a project is very little compared with the total investment—and could well be the wisest expenditure of all.

Finding Competent Assistance

There are many consultants and planners who list themselves as experts. Unfortunately, not all of them are competent. Consulting requires extensive experience in a particular field, a strong educational background, and the ability to communicate effectively both verbally and in writing. Further, the consultant must have an analytical mind and be able to translate findings into understandable, practical action plans for the client. Therefore, to avoid hiring the wrong person, you must do a thorough job of checking the references of the particular consultant (not just the firm he works for) you are considering.

Some consultants and consulting firms are listed in the Yellow Pages of your telephone book. You will find specialists in all phases of the business, including overall management assistance, personnel, and facilities planning and design. There are also accounting firms that handle hotel and restaurant accounts, with two firms specializing in the hospitality industry:

　　—PricewaterhouseCoopers

　　—Deloitte & Touche

Both of these are large, international in scope, and have offices in most of the major cities. Another source of information is your local or state restaurant association. They generally maintain a file on people or firms who are reputable. You can also get help from the Small Business Administration Office and possibly from your local Chamber of Commerce.

Still another resource is SCORE. Figure 10.2, appearing at the end of this chapter, is an excerpt from a manual published by SCORE (Service Corps of Retired Executives), with regional offices located across the country. SCORE is a volunteer organization made up of individuals who have years of experience in executive positions, including those who have been involved in the restaurant industry. So feel free to contact them as an invaluable source for providing answers to your questions—from cash flow issues to internal control.

Once you choose a consultant, you must evaluate what you find. There are certain steps that should be taken to be sure that your project receives proper attention. First of all, you want to be sure that you have defined your plan. Before any consultant can work effectively with you, that person must have a full understanding of the task to be performed. Sometimes it is even wise to consult with someone to identify properly just what is to be done.

You should develop a program related to your needs and the needs of the project. It should take the form of an outline of just what you want to accomplish, and should include a time frame for completion. Nothing in this program will be "carved in stone," but it will provide a logical starting point for you.

Questions to Ask Before Hiring a Consultant

Once you develop your outline, you are ready to contact various consultants to assist you. Depending on your particular project, this can include architects, management, human resources, or kitchen planning experts. Once you have located the consultants, prepare a list of questions to establish credibility and expertise before proceeding beyond an initial interview. The following are examples of the kinds of questions you may want to ask prospective consultants. These questions should serve as a starting point for you:

- What is the particular specialty or specialties of your firm?

- Have you had practical experience in restaurant operation? Where? When? How long?

- Do you have a schedule of services offered? Do you have biographical sketches of yourself and your key people?

- If you are awarded a contract, who will do the work?

- Have you done this type of task before? Where? Who for?

- What is your fee arrangement? Do you write open-end (no-limit) contracts, or will you guarantee a "not to exceed" price?

- Will you present a written proposal? Do you require a retainer?

- Can you provide a list of present or former clients who can be contacted for verification of your work?

- What is your educational background?

- What changes are occurring in this industry? How have you kept up with these changing events in the industry and in business generally?

You should then check the references that are submitted to you. In addition, it is very important for you to check with clients whose names *are not* submitted. You can identify them by pursuing the consultant's client list. If such a list is not available, you might check with your restaurant association for information regarding other projects completed. Sometimes the association people are reluctant to endorse or criticize anyone, but you may be able to get names of persons with whom you can check further. Careful checking will ensure that you do not spend money for services that may not satisfy your needs.

Getting Maximum Benefits from Consultants

Carefully read the proposals submitted on work to be done. In evaluating their content, be sure they cover your original outline, including any modifications you have made. In addition:

- Be certain that all of your work requirements are covered. A good proposal should have the total job broken down by phase, with estimates as to the time required for completion of each phase, and for the total job.

- The proposal should state clearly what is expected as a final result (e.g., a written report, hands-on assistance, and complete drawings, including specifications). Proposals for kitchen plans should be coordinated with your architect and construction group to assure that each person, including you, knows each other's specific responsibility.

- Starting and completion times should be indicated.

- Fee and expense structure should be spelled out clearly, along with an estimate of the total cost. Any necessary retainer amount should be specified.

- If the proposal has not been prepared so as to constitute a contract, then a separate document constituting a contract should be drawn up with the proposal attached as an exhibit.

To summarize, the proposal should spell out each and every element of your deal: what work is to be done, how it is to be accomplished, how long it will take, who will do it, and how much it will cost. If you expect a thorough proposal, then you must also accept the responsibility of communicating your desires to the consultant. That communication must be as complete as the proposal you hope to receive concerning the job that you want performed.

Competent Consultants Should Be Experienced Specialists

Those of us who have worked in the food service industry for any length of time are by nature "jacks of all trades." And that is as it should be, because the unusual nature of the restaurant business demands it. Every operator's day will be filled with a variety of tasks that include buying and receiving merchandise, actually preparing food or at least overseeing that preparation, checking yesterday's receipts, planning future menus, examining the last period's financial statements, fixing a malfunctioning dishwasher, interviewing prospective employees, etc.

Experienced consultants are familiar with these routine tasks and are fully aware of the demands on the time of restaurant managers. Furthermore, they have taken the time and steps necessary to become specialists in certain specific areas of the business. There are two major areas in which consultants offer valuable services.

1. *Management Services.* This is a very broad category that includes several different but interrelated disciplines:

Financial Management and Control

☐ Design and implementation of internal control systems for proper management of expenses and income.

☐ Feasibility studies, including market research and site selection, to provide a basis for decision making regarding future investment in expansion or development for new business. Included would be the development of programs to be followed by designers and planners.

☐ Financial analysis of present business as related to realization of potential profits. This would probably include assistance in the area of financial projections and operating budgets.

☐ Business evaluation and appraisal of business value. This is a highly specialized area that requires far more than the application of a multiple to a few years of average earnings. This process also requires a detailed study of the industry, financial analysis of the particular restaurant, and a sound forecast of the potential earnings from accounting history and economic data.

☐ Complete analysis of all phases of restaurant operations, including menu evaluation or development, and the overall pricing structure for both food and beverage business. Food production and labor cost control to include purchasing, receiving, preparation, service, and the analysis of those cost and expense items necessary to make it all work together for profit.

Personnel Administration

☐ Development of personnel policies and procedures, training manuals, and programs.

☐ Assistance in the development of organization and staffing plans.

☐ Development of policy and procedure manuals, standard recipe files, purchasing and receiving guides, sanitation manuals, and operating checklists.

2. *Food Facilities Design Services.* This relates to the design of the physical plant and includes several different but related activities:

☐ Development of preliminary plans to fit the food service program, as developed in keeping with proposed operating policies.

☐ Preparation of a budget estimate for food service equipment for use in line with the overall project cost estimate.

☐ Preparation of contract drawings, including selection of proper equipment. Interface with architects, engineers, and owner to assure delivery of a totally acceptable project.

☐ Preparation of bid specifications for equipment and evaluation of bids as received.

☐ On-site supervision during and following installation to ensure contractor compliance with all contracts as let.

☐ Tabletop design, including china, glass, and flatware. Consultation regarding type and necessary quantities of pots, pans, and small utensils.

There is ample opportunity for a restaurant operator to secure assistance in any area where help is needed. Unfortunately, some people tend to view a consultant as someone who will look at a business and prepare a report that will never be used. Although that may happen, it is usually not the fault of the consultant.

If you engage the services of a consultant, you should know precisely what you want done and exactly how you intend to follow up on the consultant's work. It is far less expensive to use a consultant for a given project than to carry one or more persons on the payroll for staff assignments. Further, if your business has no extra people for the staff work assignments, there is no way that these necessary tasks will ever be accomplished. When these conditions exist, you are very likely depriving yourself of much-needed profits.

STARTING AND RUNNING YOUR OWN BUSINESS

Presented by

SCORE®

Sponsored by
the U.S. Small Business Administration

"COUNSELORS TO AMERICA'S SMALL BUSINESS"

PREFACE

This manual was written by members of SCORE (Service Corps of Retired Executives, Houston, Texas). These men and women have had many years of experience in executive positions. Some have started and managed businesses of their own—all have years of experience in solving problems and making policy decisions at all levels of business management. The purpose of this manual is to provide simple, easy-to-understand, yet reasonably complete information pertaining to the basics of starting and running a small business. We have attempted to cover as many aspects of business as possible within the framework provided.

The manual is structured along the lines of the steps which must be taken to organize and start a small business. First, the personal factors the potential owner should have are discussed, followed by an examination of the management and organizational skills required and human resource requirements. Then there is a review of the factors to consider to determine if the product or service is feasible and how to market and sell the product or service. This is followed by a discussion of the various options as to how the business could be organized and what the insurance, permit, and license requirements are and concerns that must be addressed. With these preliminaries covered, the discussion turns to determining the capital needed for the venture and the sources of such funds. We then consider the recordkeeping requirements of a small business. The discussion closes with a review of what goes into a business plan and the benefits it will provide over the life of the business.

In addition to being a reference manual to the seminar, this manual is also intended to provide information and guidance for use in SCORE counseling. The limitations resulting from the space in this manual do not permit in-depth discussions of each important area. Therefore, to realize the maximum benefits and working knowledge of all that is covered in this manual and discussed at the workshop, the addition of SCORE counseling is a must. It is only through counseling that areas of concern or questions can be dealt with in a complete fashion and you can draw on the vast experience of your SCORE counselor. SCORE counseling is provided without charge to the new or established business and can be obtained or at your place of business.

Note: The manual contains various figures that change with the law (taxes, state laws, city ordinances, etc.) and it is wise to check on any figure before using it.

The following is excerpted from the manual and is reprinted with the permission of SCORE, Chapter 37.

There are many volunteer organizations in our country that are important in the operation of many of our institutions including hospitals, schools, and nursing homes. One such organization is SCORE, the Service Corps of Retired Executives. SCORE, in conjunction with the U.S. Small Business Administration, works with small business persons actively engaged in a business or with persons thinking about starting out in a new one. SCORE has a total of ten active regions in the country. Within each region there are more than forty districts comprising some 300 chapters. Some chapters have satellite operations and when added to the total there are over 400 SCORE listings in local telephone books.

The organization provides services to the small business community in various ways:

- They provide counseling by members who have had active experience in the particular business in which a client may be interested. Such sessions are normally scheduled and held in the SCORE Business Information Center.

- Each chapter maintains a library of more than 250 titles covering all sorts of businesses as part of The Business Information Center. Not all chapters have business information centers but each SBA district has at least one, so the number is roughly fifty of "BICS." Access to this fine source of research material is available to all. The material is in printed form and on videotape. In addition, there are computer stations with a wide variety of computer software programs designed to assist in the development and management of small business. These stations are accessible to all clients who visit the SCORE offices. The computer stations provide template applications for the start-up business and existing business development needs. Integrated software uses various word processing, spreadsheet, and database applications.

- Field counseling is provided by counselors who will travel to a particular business upon request by the owner. These sessions may cover a number of subjects including cash flow, marketing, advertising, labor shortages, internal control, and organization. The field counselors are experienced in the particular business and can often offer valuable help to a client.

- The chapters offer prebusiness seminars as well as advanced seminars dealing with specific subjects of interest to prospective and present business owners and operators. These seminars offer a short course in many subjects that are of concern to the small business community.

  - What it takes to run a business

  - Steps to help get your business started

  - How much money you will need

  - How to determine market potential

- With restaurants—how to choose the right format

- Where to find financing for your restaurant, whether you are starting a new one, refinancing an existing one or looking to start a second or third operation

- What lenders want to know about you and your business

- How to develop a business plan

- How to establish and maintain business records and the importance of doing so

- Management techniques

- Regulation, licenses, and taxes that impact on your restaurant

- The matter of business insurance—how much is necessary and why it is so important today. How much might it cost and how will it affect the bottom line?

- Open question-and-answer sessions that always encourage discussion of topics that are interesting to everyone.

Of utmost importance to the restaurant owner is the fact that all of this service is free of charge. It is provided under the auspices of the SBA and with the efforts of the many highly qualified volunteer counselors with SCORE.

Chapter 11

How to Make Advertising and Promotion Dollars Pay Off for You

Table of Contents

Chapter 11

How to Make
Advertising and Promotion Dollars
Pay Off for You

It is virtually impossible to start a new restaurant operation in today's highly competitive world without advertising. And unless you are very lucky, you will also need some sort of sales promotion program to sustain a consistent flow of business. As with any other kind of business, the *successful* restaurant operator is the person who "makes things happen."

HOW MUCH SHOULD YOU BUDGET FOR PREOPENING ADVERTISING?

If you are contemplating opening a new restaurant, you should include the cost of advertising in your preopening expense budget. One way to estimate your dollar needs is to rely on the average cost of advertising expense for all restaurants. This average is expressed as a ratio to sales and amount per seat, and can be found in *Restaurant Industry Operations Report for the United States,* published annually by the National Restaurant Association in cooperation with Deloitte & Touche, LLP.

For example, the 1987 study indicated that the average profitable restaurant serving food and beverage with a check average per person of $10 and over, spent an average of $144 per seat for marketing (includes advertising), or 2.1 percent of total sales during 1987. Average income and expense per category will vary in different parts of the country. Most, if not all, state associations will publish statistics related to their state and various cities in the state.

To go back to the question of how much money is required for preopening advertising, we could start with the national averages as noted above. If the national average for food and beverage restaurants is 2 percent, and you are planning to open such a restaurant, you will probably need at least twice that much, or around 4 percent or 5 percent of the first year's estimated net income for advertising and promotion. The business will provide some of that expense from income, but there will be a *cash* need of at least one-half of that amount to cover preopening expense and ongoing expense during those months when the business is new.

As an example, if you are opening a new place and forecasting $700,000 of net income in the first year, you should plan on spending $35,000 for advertising and promotion during that time. Your cash needs for those expenses before and shortly after you open will probably be about $20,000.

Too many people try to open restaurants on a shoestring. If you want to give yourself every possible chance for success, then be sure you have sufficient capital to open and operate until your business becomes established.

HOW TO SELECT AN ADVERTISING AGENCY

There will be no problem finding an advertising agency. As a matter of fact, some—like all other purveyors of goods and services—will find you. As soon as the news regarding the impending opening of a new restaurant hits the street, the various suppliers start calling on the owners of the project. And some of them will be concerned with supplying promotional know-how, including advertising.

Advertising is usually quite expensive, but it is a necessary part of your success. Because of this, it is important for you to be very careful in your selection of an advertising agency.

Because you are advertising to attract customers to your restaurant it is necessary to know as much about your market population as you can. This will allow you to direct your advertising toward specific segments of the market. For example:

- You will need to know their sex, age, educational level, where they live and work, what kind of work they do, what routes they use to drive to and from work, and how many of them use bus, train, or van pools for transport.

- You will need to know, based on the foregoing, how best to reach these prospects, and which of the various media will do the best job. You have many choices of media to choose from, including television, radio, newspapers, direct mail, billboard advertising, and signs on taxis and buses.

The more information of this kind you have, the more intelligently you will be able to talk with and evaluate agencies and the services they sell. By now, it should be very clear to you that each of the chapters in this *Guide* fit together to make up one big picture. (If you have on hand some good market research data gathered during the planning stage, it will be just what you need at this time for planning your advertising campaigns.)

Some people will probably wonder why it is important to use an agency anyway.

"We'll just write our own copy and contract directly with the media of our choice, and that will eliminate the middleman," they say, "and we will save a whole lot of money in the process." Well, maybe. Such a statement could be true if the person is skilled in advertising techniques. If not, the result could be just the opposite. Take, for example, the following:

- Consider a thirty-second television spot on a local station that sells for some $2,000 to $4,000. If you buy a spot that is seen at the wrong time and on the wrong program, the major portion (or all) of the expenditure may be wasted.

- On the other hand, if you use an expert, he should be able to put the same ad in the proper place—creating enough business to pay for both the ad and his fee—and deliver solid profits for your restaurant.

When selecting an agency, find one that is active in the restaurant industry. It will be more aware of your special needs and will be better able to tailor the program to reach your target market. Remember, it always pays to use a professional's help in something as critical as an advertising campaign.

How to Ensure Success from Your Advertising Campaign

As mentioned, if you want to have a strong dollar return from your advertising outlay, you should first construct a budget. Furthermore, when contemplating the use of newspaper ads, remember that there will be an expense for the artwork and layout plus the expense of setting the type.

Caution: Don't ever run a newspaper or magazine ad without first receiving a proof from the media. And read the proof very carefully to be sure that it says what you want it to say, and that it is free of spelling and punctuation errors. Also, if you can plan your advertising campaigns in advance for a given period of time, you will be less apt to find yourself in a hurry to meet a deadline and will reap far better results overall.

Here's a sample of what your budget should look like:

Newspaper Advertising Budget

Newspaper	Frequency of Ad
Circulation—250,000	2 times/week
Length of Promotion —	6 weeks
Cost of Ad —	$150
Total cost of advertising:	
6 × 2 (twice/week) × $150 =	$1,800
Coverage—6 × 2 × 250,000 (cir.) =	3,000,000 (persons)

If you are using an agency, you will find that it will base its charge on an hourly rate, or as a percentage of the total ad cost. Measuring results against promises means knowing precisely what you contracted for, and maintaining a record of what you actually received. It is very easy to "lose" money on service contracts such as these. Therefore, good recordkeeping is a must.

Advertising Media—and How to Profit from Them

There are many other ways, besides newspapers and TV, that you can use to advertise your restaurant:

- *Billboards and Posters.* Billboard ads can be a very effective means of advertising. You should make certain, however, that they are located on streets and highways traveled by people who are in your market area. Posters can be placed on buses, subways, or taxis. Both should be colorful and eye-catching. Also, they must be brief so as to be read quickly.

- In many areas this kind of advertising can be quite expensive. In addition, to carry impact, they must be changed from time to time, and the cost of artwork, paper, labor, etc. can become quite high.

- *Direct Mail.* This is a good form of advertising that can be planned to reach your specific market area. You can buy mailing lists from various sources such as list brokers, but the best lists should come from your own files. You should use it for the purpose of informing your steady customers of the various promotions you are planning to run.

- *Sample Menus.* It is a good idea to have an inexpensive mini version of your regular menu available to give to your guests. Often diners will ask for a menu to take home, and the miniature is an excellent—and cheaper than handing out your regular menu—way to advertise. You don't have to wait for people to ask for one either. Offer one to each departing guest.

- You can also make personal calls on various office buildings, hospitals, or plants to introduce yourself, invite people to visit your restaurant, and leave a menu. With this method, you don't cover as much ground as a newspaper ad would, but you will be amazed at the response you'll get from the personal effort.

- *Radio.* Spot ads on radio will reach many people. Remember, though, that people listen to a particular station because it offers the kind of programming that suits their taste. For example, it might be all news, or country-western music, or talk shows, or a Dixieland band.

- Therefore, if you are placing an ad on the radio be sure you are on a station that will reach your target market. Deciding on the "right" station and the "right" time will take considerable research or the advice of a pro—or it might even take both. The radio is a companion for many people at specific hours of the day—in the morning while getting ready for work, at the breakfast table, and in the car while spending a lot of time in rush-hour traffic—so keep that in mind when using the radio as an advertising media.

- *Telemarketing* is a medium that might be considered. This could possibly be a way to reach companies, groups, conventions, etc. for catering services. It could also be directed toward party and event planners.

- *Your Own Web Site.* The World Wide Web (www) is now being used throughout the country. One has only to access the Internet to see how many restaurants are advertising this way. They can be found in all of the major cities and are evidently successful. The NRA Operations report makes note of the widespread use of the Internet for a host of ways to reach consumers and convey information about menus, credit plans, hours of operation, location, etc.

HOW TO PROMOTE YOUR RESTAURANT

When and how often should you promote your restaurant? The answer is *always*! There are two kinds of promotion. First, there is unplanned or ongoing promotion, which is constant. For example, you are promoting your restaurant when you serve good food in pleasant surroundings in a friendly and congenial manner. Your own personal affability and charisma will attract customers to your place.

In addition, all of the techniques and ideas espoused in this *Guide* are ways to promote your business! How? Through good and intelligent management. The kind that encourages and motivates every employee to work at producing top-quality food, drink, and service, which in turn makes a *promoter* out of every happy diner who enters and leaves your restaurant. For a restaurant, there is nothing like a good reputation and word-of-mouth advertising.

Second, there is planned or occasional promotion. Running promotions can be one of the real fun things the imaginative and creative operator can do. Also, there is a thrill to be realized from watching a successful promotion develop increased sales and profits for your restaurant. It is like what a salesman feels when he "closes" a sale. It is the time when you can see the actual result of your creativity, imagination, and hard work pay off. Of course, there is not much you can do about economic trends, massive changes in product cost, crippling legislation, or labor strife that affect your business. But you can make something happen in your own little corner with some well-thought-out promotion plans.

Reasons for Running Promotions

Running promotions is a must in today's heavily competitive marketplace. Here are a few reasons why they are so important:

1. They will let people know about your restaurant—and what it has to offer. One of the best ways to get business is to ask for it.

2. You can increase the sale of certain items by advertising "come-ons." For instance, you may offer free hors d'oeuvres to increase your early-evening cocktail business.

3. Your business may be local and you may want to reach out for some transient business in a market that you have failed to penetrate.

4. You may need to promote to compete favorably in your own market area.

5. They may help you pick up extra sales on slow days of the week.

SALES PROMOTION TECHNIQUES

Coupon Redemption

Coupon redemption is probably the biggest—and most widely used—promotional device in the country. There are billions distributed every year as promotions for all sorts of products. In the restaurant business, the usual forms of coupon promotions are either to offer something such as "a free chicken dinner when one is bought at the full price," or to offer something free such as "the first drink on the house."

Here's how they can pay off for you. You run an ad in the local paper with a coupon that entitles the bearer to one free chicken dinner when one other dinner is purchased at the regular price of $9.95. Suppose the food cost to you on this dinner is 25 percent, or $2.49. Therefore, if you sell one and give one free, your total cost on the two dinners is still only 50 percent. And if you sell anything else such as a drink before dinner or a carafe of house wine (which is almost certain), your total cost will be reduced further. In the meantime, if the promotion is well received, you will be creating traffic and introducing new diners to your restaurant.

Complimentary first drinks in the cocktail lounge for all dinner guests is another traffic-builder designed to bring people to the restaurant.

Sampling

This technique consists of offering bite-size selections of items from the menu. For example, you might offer your patrons new items that you are introducing on the menu.

Complimentary Food and Beverage

There are always times when it pays to "pick up the check," or offer something complimentary like a bottle of wine with dinner when certain important people visit your place of business. "Important" could mean anything from persons in high places to a couple of your very good customers celebrating a wedding anniversary. Keeping an eye out for these kinds of situations and then doing something appropriate is always good for business. Therefore, it is beneficial to find out when your regular customers are celebrating birthdays, anniversaries, or other special occasions, and keep this information in your promotion files for future use. "Fine," you may say, "but how do I go about getting this data?"

The best way to determine birthday or anniversary dates celebrated by your customers is to pay attention to those kinds of parties when held in your restaurant. At that time, you can get the necessary information from the guests and make the necessary notes in your suspense file. Then you will be ready for the next time that date rolls around. Furthermore, a card from you with a suggestion that they celebrate the occasion in your restaurant will be a big plus for you. If you think that "more is better," then you can offer a free bottle of wine or a cake when they dine with you. And, if possible, be sure you are in the restaurant and make the presentation personally, as it will have more impact and help your overall sales program.

Knowing your customers personally will often lead to listening about birthdays, anniversaries, or other special occasions. When you are highly visible in your restaurant, and when you make the effort to meet and visit with your guests, you are bound to pick up plenty of information about their personal lives. Don't overdo it by spending too much time with any one guest, however. It is better if your contacts are friendly but brief. Just make sure you keep notes so that the information you get isn't lost or misplaced.

One more idea. Give out a free drink or other complimentary item for persons born under the current astrological sign. Stage this promotion each time the sign changes and enter the names, addresses, and birthdates in your file for future use.

One restaurateur keeps a card file in a rather inconspicuous place in the dining room. Each card tells him something about his customers. For example, if they have been traveling—where and when; information about birthdays, anniversaries, etc.; their hobbies or other particular interests; where they work and live; if they have children—whether they are at home, away at college, on a new job, etc. He picks up the information through casual conversation from his guests when they visit his restaurant. And he never fails to make a note of any helpful information he can get. This is a great technique for opening a short conversation. It will greatly impress your guests with your apparent interest in them.

Marking an Occasion

When a customer leaves the restaurant, the host or hostess selects a rose from a bouquet on the maître d's station and presents it to the customer who is celebrating a birthday or anniversary. Although roses are not inexpensive, it is still a nice touch. And the cost is budgeted right along with the other expenses of the restaurant.

Happy Hours

Many cocktail lounges employ this promotion, which generally consists of either discounting the price of drinks or offering two drinks for the price of one. The hours for the promotion are specified, and are usually something like 4:00 P.M. to 7:00 P.M., Monday through Friday. The most successful of the plans is the one linked to the number of visits to your restaurant. For example, a free meal could be offered after a customer has been to the restaurant six times. Or a complimentary bottle of wine could be offered to the diner who after three visits brings an additional guest or guests to the restaurant.

This kind of promotion can be announced internally in your restaurant by including it on table tents or in a promotional handout. Before starting such a program, be sure to give some serious thought to how you will control it.

Salute to Some Charity

(Those persons who make a certain stipulated contribution to the named charity)

What to Do:

In cooperation with officials of the charity, devise a method whereby donors (certified by the charity) receive something complimentary at your restaurant.

For instance, a complimentary carafe of wine could be offered with dinner for two when evidence of a stipulated donation amount is presented by the customer. If there are no legal barriers, you might even have your wine purveyor share in the cost (and the publicity).

Support Your Local Sports Team

(Any local team, amateur or professional—football, baseball, basketball, hockey, soccer, etc.)

What to Do:

Offer a discount for selected dinner menu items to diners who present the ticket stub from one of the games you are promoting. These stubs could be valid only for the week (in the case of football) following the game, or for the entire season if you wish.

The promotion could be announced via newspaper, radio, posters, etc. Additional gain can be realized if you are active in such civic groups as the Chamber of Commerce or local Team Booster Club and do some personal promoting with those groups. In addition, you could ask for a place on one or more of the meeting agendas and make the announcement at those times.

Saluting the Zodiac Sign of the Month

(Those persons born under the sign that corresponds with the current month)

What to Do:

Offer a free cocktail or after-dinner drink to those persons born under the current sign. Any form of identification such as driver's license can be shown. The main idea here is to create traffic and bring new customers to the restaurant.

Announcement can be made through newspaper or radio advertising, etc.

Be sure you record the names, addresses, and birthdates in your birthday file. This is a good way to build up a list for later promotions. You can encourage new business by mailing out birthday cards to your customers.

Chapter
12

How to Get Top Benefit
from Tax Savings and Shelters,
and Build Financial Security

Table of Contents

Chapter 12

How to Get Top Benefit from Tax Savings and Shelters, and Build Financial Security

There are numerous smart, legal ways that you can use to protect your profits and build personal wealth. Unfortunately, many restaurants don't take advantage of them and get into serious financial difficulties as a result. Of course, not all of these strategies are well known. To help you, we have included a small sampling of the benefits to which restaurant owners can legally help themselves.

When businesspeople talk about tax deductions, the topic always involves credits having cash value that will drop right down to the bottom line. Although this is true and the major reason for securing as many deductions as possible, there is also another benefit to be derived from tax savings. In a tight labor market like the one in 1998 with the unemployment rate hovering around the 4.0 percent rate, recruiting and holding employees becomes a monumental challenge. Tax savings usually result from policies that incorporate things like health plans, complementary meals, uniforms, and any other items that have a tendency to slow or eliminate employee turnover. These policies may be even more beneficial by slowing turnover, which in turn may lead to more consistency in food and beverage preparation, increased customer satisfaction, and increased sales and profits.

IMPORTANT: Some of the ideas given in this chapter involve legal and tax areas that are best discussed and implemented with the help of a professional adviser.

HOW YOUR RESTAURANT MAY BE ABLE TO PAY YOUR LIVING EXPENSES—TAX FREE

You may be able to set things up so your restaurant business pays your everyday household expenses—rent, mortgage payments, utilities, repair costs, and so forth. Basically, all that's required is that

✔ Your restaurant operation be incorporated;

✔ The household be located on the premises;

✔ You need to be close at *all* times for the smooth running of the restaurant; and

✔ The corporation makes it a formal requirement of your employment that you live on the premises.

The big tax payoff is that if these conditions are met, what your restaurant corporation pays for your living expenses is fully deductible by your corporation and tax free to you. This could be the equivalent of a tax-free salary increase of many thousands of dollars.

If any of this sounds familiar, it's because this tax break for living expenses is the same break that allows your corporation to provide you and your employees with tax-free meals. Of course, you can be sure the Internal Revenue Service will take a tougher position on tax-free household expenses than it does with meals—many more revenue dollars are at stake. Nevertheless, taxpayers can and do prevail.

> Jack and Jill own a restaurant named *On the Hill, Inc.* They have a home adjacent to the restaurant and it is their only residence. This is a new venture and they want to personally supervise the restaurant and be able to respond quickly if something should require their immediate attention. Either Jack or Jill is on hand in the restaurant at all times, and should it be necessary to call in the other, each one feels it important for that person to be able to respond as quickly as possible. These people start work at 5:00 A.M. daily and usually work until the restaurant is closed and cleaned at about 10:00 P.M. They maintain a small staff and they—Jack and Jill and the employees— take their meals on the business premises, and the corporation picks up the tab for the meals. They have claimed a deduction on the meals and a portion of their living expenses.
>
> Will the IRS allow this deduction? Only the IRS knows, but it is not illegal to try and who knows, they might win.

Will the government permit you to take advantage of this tax-free break for living expenses? Only the government itself knows the answer. Much depends on the facts and circumstances of your own individual situation—and you and your professional adviser are the ones best suited to make that judgment.

HOW TO SET THINGS UP SO THE RESTAURANT PAYS PERSONAL MEDICAL BILLS

Owners of incorporated restaurants are in an especially strong tax position. *Reason:* Besides being restaurant owners, they are also employees of their restaurant corporations. And corporations can give fringe benefits to employees. This means that the corporation can pick up the tab for many of the owner's everyday family expenses—either tax free or tax deferred. (Because they are self-employed, restaurant owners may get similar breaks; see the next section). Here's a prime example of tax-free medical payments.

> Smith's restaurant corporation sets up a health plan. The corporation contributes to the plan by paying health insurance premiums on a policy covering Smith and other employees. The premiums are fully deductible by the corporation as a business expense and tax free to Smith. Benefits paid by the policy are also tax free to him. In effect, the plan turns money Smith might ordinarily receive as fully taxable salary into tax-free medical payments.

This is an allowable deduction and can be important in attracting and keeping employees. The one factor that must be recognized is that a plan such as this must be in writing, maintained on a nondiscriminatory basis, and made known to all employees. Whether it is prudent for your restaurant is for you and your business adviser to decide.

HOW A RESTAURANT CAN PAY THE OWNER'S LIFE INSURANCE PREMIUMS

> Every restaurant owner would like to get top insurance protection at an affordable cost. A traditional winner here has been split-dollar insurance.
> The typical split-dollar setup works as follows:
>
> Your restaurant takes out cash value life insurance on your life. Each year it pays the portion of the premium equal to the increase in the policy's cash value for that year. You pay the remainder of each year's premium costs—if any. And you get to name the beneficiaries and reap the following benefits:
>
> - After a few years, your annual premium costs are little or nothing. For example, your average yearly cost of insurance protection can be much less than comparable term coverage.
>
> - The policy really doesn't cost your restaurant anything. *Reason:* The policy's cash value belongs to the restaurant. So it eventually

gets back every penny it lays out from the policy's proceeds. Meanwhile, you are, in effect, receiving an *interest-free* loan from your restaurant.

Tax Result: Your restaurant gets no deduction for the premiums it pays. But you must pay tax on the value of the insurance protection you receive, less your share (if any) of the premium. Even so, after taking taxes into account, your cost for this kind of insurance protection is extremely low when compared with other life insurance setups.

But some owners take their basic split-dollar setup one step further. They turn the low premiums into no premiums by using a variation called the bonus split-dollar plan.

In this setup, your company pays the *entire* premium. You don't pay anything at all. The portion of the premium that you would ordinarily pay is charged to you as compensation. Because it's compensation, the restaurant gets a deduction for it. (Although you have to pay tax on this, as explained below, it should be much less than the premium you would otherwise pay.) And your restaurant still gets the cash value. This raises the following question and answer.

Question. But that's the problem. Because the restaurant is paid the cash value, won't my family be receiving a lot less insurance protection?

Answer. True, your actual insurance coverage is always less than the face value of the policy. As the cash value of the policy goes up, so does your restaurant's portion of the proceeds.

➡ **Result**: Your insurance protection goes down gradually as the years pass. This may be acceptable if your need for such protection will also diminish. But if not, here's what to do. Have the policy pay the dividends. Use these dividends to buy additional insurance up to the amount of the policy's cash value.

Any excess dividends can be used to lower the premium payments by the restaurant. (Whether used to pay premiums or buy additional insurance, the dividends are taxable to you.)

➡ **Result**: Your restaurant still recovers its loan, but now an amount equal to 100 percent of the face value of the policy is available to your family. And by using bonus split-dollar, you not only get additional coverage, but you also get it at a lower cost. Your restaurant is paying your part of the premium as well as its own. Of course, the additional payment by your restaurant is taxed to you just as if you had received a bonus. But if you had made your portion of the premium payment yourself, you'd probably be out-of-pocket more than twice as much. Let's look at the next example:

Your portion of the premium is $500 and you're in the 40 percent tax bracket. If you pay the premium yourself, you are out-of-pocket $500. But let's say your restaurant pays the $500 premium and charges it to you as compensation. You're out-of-pocket $200, the tax on $500.

➡ **Result:** You've saved more than half the cost of having your restaurant pay your portion of the premium.

Another Benefit: Unlike some other compensation plans, it is not necessary to get government approval of your split-dollar setup. Here's what to do:

If you are interested in split-dollar insurance, see your insurance and tax advisers. Split-dollar does not require a special type of policy; ordinary life insurance is almost always used. But there are all sorts of variations to the way you and your restaurant share the insurance costs. Your advisers can help you decide which method would be best in your situation.

HOW TO GET A BIG TAX BREAK FOR SUPPORTING YOUR PARENTS EVEN THOUGH THEY'RE NOT YOUR DEPENDENTS

A successful restaurant operation is often a family affair, with some or all of Father, Mother, and the older children doing their part. But then who looks after the little ones while the rest of the family is working? Frequently, it's Grandma and Grandpa, or other relatives.

Even though this help may add up to a tidy sum over the course of a year, you still may not be able to claim your older relatives—let's say your parents, for example, as tax dependents. But Grandma and Grandpa may make a valuable contribution to the business and then you could appoint them as directors. You could then pay them for services rendered to the corporation. As directors, they would be entitled to the same fees as other directors.

HOW PUTTING YOUR SPOUSE ON THE PAYROLL CAN PAY OFF IN THOUSANDS OF DOLLARS IN EXTRA DEDUCTIONS

The owners of many family-run restaurants may be missing out needlessly on tax deductions. With a simple change in their payroll setup, they may be able to pick up $4,000 or more in extra deductions. Here's a typical example:

Mr. Brown owns a restaurant and Mrs. Brown works at home, but two or three times a week she comes into the restaurant to help with the bookkeeping. She also fills in when anybody on the staff is out sick or on vacation.

Mr. Brown has never paid Mrs. Brown a salary for the work she's done. He figures there is nothing to gain by paying her a salary. The money simply goes from his pocket to hers. Nor does he pick up any tax advantages. They file a joint tax return. So half of his income is taxed to her and vice versa, regardless of who earns it.

Mr. Brown is right about the joint return, but that's only part of the tax story. There's a basic tax strategy: Mr. Brown should put Mrs. Brown on the restaurant payroll as a restaurant employee. That way, the Browns can claim two new deductions on their joint return that they are not entitled to now.

➡ **Result:** A lower taxable income on the Browns' joint return.

HOW TO NAIL DOWN TOP TAX DEDUCTIONS WHEN YOU TAKE YOUR SPOUSE ALONG ON A CONVENTION OR BUSINESS TRIP

Let's say you and your spouse are going to attend a restaurant convention or trade show. As long as your primary reason for the trip is restaurant business, you are entitled to tax breaks—even though you take a vacation side trip.

Your Expenses. You can deduct your cost of getting to and from the convention site. In addition, you are entitled to deduct your lodging and incidental expenses but only 50 percent for meals and entertainment while at the convention. The cost of any vacation side trip is, of course, a nondeductible personal expense.

Your Spouse's Expenses. Her expenses are also deductible if she's your partner in the restaurant business.

➡ **Reason:** The tax rule is that a spouse's expenses are deductible if the wife's presence on the trip has a bona fide business purpose, but if your spouse is not involved in the restaurant and she's just coming along to keep you company and do some vacationing, her expenses are not deductible. Nevertheless, you are still entitled to these government tax-cutters.

Despite the tough general rule, the government may allow you to deduct all of the cost of your spouse's transportation and a portion of your meals and entertainment.

Getting There and Back. Let's say you and your spouse are flying to a convention. If you travel by air and get a bargain rate for two travelers, you can still deduct what it would have cost you to go alone.

And it's even better if you drive to the convention. Then the entire cost of your transportation is deductible!

➡ **Reason:** You would have spent the same amount whether or not your spouse accompanied you.

Meals and Lodging. As with your airfare, you can deduct the cost of a single room even though one-half the cost of a double room is less. However, there is a tax-saving exception. You may be able to deduct 50 percent of your spouse's meals when she comes with you to a business lunch or dinner. It can be strictly a social affair. The government requires that the atmosphere be quiet and conducive to business—it's not necessary that business actually be discussed.

SOME DOLLAR SAVING WRITE-OFFS RESTAURANT OWNERS COMMONLY OVERLOOK

What restaurant owners may not be aware of is that some of the smaller items (with a life longer than twelve months) they buy for their restaurants also qualify for the write-offs. And although the write-offs for each of the items may be much smaller than the one for say, a convection oven for their kitchen, all those write-offs can add up to big tax savings.

Here are eleven of the commonly overlooked tax-savers that are generally available to restaurant owners the first year that the property is put into use.

> The regular investment tax credit is generally unavailable for assets purchased after 1985. The new tax laws allow a maximum write-off beginning in 1997 for purchase of equipment ($18,000) or a car ($3,160). The pre-1986 credit was calculated on a percentage basis.

1. Movable wall partitions qualify for the write-off if they are not made a permanent part of the building.

2. For customer seating.

3. Wall-to-wall carpeting is generally ineligible for the credit, but is eligible when the carpeting is fastened to wood strips that are nailed along the wall.

4. Wall panel inserts designed to hold condiments and beverage bars may both be eligible.

5. The cost of updating or redecorating a restaurant's dining room and kitchen may qualify for the investment credit.

6. Special electrical or plumbing connections qualify if they are necessary for and used directly with specific items of equipment.

7. Vending machines, such as those that dispense cigarettes, are eligible, but this may change due to pending legislation on smoking.

8. Outside restaurant ornamentation, like false balconies, qualifies. The ornamentation must be nonessential to the operation or maintenance of the building.

9. Display racks and movable shelves are eligible.

10. Lighting used to illuminate the exterior of the restaurant (though not the parking lot) qualifies.

11. Floor tiles applied with adhesives qualify for the write-off.

Equipment purchased for use in a restaurant could possibly include items that are used in connection with the restaurant business, like a stereo system, intercom system, or fire extinguisher and qualify for the same reasons kitchen equipment does.

> **IMPORTANT:** This is not a complete list of restaurant purchases that can qualify for the write-off. There are many more. So where there's a question about a particular item, be sure to check with the restaurant's tax adviser.

WHY LEASING PROPERTY TO YOUR RESTAURANT MAY BE A GOOD WAY TO NAIL DOWN TAX-SHELTERED PROFITS

Restaurant earnings paid out as dividends are taxed twice—once at the corporate level and again at the individual. They are not deductible on the restaurant's return. That's why the owner of a corporation wants to grab each and every opportunity to pay out corporate earnings that the corporation can deduct. For instance, a bonus that is tied into restaurant earnings is deductible as a reasonable expense. Here's what to do:

If your restaurant corporation is about to buy a building or piece of equipment, maybe it should think about leasing instead—from you. If the lease is based partly on restaurant revenue, the rents paid to you are, in effect, deductible earnings. The following is a typical situation.

> Country Kitchen, Inc., needs a banquet facility. Instead of Country Kitchen buying the building, the restaurant's shareholders, Mr. and Mrs. Polk, buy the lot, build the new banquet hall, and then lease it to the restaurant.
>
> Under the terms of the long-term lease, Country Kitchen, Inc., pays the Polks an annual $45,000 plus a percentage of the restaurant's annual gross revenue. And the restaurant takes a deduction for the full amount—fixed payment plus percentage. (Over the course of the lease, the gross revenues of the restaurant should grow, and the percentage payments should grow along with it.)

Will this kind of lease arrangement be tagged a disguised dividend by the government? Not as long as certain guidelines are followed. There must be a legitimate business purpose behind the leasing arrangement (e.g., the restaurant cannot secure reasonable finance terms on its own). And the lease terms must be reasonable. Percentage leases are common in commercial real estate but you can't go overboard.

You must deal with your corporation at arm's length. This means the rent terms must be comparable to what you would be able to negotiate with an outside tenant.

Ask Your Adviser. To get an idea of what the guidelines are in these types of lease arrangements, your tax adviser may want to take a look at a recent case, *Roman Systems, Ltd.,* which is the subject of the following article.

CREATIVE LEASE SETUP LEADS TO BIGGER DEDUCTIONS

It is not uncommon for a restaurant corporation to have trouble obtaining a lease on its own. Landlords often want the restaurant's shareholders to assume personal liability for the lease. One restaurant figured out how to bypass the problem in a way that allowed the restaurant to pass earnings to its shareholders free of corporate income taxes.

> *Case.* Roman Systems, Ltd., a restaurant corporation, was unable to enter into a lease.

> ➡ **Reason:** Roman Systems credit was not good enough, and four of its six shareholders were unwilling to guarantee payment of rent.

> *Plan of Attack.* The two willing shareholders formed a partnership, Two Romans, and entered into the lease with the landlord. Roman Systems then sublet the restaurant from Two Romans for a higher rental than the partnership paid to the landlord.

> ➡ **Result:** The partners were personally liable to the lessor, but in exchange for assuming this risk, they received extra rent from Roman Systems, Ltd.

The corporation took a deduction for the higher lease payments to Two Romans, but the Internal Revenue Service argued that the rent paid to Two Romans did not reflect the fair market value of the leased building. According to the Internal Revenue Service, the fair rental value—determined by arm's-length bargaining between strangers—was the amount that Two Romans paid the lessor. So the excess rental was not really rent. It was a way to siphon off the corporation's profits to the two risk-assuming partners.

➡ **Result:** No deduction for the excess—but the Tax Court said the rent was fully deductible because

The fair rental value of the building is not determined solely by the rent paid by Two Romans.

➡ **Reason:** The lessor undoubtedly would have charged the corporation a higher rent because it was a higher credit risk. What's more, the rent charged Roman

Systems by Two Romans was in line with the rent paid by other restaurants. Because the sublease had a legitimate business purpose and the amount of the rent was reasonable, Roman Systems can deduct the full amount of rent paid.

The time allowed for depreciation of an improvement to an existing building has now been lengthened to thirty-nine years, which is a very long time. There may be a benefit to this change. Suppose you are in a building that is in need of improvement and this improvement would enhance your business. If the landlord will not make the improvement because of the foregoing, you might suggest the following: that you would make the improvements as a part of the restaurant expense in exchange for a lowering of the rent you pay. Before making any deal, you should talk with your tax adviser.

HOW TO PUT MONEY INTO YOUR RESTAURANT NOW SO YOU CAN GET A TAX-FREE REPAYMENT LATER

Your incorporated restaurant may need some cash. It could get the money from a bank—but the interest rates would be too high. So, instead, you loan the necessary money to the restaurant and benefit from a tax savings. If the transaction is a bona fide loan and you handle things right, you will pay no tax on the restaurant's repayment. *You will owe tax on interest you receive.* Otherwise, the government may say your *loan* is really a capital contribution. That would make the repayment a fully taxable dividend.

Let's look at the following example of a winning case.

> Mr. C—the president and sole owner of C, Inc.—loaned his company money and charged interest. The company used the advance to buy inventory in quantity at bargain prices. The company's debt was evidenced by a demand note, which made C a general creditor of the company. The company made repayments of the principal and also paid interest on the loan. He reported the interest as interest income on his return and the company deducted the interest on its income tax return.

The government said the transaction was a contribution to capital, so the repayments were taxable dividends to C. This was a taxpayer victory because a Federal District Court said that the advance was a loan, not a capital contribution. The company had a valid business purpose for borrowing from C instead of a bank. And C was not putting his money at risk. He was a general creditor of the company—the company was considered a good credit risk by the banks. Granted, there was no fixed period for repayment and no collateral, but those facts are not that important. C controlled the company and he knew he would be repaid.

HOW TO AVOID A GOVERNMENT HASSLE

When you set up the loan to your restaurant corporation, keep an eye on the following points. They are the factors the courts say work in your favor. They are characteristics of a debt and help you to nail down loan tax treatment.

- Note signed by the president in his capacity as an officer of the corporation

- Nonsubordination to claims of other creditors

- Market interest rate and fixed maturity date in reasonable future

- Nonconvertibility into stock

- No voting rights

- Ratio of debt securities to stock must be reasonable

- It is imperative that a note between the parties be created

This leads us to the question of: What's a reasonable ratio? Three to one is usually considered safe, but this is only a rule of thumb and the same is true of the other factors. There's no absolute guarantee that the presence (or absence) of any of these factors will decide the issue. So you'll want to get expert advice before making a loan to your company.

HOW THE TAX LAW CAN HELP YOU GET THE MONEY YOU NEED TO OPEN ANOTHER RESTAURANT

The tax law contains a special provision for small business. Section 1244 can help restaurant owners get the capital they need for expansion. Section 1244 allows a small business corporation to issue stock with built-in protection. You can offer potential backers stock that carries a kind of tax insurance. And you can make this offer at no cost to your restaurant. Uncle Sam picks up the tab.

To see how restaurants and investors alike can profit from Section 1244, let's check out a typical situation:

> Halfpenny Restaurant, Inc., wants to open another restaurant. It must issue more stock to raise capital. Halfpenny has already lined up a number of possible investors. Brown, for example, is considering putting up $75,000.
>
> He sees Halfpenny as having plenty of long-term potential, but he's still reluctant to give the deal the go-ahead.

Here's where Section 1244 comes in. Halfpenny issues stock that qualifies under Section 1244 and informs Brown of that fact. This one move may be just the edge that swings Brown in the restaurant's favor because, with Section 1244, Brown has tax insurance:

1. If Brown sells his stock a few years down the road at a profit, he gets low-taxed, long-term capital gain treatment, but

2. If the worst happens and the investment doesn't pan out, Brown can write off his loss as a dollar-for-dollar deduction against ordinary income up to $50,000 (up to $100,000 on a joint return).

Obviously, Section 1244 puts Brown in a much better tax position. And it's exactly the kind of tax sweetener that can win investors for your restaurant.

The key question is, How can my restaurant issue stock that qualifies under Section 1244? There are some tests you have to meet.

That's it! Your restaurant doesn't have to file anything with the government but your records must show that the corporation qualifies as a small business corporation when stock was issued. Of course, considering what's at stake, you'll want to talk things over with your professional adviser before you go ahead and issue the new stock.

HOW YOU CAN WRITE OFF THE COST OF CHECKING UP ON YOUR COMPETITION

You may be thinking of making major changes in your menu. *Or* maybe you are redecorating the place. *Or* perhaps you are looking for a new chef for your kitchen. *Or* new entertainers for your cocktail lounge.

What do these situations have in common? Simply this: Before making any decision on these matters, you may want to check out what your competitors are doing. And the cost of checking out your competition may be a deductible travel expense. You can write off the cost of travel that qualifies as an ordinary and necessary business expense. This should, of course, include your automobile costs in checking up on Sam's Bar and Grill across town or Chez Pierre out in the suburbs. It may also cover your travel costs (including meals and lodging) when you go out of town overnight (but only 50 percent of meals and entertainment).

For example, here's what actually happened in a recent case.

> Mr. Russo was the manager of Garden Square Bowling Lanes. Garden Square consisted of a cocktail lounge, restaurant, coffee shop, banquet facilities, and bowling lanes. One of Russo's duties was to sign up entertainers for the cocktail lounge. He spent thirty-five Saturday evenings in one year visiting other lounges in search of talent. He also paid monthly visits to other bowling centers to check out their business operations. And Russo made trips to San Diego and Las Vegas to view bowling tournaments.

Russo's travel costs were fully deductible. The Tax Court said that the costs were an ordinary and necessary business expense for Russo because the trips had a sufficient connection with his responsibilities as manager of Garden Square.

IMPORTANT: You must keep adequate records to back up your travel deductions in case of an audit. This means a contemporaneous diary of where you travel, when, for what business purpose, and the amount of the expense, supported by receipts for your lodging and any other expense over $25.

HOW A RESTAURANT MAY BE ABLE TO GIVE EMPLOYEES BIGGER PAYCHECKS AT NO EXTRA COST

Would you like to be able to give your lowest-paid employees—dishwashers and kitchen helpers, for example—more take-home pay at no cost to you? Of course you would! And that's exactly what you can do, thanks to a special tax break. An employee or a self-employed individual with qualifying children may be entitled to a tax credit under current laws if his or her earnings do not exceed $30,095.

Your accountant (or whoever does the books) can give them the credit in advance via reduced withholding. The workers don't have to wait until they file their tax return. The result is more take-home pay without your raising their pay. Even more remarkable: If the credit exceeds what's withheld for income taxes, the worker gets an advance payment of the credit in each paycheck from the restaurant.

That's fine for them, you might say, but what about the restaurant? How does it get reimbursed for paying the advance?

Again, it doesn't cost the restaurant anything. Any advance credit it pays out is used to offset its payroll tax liability. The payments offset other income tax withholding, the employees' share of Social Security tax, and the restaurant's share of Social Security tax, in that order. If the advances exceed the restaurant's total payroll tax bill, it may either (1) uniformly reduce advance payments to all employees, or (2) treat the excess as an advance payment of its own income tax bill.

HOW TO HANDLE IT:

Your employees who qualify for advance payments file a completed Form W-5 with the restaurant. It's a simple form. Your accountant figures the amount of each employee's advance from the government's Advanced Earned Income Credit Payment Table and adds the proper amount to the employee's pay. Your accountant then notes on payroll tax Form 941 that your restaurant has made advanced earned income credit payments and deducts the advances from the payroll tax due. *Note:* An advance doesn't count as wages, so there's no payroll tax on it.

> *Question.* What if the advance earned income credit payments turn out to be bigger than the actual credit the employee is entitled to on his return?
>
>> *Answer.* That's the employee's problem. Your restaurant shows the total amount of advance payments it makes during the year on the employee's Form W-2.
>>
>> The employee is liable for any excess when he files his tax return.

Question. I pay my waiters and waitresses minimum wage, too. Will they qualify for this break?

> *Answer.* Probably not, if they receive tips, but if their wages and tips come to less than $30,095 for the year, they may qualify just like anyone else.

REMEMBER: If an employee files a Form W-5 with your restaurant, you *must* make advance payments. But it is up to the employee to file the form each year. You are not obligated to take any action until the employee does file. Of course, you may want to let your employees know about this tax break. If so, the easiest thing to do is distribute Form W-5 to the employees. It will let them know if they qualify for the credit.

WHY REFRESHER COURSES HAVE BUILT-IN TAX SAVINGS

If you're one of the many restaurant owners who each summer mix a little pleasure with brushing up on trends in the restaurant business, don't overlook the tax savings inherent in taking a refresher course. You can deduct the cost of education that's undertaken to maintain or improve your business skills. A restaurant management course is an example.

Exactly what expenses are deductible? First, you can deduct your direct costs, including books, tuition, and the like. In addition, you can deduct the cost of transportation, plus—if you must travel away from home overnight—the cost of meals at 50 percent and lodging away from home. The following situations may influence some of your decisions regarding travel.

> *Question.* Your restaurant is located in Chicago. The courses you want to take are being given in Chicago and Philadelphia. If you go to Philadelphia to take the courses, will you forfeit your deduction for travel, meals, and lodging?
>
> > *Answer.* No. You can pick and choose the education center that you prefer.
>
> *Question.* How about sightseeing? While you're in Philadelphia, you expect to do some sight-seeing and some visiting—you have a lot of friends and business acquaintances in the area. How will this affect your deduction?
>
> > *Answer.* As long as your primary reason for going is to take the courses, your deduction won't suffer. However, the actual cost of visiting and sight-seeing comes out of your own pocket—it's not deductible. On the other hand, if your primary reason for going to Philadelphia is sight-seeing and visiting, with a refresher course thrown in on the side, you can deduct only the actual cost of attending the course. Everything else—travel, meals, and lodging—is nondeductible.

For Example:

Mr. Smith, a salesman, enrolled in a university-sponsored continuing education travel program. The objective of the program was to promote interpersonal effectiveness in business and professional settings. It was not geared to any particular occupation. The program held three hours of workshops and lectures each day. And participants were free to choose which sessions they'd attend. Smith took his wife and children on the trip and he spent two hours per day at the sessions, leaving the remainder of the time for recreational and sight-seeing activities.

> **Tax Result:** Smith's trip was essentially for recreation. He spent most of his time on personal pursuits and his family accompanied him. Therefore, his travel, meals, and lodging are not deductible. However, the expenditures directly allocable to education—the tuition, books, and so forth—are deductible.

In addition to keeping a close eye on the time spent on business versus pleasure, you'll also want to keep a detailed record of all your education expenses. Although a good memory may help you pass the courses you are taking, it—without proof—won't nail down your deductions if your return is audited.

HOW TO MAKE SURE THE RESTAURANT GETS THE BENEFITS OF A CORPORATE SETUP

A restaurant owner usually incorporates to protect himself from personal liability for the debts of the corporation and to get the tax breaks that go with the corporate form. So it would be a shame if, after going to all the trouble of incorporating, the owner ends up with none of these benefits. But it happens practically every day and can mean disaster for owners. Moreover, all it takes is a few slip-ups and a court will rule that the corporation veil has been pierced.

➡ **Result:** The owner is stuck with the corporation's debts and owes a big bill for back taxes. Let's see what can occur.

Mr. Everett incorporated his retail business. Everett engaged James G. Smith to do advertising for his business. When the contract with Smith was drawn up, Everett did not mention that the business was incorporated. In fact, he personally paid the first bill. Then, Everett, Inc. had financial difficulties. The second bill went unpaid. When Smith sued, Everett claimed that he was protected from personal liability because his corporation had contracted for the advertising.

Everett did not inform Smith that he was acting on behalf of his corporation when he signed the contract. Therefore, said the court, he is personally liable for the fees—even though Everett had incorporated and Smith's services were valid corporate expenditures, *James G. Smith & Associates, Inc. V. Everett (Ap. Ct. Ohio 1982) 439NE2d932.* Most states require that the registered agent's name designated to receive process for the corporation be a current one. If not, personal liability for corporate debt may be incurred.

Don't let this happen to you. Make sure you don't end up holding the corporate bag. If you want the benefits of a restaurant corporation, make sure you look, act, and sound like a corporation. For the most part, this is merely a matter of formalities—making sure all the *i*'s are dotted and the *t*'s are crossed. As we've seen, failure to comply with these formalities can prove very costly.

ORGANIZING A RESTAURANT CORPORATION

Following are some of the more important things a restaurant owner can do to make sure his corporation is treated like one.

1. See that the articles of incorporation are properly drafted, signed, and filed with the appropriate state agency.

2. If a partnership existed before the incorporation, file a formal notice of partnership dissolution and notify the partnership's creditors.

3. Hold a shareholders' meeting and elect a board of directors.

4. The board of directors should hold an organizational meeting and elect officers, adopt by-laws, issue stock, and adopt the corporate seal.

5. Change letterheads and other printed forms and stationery to reflect the corporate name.

6. Open a bank account in the corporate name and deposit all sums received on and after the day of incorporation in that account.

7. Revise the restaurant's listings in business and telephone directories to reflect the corporate name.

8. All insurance, such as fire and public liability, should be assigned or reissued to the corporation.

9. All contracts and leases should be modified to indicate that the corporation is now the contracting party (i.e., that the restaurant owner is only acting as agent for the corporation).

10. Apply to the government for a federal employer's identification number for the corporation.

11. Be certain to keep all personal debts out of the corporation.

12. Do not pay personal expenses out of the corporate bank accounts.

HOW TO OPERATE AS A CORPORATION

1. Make sure all major transactions of the corporation are included in the corporate minutes.

2. Hold annual stockholders' meetings, elect directors for the following year, and approve acts of the directors for the previous year.

3. Keep the accounting records of the corporation separate and apart from the records of the shareholders and directors.

4. Keep the stock register up-to-date and complete with all stock certificates signed and distributed.

5. Maintain proper documentation for all of the corporation's employee benefit plans, buy-sell agreements, and the like.

> **IMPORTANT:** Some people say incorporation can be a do-it-yourself affair. There are kits you can buy that are designed to help you incorporate your business. *This is not recommended!* The laws are too complicated and the stakes are too high. Get a reputable attorney and accountant and follow their advice.

HOW TO USE A WELL-DRAWN CORPORATE MINUTE BOOK TO ELIMINATE RISKS IN THE INCORPORATED POCKETBOOK

The minute book may be one of the most important—and often overlooked—records kept by an incorporated restaurant. It contains the minutes of the board of directors and stockholders' meetings. As an owner of your restaurant corporation, you have control over the corporate minutes. Carefully drawn and recorded, they can back the restaurant up when settling differences with the Internal Revenue Service.

Here are some areas that are particularly susceptible to investigation by the government. Your corporate minute book can help make the difference.

- *Restaurant-Owner's Compensation.* Is it reasonable? The minutes can state that the salary paid to an owner-employee of the restaurant corporation is based on both his ability to run the day-to-day business of the restaurant, and on the responsibilities he assumes. Minutes can also justify salary increases by spelling out increased productivity and exceptional managerial skills.

- *Corporate Leases.* To help nail down the restaurant's deductions for rent, a

corporate resolution formally approving the terms of the lease should appear
in the minutes, together with a copy of the lease.

- *Accumulation of Earnings.* Are they unreasonable? Generally speaking, many
restaurants don't have this concern.

  ➡ **Reason:** A restaurant can accumulate $250,000 of earnings with-
  out being hit with a penalty tax. But a larger restaurant operation
  may be faced with the problem *unless* it can show a valid business
  purpose for the over $250,000 accumulation. The minutes can set
  out the precise reasons why the accumulations were necessary
  (e.g., restaurant expansion, working capital, or protection of the
  business during slow periods).

- *Retirement Plans.* Including your restaurant corporation's qualified profit-
sharing or pension plan in the minutes provides an examining agent with all
the firsthand proof he or she needs to see how the plan is set up and operating.
The minutes can indicate that the plan is for the benefit of all the restaurant's
employees and doesn't discriminate in favor of the restaurant owner.

These are just some of the situations where well-drawn minutes can play a vital
role. There are many others. For instance, the minute book can reflect the basis of
the corporation's group-term insurance plan, and any deferred compensation plans
for the restaurant owner. Minutes can specify what and who are covered by the
restaurant's medical reimbursement plan, and the justifications of any buy-sell
agreement covering retirement, death, or disability of an owner-employee of the
restaurant. And minutes are particularly useful in establishing the arm's-length
character of business transactions between, say, your restaurant corporation and a
shareholder.

However, minutes won't come to the rescue of a corporation that says one thing
in the minutes and does exactly the opposite. The Internal Revenue Service will look
through form to the substance of corporate activity when it challenges a deduction.
To avoid problems, draw your minutes accurately and precisely. Let your tax adviser
look them over before they are recorded to make sure their language squares with
the corporate and tax results you want—or are required—to attain. And make sure
they are not just paid lip service.

Index